Praise for Sustainable Ambition

"In *Sustainable Ambition*, Kathy Oneto presents a revolutionary approach to achieving goals without sacrificing well-being. A must-read for those seeking a more holistic and fulfilling life."

—**Greg McKeown,** author of *New York Times* bestsellers *Essentialism* and *Effortless*

"Ambition looks different for all of us, and it looks different at new points in our lives. In this encouraging book, Kathy guides us all to find a sustainable path where we can achieve great things and love our lives too."

—**Laura Vanderkam,** author of *Tranquility by Tuesday*

"Just as becoming indistractable requires mastering your focus, living with sustainable ambition demands aligning your goals with intention and resilience. Kathy Oneto's method is a road map for anyone seeking to achieve success in a way that energizes rather than depletes you. This book is a game changer for moving beyond the noise of productivity hacks and designing a life of purpose and fulfillment."

—**Nir Eyal,** author of *Indistractable: How to Control Your Attention and Choose Your Life*

"For someone, like me, who has struggled with burnout while pursuing ambitious goals, this book feels like a revelation and permission slip all in one. Through her compelling framework of Right Ambition, Right Time, and Right Effort, Kathy Oneto offers a practical and deeply human approach to achieving what matters most—one that works with our natural rhythms rather than against them, like any sustainable system in nature. Her method highlights a profound truth: being ambitious doesn't have to mean constant striving—we can pursue our dreams while protecting our energy, honoring our need for renewal, and finding more joy in the journey."

—**Jen Fisher,** best-selling author, podcast host, and global expert on well-being at work

"Ambition is a long game. Kathy Oneto's *Sustainable Ambition* is both aspirational and practical, guiding you to make choices and pace yourself to pursue goals on your timeline so you can live sustainably and succeed your way. An essential read for anyone who wants to build a fulfilling career and a life with purpose and resilience."

—**Dorie Clark,** author of *Wall Street Journal* bestseller *The Long Game* and executive education faculty at Columbia Business School

"Most people think 'sustainable ambition' is an oxymoron. Kathy Oneto busts that myth in her engaging, practical, and transformational book. Read it and learn how to have significant impact on the world while enjoying your life while you are living it."

—**Pamela Slim,** author of *Body of Work* and *The Widest Net*

"*Sustainable Ambition* is a must-read for anyone who's feeling the burn of hustling harder or sick of straining to meet someone else's definition of success. It's time to take back your time and live on terms tailored to you. Kathy Oneto shows you how to dream big, live well, and leave a legacy that's uniquely and distinctly yours."

—**Bonnie Wan,** bestselling author of *The Life Brief* and *Ad Age*'s 2022 Chief Strategy Officer of the Year

"*Sustainable Ambition* is the book to read when you're ready to make conscious choices to live like you mean it. Life's short, and Kathy helps us prioritize what really matters while we're fortunate enough to be here. This is a must-read for those who want to live spectacularly alive lives."

—**Jodi Wellman,** founder of Four Thousand Mondays and author of *You Only Die Once: How to Make It to the End with No Regrets*

"Yes! Ambition is a good thing! And being ambitious in a sustainable way is an even better thing. *Sustainable Ambition* offers an insightful, strategic approach to finding the sweet spot in Right Ambition, Right Time, and Right Effort."

—**Margaret Andrews,** Harvard University instructor and founder of the MYLO Center

"*Sustainable Ambition* is that rarest of books about success and achievement: a curious, nuanced engagement with our desire to be more and do more with our lives—and the hazards that come with that pursuit. Oneto ventures beyond the usual boilerplate about work-life balance or slowing down to offer an alternative path that acknowledges the joy that comes from challenging ourselves *and* the difficult choices we must make along the way. By embracing how goals and interests evolve as you learn and grow, Oneto delivers practical guidance on discovering what matters most to you, navigating the tensions inherent in a rich life, and pacing yourself for a long life lived ambitiously."

—**Tara McMullin,** writer, critic, and author of *What Works*

"In a world where options are limitless, but time and energy are finite, it takes deep reflection and a sound strategy to make your aspirations a reality while also maintaining joy throughout the process. Enter *Sustainable Ambition*. In her action-driven book, Oneto packs in critical insights to consider on the path to success and provides the road map for going the distance with sustained enthusiasm. While passion, drive, and focus are the keys to making your life goals a reality, recognizing how to prioritize, be resilient, and think holistically are the fuel that will ensure you find both achievement *and* fulfillment throughout your entire journey."

—**Dawn Graham,** PhD, author of *Switchers: How Smart Professionals Change Careers and Seize Success*

"*Sustainable Ambition* challenges you to be as strategic about your life goals as you are about your career. This personal and professional development guide offers a road map for successfully navigating modern work life without falling prey to overwork and burnout."

—**Timothy Galpin,** PhD, senior lecturer in strategy and innovation at the University of Oxford Saïd Business School

SUSTAINABLE AMBITION

● ● ●

How to Prioritize What Matters
to Thrive in Life and Work

KATHY ONETO

GREENLEAF
BOOK GROUP PRESS

This publication is designed to provide accurate and authoritative information in regard to the subject matter covered. It is sold with the understanding that the publisher and author are not engaged in rendering legal, accounting, or other professional services. Nothing herein shall create an attorney-client relationship, and nothing herein shall constitute legal advice or a solicitation to offer legal advice. If legal advice or other expert assistance is required, the services of a competent professional should be sought.

Published by Greenleaf Book Group Press
Austin, Texas
www.gbgpress.com

Copyright © 2025 Kathy Oneto

All rights reserved.

Sustainable Ambition® is a trademark of Kathy Oneto
Consulting & Coaching © 2023–2025. All rights reserved.

Thank you for purchasing an authorized edition of this book and for complying with copyright law. No part of this book may be reproduced, stored in a retrieval system, or transmitted by any means, electronic, mechanical, photocopying, recording, or otherwise, without written permission from the copyright holder.

Distributed by Greenleaf Book Group

For ordering information or special discounts for bulk purchases, please contact Greenleaf Book Group at PO Box 91869, Austin, TX 78709, 512.891.6100.

Design and composition by Greenleaf Book Group
Cover design by Greenleaf Book Group

Publisher's Cataloging-in-Publication data is available.

Print ISBN: 979-8-88645-294-5

eBook ISBN: 979-8-88645-295-2

Audiobook ISBN: 979-8-98530-935-5

To offset the number of trees consumed in the printing of our books, Greenleaf donates a portion of the proceeds from each printing to the Arbor Day Foundation. Greenleaf Book Group has replaced over 50,000 trees since 2007.

Printed in the United States of America on acid-free paper

25 26 27 28 29 30 31 32   10 9 8 7 6 5 4 3 2 1

First Edition

Contents

INTRODUCTION 1

PART I: THE SUSTAINABLE AMBITION METHOD

Chapter 1: Become Consciously Ambitious 15

Chapter 2: Reclaim Personal Success and
               Ambition as Your Own 39

PART II: RIGHT AMBITION

Chapter 3: Discover What Is Meaningful
               and Motivating to You 63

Chapter 4: Make Your Ambitions Yours 93

Chapter 5: Navigate the Ups and Downs of Ambition 115

PART III: RIGHT TIME

Chapter 6: Define Your Life and Work Ambitions Now. 141

Chapter 7: Plan in Arcs, Pacing Your Ambitions 161

Chapter 8: Navigate the Tensions across Ambitions 181

PART IV: RIGHT EFFORT

Chapter 9: Prioritize Your Effort. 207

Chapter 10: Sustain Your Effort and Yourself 227

Chapter 11: Allow Yourself to Live and Work Sustainably. 255

PART V: PRACTICING SUSTAINABLE AMBITION

Chapter 12: Find the Sustainable Ambition Way. 273

CONCLUSION: Choose What's Possible beyond
                  What's Next 297

ACKNOWLEDGMENTS 303

SUSTAINABLE AMBITION TOOLS AND RESOURCES 307

GO DEEPER WITH SUSTAINABLE AMBITION 311

SUSTAINABLE AMBITION QUICK REFERENCE 313

RECOMMENDED READING 315

NOTES 319

ABOUT THE AUTHOR 335

Introduction

• • •

It had been eleven beautiful days in the Colorado backcountry. Epic scenery. Amazing vistas. A once-in-a-lifetime crossing of the Continental Divide. I took a heavy step heading down the trail, eager to get to our end point for the day.

Zing! My foot screamed. *Oh my gosh! There it is again. What is going on?!*

Pain shot down the front of my right foot, from the ball toward the end of my big toe. I tried to place my foot differently, lifting my toes and shifting weight to the outside, knowing full well doing so could lead to other physical problems. It didn't matter. The zinging continued now with every step.

My friend and I had been hiking for eight hours that day in the middle of our three-week backpacking trip on the Colorado Trail. While it had been thrilling to challenge myself to take on this endurance hike, the foot pain made me reconsider. It was excruciating, and I lost it. My mind swirled.

I smell! My feet are killing me! I packed too much! The trail has gotten ugly! What was I thinking signing up for three weeks out here?

We still have thirteen days left! What am I going to do? Grumble, grumble. Pout, pout. Stomp, stomp. *Oww!*

At that moment, I was at a crossroads. Could I stay committed to this goal and see it through? Was it worth it to endure the pain, carrying a twenty-five-pound pack, all for the glory of saying I completed the trail? What trade-offs was I making in doing so? Was it possible to even make a change at the halfway point, or was I locked in? Plus, at this juncture, was I still even enjoying the adventure?

That evening, we also stood at a crossroads, literally at a fork in the trail. Go left and head toward hot showers. *Oh yeah. That sounds good!* Go right and stay on track with our goal and on schedule so we'd finish in time. *If I have us go the other way, it's going to throw us off. I don't want to screw up our chance to complete the trail.*

I was conflicted, but we had to decide which path to take. Hot showers or stay on track?

Moments of questioning. Moments of choice.

Such moments can range from the small—choosing which physical path to take—to bigger life decisions we initially pursue with confidence, thinking we know what we want. Our choices seem well founded at the time. But later, we can have moments of realization. A shift happens. We change. The environment changes. We and our thinking evolve.

We end up asking, *How did I get here? Do I still want this? Is it worth the effort and the compromises I'm making to continue with my pursuit?*

I've heard such questioning time and again from friends, podcast interview guests, and coaching clients. Many of you have likely had those moments, when you recognized a shift, a feeling of being off, or a desire to change and wondered—or are currently wondering—what you want now or where to go next.

I've experienced such moments too. I hit a point in my forties where, despite my best efforts to be on top of my career, I took a job because I thought I should, realizing once I was in the role that it wasn't the right fit. My body rejected that ambition. But when I left, I felt lost. *What now?* I have put off ambitions, like living abroad, not knowing how I could possibly pull them off. I've let my job take over my life and put in too many hours, working myself to exhaustion while not prioritizing enough time for important relationships.

This all happened even though I started to ask questions in college about success, ambition, and navigating life and work, and then later as I entered adult life on my own. For decades, I've been asking and searching for the answers to inquiries like these: What is success for me? Where do I want to contribute in this world? What choice will I make at this time to allow room for both my career and the life I want to lead? How can I pursue my ambitions and not destroy myself? Pondering these led me to become a coach, start the *Sustainable Ambition* podcast, and conduct research for this book.

Many of us end up feeling unfulfilled at times—like we're not able to put time and energy into what truly matters to us, despite doing a lot across both our life and our work. We can be busy and rushing around, yet feel unsatisfied, stretched thin, or depleted. This can include those of us who are ambitious but aren't just wanting to strive in our careers. We're committed to what we want for our lives, too.

It can be disorienting when we realize we want something

more and our world shifts on us, times I call "inflection points." In the discomfort, we often think we're the only ones who must feel this way. Yet it's normal and common to feel like the algorithm around life and work doesn't add up anymore, prompting us to rethink what we want and how we live our lives. As a coach working with people navigating these life and work transitions, I continue to hear such revelations.

In such moments, many think they have lost their ambition, and perhaps some do for a time. But often our ambition has a rebirth. We realize we do want to be ambitious, but our ambition looks different now. For some, external motivators like a new job title or a higher salary don't cut it anymore. We don't want to accept that work can't be compatible with our lives and that we have to put our personal lives aside at the expense of work. We look for new ways to define success that better fit how we want to live our lives.

It's why I often hear statements or questions like:

- "I still have ambitions, but the traditional measures of success no longer motivate me. I want to be engaged, driven, and excel at work, but I want space for my life, too."

- "I'm not ambitious like I used to be. Something's shifted. Is that okay? What does that say about who I am? How do I move forward from here?"

- "I don't mind working hard in pursuit of my goals, but I need a way to keep myself in check and not fall into burnout, as I've done time and time again."

The practice of Sustainable Ambition, as outlined in this book, is for those of us asking such questions, who want to be successful on our terms, to craft our lives in the ways we choose, and to achieve what we want while maintaining our well-being. Ultimately, we want to feel fulfilled and to flourish. While we recognize that meaningful work is an important part of that, we know that broader ambitions feed our happiness. Life pursuits matter too.

We want to know that where we're putting our time and effort is worth it. We want what we're pursuing to feel energizing, not depleting, and to feel comfortable either leaning into that energy or dialing it back without beating ourselves up. In the end, we want to stay resilient so that, over time, we can put effort into what is truly important to us.

And when the questions come up again, we want to be in a position to make more conscious choices for ourselves. Do we continue forward, or do we change course? Sustainable Ambition invites us to make these decisions with more awareness and to understand the trade-offs we're making. It helps us know if we're investing our limited time and effort against what is meaningful and matters most to us.

On our backpacking trip on the Colorado Trail, my friend and I made choices for more joy and sustainability. On day eleven, we took the fork in the path that led us to those hot showers and a bed for the night, building up our resilience to carry us forward in the days ahead. We also chose to end the hike early, not completing the trail or the twenty-one days after all. We realized we weren't enjoying the terrain and hiking much at the end and felt we had achieved what we had set out to do. We were personally satisfied and fulfilled with what we had accomplished. We didn't need to push for more miles on the trail, and rather pushed for recovery and fun instead, celebrating our trek being tourists back in Denver.

You can be in a position to make such choices too. But to do so, you need a better way to make such decisions, and you need to know yourself. I want to offer you a better way to achieve what you long for: to pursue and put time and energy into what you want and what matters most to you across your life and your work and to feel fulfilled without compromising your personal life or your well-being.

THE SUSTAINABLE AMBITION METHOD

For those of us who are ambitious about our lives and our work, we are likely to have more that we want and need to do than our finite time and energy will allow. To achieve our goals and avoid exhaustion, we need a better way to manage the tensions we feel across all our demands and to manage our limited effort, so we remain motivated, focused, and sustained. To navigate these conflicts and to pursue our goals and dreams with resilience, it helps to be more consciously ambitious and to direct our life and work ambitions wisely by aligning the right ambition at the right time with the right effort.

This is the foundation of the Sustainable Ambition Method that I've created, drawing on what's worked for me; academic research; interviews with experts, authors, and friends, both one-on-one and as guests on the *Sustainable Ambition* podcast; and work with my coaching clients. The method provides ways to get clear about our Right Ambition, Right Time, and Right Effort and asks us to use self-defined success as our guide, to make courageous choices across life and work, and to accept that to find sustainability is a constant, personal practice in effort management. By doing so, we can pursue our goals and dreams in a way that is fulfilling and manageable over the long term rather than all-consuming in a way that leads to exhaustion, burnout, or making sacrifices in important areas of one's life.

You may be wondering—*how do I figure out what I want? What does fulfillment mean to me? How do I determine what matters most to me now, and is it worth it to put in the effort? How can I allow myself to shift priorities to other ambitions I hold at this time or dial down my ambition at this stage of life? Or how can I be ambitious and not give up important aspects of my life or not feel like I always have to give 110 percent and jeopardize my well-being?*

These aren't easy questions to answer. Time-management techniques and productivity hacks don't provide foolproof solutions; they simply suggest how to use our finite time and energy more efficiently and squeeze more out of us. Unlike these approaches, the Sustainable Ambition Method encourages embracing a new mindset that redefines success and ambition and guides you in addressing the two sides of ambition: aspirations and effort. The method points toward identifying what internally motivates you to drive your effort rather than allowing the external world to determine your success and ambitions. It helps you see what it is time for *now*, to focus your effort and encourage you to put appropriate structures in place to make your effort sustainable. And it emphasizes becoming more discerning about how you use your effort and energy and build resilience to sustain yourself while you stretch for your goals. It's a more rewarding, realistic, and resilient approach to achieve personal success and integrate life and work.

The Sustainable Ambition Method is different, and it is available to you. I've heard people, upon hearing this term alone, say,

"Ooh, that's interesting. I love that!" More conversation uncovers why it sparks and resonates with them. I've had others tell me that just knowing the concept of Sustainable Ambition has changed how they view their lives and work and how they make decisions. I've had a person come up to me after a speech and say, "You've changed how I'm thinking about my life now, and I'm going to realign my ambitions and make sure what I say yes to sets me up for sustainability." My coaching clients and workshop participants have found the concepts and exercises help them achieve more clarity, give them permission to view success and ambition differently, and guide them to put in place more realistic approaches to sustain themselves.

My hope is you can do the same by embracing the method too.

WHAT'S INSIDE

Sustainable Ambition offers a strategic approach for how to pursue your professional and personal goals in a way that is fulfilling and manageable over the long term, rather than becoming all-consuming to the point that it compromises other important aspects of your life or leads to burnout. In addition to being a coach, I've been a strategist over the course of my career, conducting research, developing insights, and creating models and plans to help companies and people move forward. This book bridges my two worlds, embedding strategic practices in the method.

Sustainable Ambition lives at the intersection of three interconnected components: Right Ambition, Right Time, and Right Effort. In the book, I provide background on each part of the method and offer practical strategies, exercises, and tools that will help you motivate, focus, and sustain the effort you invest in your ambitions and goals. In Part II, "Right Ambition," you get clear on what personally motivates you, so you can ground your ambitions in what matters to you, uncover what drives your energy, and define what success means to you. In Part III, "Right Time," you learn how to prioritize your life and work ambitions now and get tools to determine where to focus your effort, how to pace your ambitions over time, and how you might fit in goals and dreams that are important to you. In Part IV, "Right Effort," you learn how to be discerning about when to put in the hard work and when to rest and recharge along the way to avoid overwhelm and exhaustion.

My aim is that, by the end of this book, you'll embrace a new mindset and be armed with this new method to consciously define success for your life and work on your own terms. You'll have a surefire approach to reclaim your ambitions as your own and a practice you can return to again and again. You'll be able to identify meaningful, motivating goals at any life stage, prioritize what matters most to you across life and work, and achieve personal success with more resilience.

With this new mindset and method, my intent is also to put you in a position of power and choice. My mission is to help people attain more fulfillment and satisfaction in their life and work pursuits, helping them to step into and embrace new ambitions with more joy and ease and less angst. As part of this, it's important to me that people realize the progress they seek, so they can step more fully into who they are and who they want to become. My hope is that you'll feel like you can make choices about how you want to use your time, effort, and energy with more acceptance and peace rather than frustration and stress.

Some people may choose to either go all-in or check out instead of stepping into the practice of Sustainable Ambition, assuming that sustainability isn't possible. I believe it's better to dial in our ambitions to get them right, because we're more likely to thrive if we get them *right* than if we take the other approaches. This is the better way.

To be sure, societal structures and organizations play a role in how sustainable our life with work can be. Yet I don't want us to wait for these factors or players to get their act together and put in place legislation or programs that would benefit us all. A case in point: the movie *9 to 5*, which featured three working women played by Jane Fonda, Lily Tomlin, and Dolly Parton, and championed practices like on-site childcare and job-sharing roles, came out in 1980, forty-five years ago. Sadly, not much progress has been made on these fronts. While organizations need to do their part, we do, too. That's where I focus—on arming you with tools to support what you *can* control.

There is one way we can make a bigger difference. While each of our Sustainable Ambition journeys is unique, the more people who embrace these practices, the easier it will become for all of us to thrive in life and work. Those who have embraced Sustainable Ambition have shared that they feel hopeful, optimistic, and confident that if they continue to use the method and check in along the way, aligning the right ambitions at the right time with the right effort, they can dance with the ebb and flow of their ambitions and find it possible to live the life they want—sustainably.

My hope is that Sustainable Ambition will do the same for you and be a mantra that can guide you, because you don't have to remain unfulfilled with your life and work or feel overwhelmed by all you feel you must do. You don't have to feel like you've missed out because you chose to focus more on your life than your work ambitions, or like you're constantly driving while never dedicating time to what feeds your well-being. You can choose a better path to achieve what you want. Because with Sustainable Ambition, you can dream big, shape the life and work you want, and thrive.

> **SUPPORT FOR YOUR JOURNEY**
>
> I'm excited to start this journey with you. I'd like to know about your ambitions and goals, what's important and matters most to you now, and what challenges you might be facing to make things sustainable for yourself. Get in touch and find resources and tools to support you along the way at SustainableAmbition.com/sa-book.

Part I
The Sustainable Ambition Method

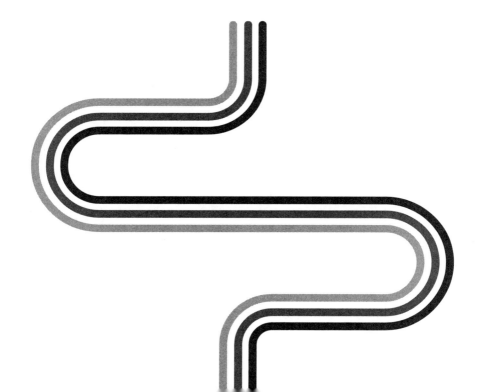

Chapter 1

• • •

Become Consciously Ambitious

"I took this job here at the agency looking for better work-life balance," I said with a smirk, a tilt of the head, and a slight shrug of the shoulders.

"Ha ha ha ha!"

I stepped back, startled, as a barrel of laughter roared at me. I hadn't meant to tell a joke, but the female colleagues who surrounded me knew what I had longed for was, well, laughable, ludicrous even. They chuckled and shook their heads. After a moment, I joined them with a knowing smile. I knew better now, four years into working at this global branding and design agency. As a vice president of brand strategy, I had experienced the exhausting grind of agency life. The drive for billable hours. Relentless client demands. Too few people. Work-life balance—what an absurd idea. What a naive thought.

I had joined the agency after two and a half years at a start-up, where I was the first employee of an incubator's natural food venture. I helped create the business and brand, launch it into the world, and secure national distribution with two retailers. The start-up was an environment with a lot of responsibility and demands (wear all the hats!), but limited resources. No problem. I was an ambitious, committed, hard worker. I loved bringing a company and brand to life in a space that had purpose—healthier food so people could lead healthy lives. I didn't mind getting my hands dirty and executing, so I got the work done.

The downside in that environment was that I wasn't adept at managing my effort. In fact, I gave far more than I had to give, and after only two years, I wound up feeling depleted and burned out.

That's one reason I decided to try working at the branding and design agency. I thought it would be less demanding to work at a more established organization—a place that was well past the start-up phase and wouldn't be plagued by limited funds and resources. Again, naive. Silly me. I hadn't done sufficient homework.

Perhaps not surprisingly, my working patterns didn't change either. Just as I had at the start-up, I continued to dig in and get the work done at the agency. For a long time, I loved the challenge and strategic nature of my work, and I willingly put in the effort the job demanded. Other circumstances were at play at that time too, as I worked there through the 2008 Great Recession. It wasn't a time for exploration and being out on the job market.

At some point, though, I started to feel my ambitions shift. I was still committed to my purpose of supporting clients' success, but a new vision for how I wanted to shape my life and work was taking root. In my early forties, I was still ambitious, but I wanted to apply my effort to new possibilities, have more ownership over my work, and have more flexibility in how I managed my days to better suit how I work best and to have time to care for aging parents and for other responsibilities.

I also didn't want to keep up the pace. I was being called toward both a new way to work and a desire to control my effort. For starters, I longed to take a sabbatical. I had worked full tilt for eight years, so my energy reserves were low. I needed a break. I didn't have much mileage left in me.

What had I learned up to that point in my life and eighteen-year career? First, that I had more energy to give to my work when it aligned with my personal vision and with what fulfilled and satisfied me. Second, that my career would have chapters, as I explored different experiences and sought to find alignment with the work that truly motivated me at the moment. Plus, I knew that my work wasn't the only activity in my life that I found rewarding. Ambitions I pursued outside of work, such as running marathons and doing triathlons, were just as important to me as my day job.

And finally, that while the environment in which I work is important, my employer wouldn't create work-life balance for me. As a hard worker who wants to craft a life with many activities, I needed to take responsibility to shape my life and work to create a different experience for myself. I needed to become more conscious of both my ambitions and my effort if I didn't want to find myself constantly in a state of being overextended and exhausted.

WORK-LIFE BALANCE IS ILLUSIVE, ELUSIVE, AND A LOSING BATTLE

Buckle up, because here we go. I'm sorry to break this to you, so I'll let Alain de Botton, best-selling author and cofounder of the School of Life, do the job and share the bad news. "Work-life balance is a myth. . . . You have to make choices, and therefore sacrifices. Having it all exists only in the mind of [former Facebook chief operating officer] Sheryl Sandberg," he said in the magazine *Kinfolk*.[1]

See, that thing called work-life balance that I had looked for and you've searched for—for most ambitious people who lead full lives, it's a losing battle. You have strived for something that isn't real and is impossible to attain. Frankly, even Sheryl Sandberg agrees, saying in an interview on the *Makers* series from PBS and AOL: "So there's no such thing as work-life balance. There's work, and there's life, and there's no balance."[2]

Wait, what?! I get it. You may be just like me, my coaching clients, and my workshop attendees: We all try our best to juggle our multiple ambitions across life and work, yet we can't continue to always push and drive, even if we are committed to our goals and what we want for our lives.

We think: *It must be how I'm managing my time. I must need better productivity practices. I need to be more disciplined.* So we try different time-management methods. We think technology and apps or paper planners will make us organized and efficient. We read books like James Clear's *Atomic Habits* to optimize our behaviors and Greg McKeown's *Essentialism* to get into the correct mindset and focus on doing less. If we can afford to, we outsource our to-do list. We seek out convenient solutions to save any amount of time, like relying on the likes of Amazon to deliver anything we need to have at our fingertips.

To be sure, these tactics can help. But still, we struggle and continue to be overwhelmed. It's why I often hear—with exasperation, defeat, and yearning—"I want to feel more balance between my life and work!" When I share my point of view, people aren't happy when I tell them they've chased the wrong outcome and that they'll continue to be disappointed.

They, perhaps just like you, wonder in disbelief, *What?! Why?! What does that mean if I want to be ambitious at work and in life but not have it be all-consuming?*

Let me explain.

The problem starts with the term itself, which is fundamentally flawed. "Work-life balance" creates the wrong mindset, and mindset drives our beliefs, what we perceive, and how we respond. The work-life balance mindset sets an unrealistic expectation that leaves us continually frustrated and disappointed. But it's the only term we've been given as a reference point for managing all we want to do across life and work.

The image that comes to mind with *balance* is that of a scale in perfect alignment with two sides of equal weight—work on one side and life on the other. The reality is that these two sides are rarely in equilibrium. The term suggests a steadiness and an evenness, but we don't live in a static environment that always allows work and life to be in equal parts.

Instead of a scale, I imagine a sailor who navigates a boat through a rough, unpredictable sea to get from one point to another. It requires attentiveness and adaptability. The sailor constantly makes course corrections and adjustments to the sails to keep the boat stable and avoid capsizing while progressing forward to the destination. In truth, for most of us, this type of instability is what we experience pretty much all the time. While we yearn for simplicity and a calm balance of activity, in today's dynamic world, achieving alignment between life and work calls for practice and constant adjusting. When we notice that we aren't in balance, instead of recalibrating, making choices, or building resilience, we get frustrated at its elusiveness.

Another problem with the balance mindset is that we often view the alignment between life and work as hard boundaries, as opposed to dials. We want strict lines around life and work, but hard boundaries aren't effective, and don't fit with today's reality. For better or worse, many professional jobs today blur life and work, given our twenty-four-hour, always-on culture and more flexible work styles. Plus, work can be demanding, as can life. Work will run into life just as life runs into work. To think you'll always be in balance, with strict boundaries, doesn't put you on a path to prepare for reality.

A final problem with the term "work-life balance" is that it puts work first. When I speak about *work* in this context, I mean activity tied to one's occupation or profession, even if you view it as a job, a career, or a calling. As much as meaningful work can contribute to fulfillment in our life, we can get tripped up when we feel that we must put work first. Work isn't always the activity that should be primary. And it's helpful to recognize that work fits into the vessel of our life. Putting work first can imply that life must accommodate work to find balance rather than looking to make work align to one's life. At the start of 2022, I was happy to see that Thrive Global, a well-being company founded by Arianna Huffington, came to the same conclusion. It shifted its terminology from "work-life integration" to "life-work integration" and agreed to do away with the term *balance*: "Our work and our lives are always integrated, so acknowledging that truth in the way we talk about our lives makes it easier to sustain."[3] Right on.

Life comes first—your life. How can we align our work to our lives rather than think that our lives need to bend to our work? What I like about the shift to life first is that it also shifts the sense of responsibility. When I speak with people about work-life balance, I sense they have an expectation that some magical force or their employers should create work-life balance for them. That's a problem. To be sure, a part of the equation resides with employers, but part of that equation resides with us too. We can't abdicate responsibility. Employers don't control us or our lives.

> As much as meaningful work can contribute to fulfillment in our life, we can get tripped up when we feel that we must put work first.

In the end, this problematic societal term and the associated mindset that drives how we respond can keep us in a losing cycle and result in constant disappointment. Work-life balance is a false expectation that simply can't be met.

I can understand if I've frustrated you with this perspective. So let me reassure you—I am an advocate of sustainable practices. That's why I wrote this book and why you should read it! Yet I am also someone who wants you to be realistic and approach the task at hand—aligning your life and work to make it all more manageable—in a way that will help you achieve it and reduce frustration.

See, we have a choice when it comes to work-life balance: Either we can stay discouraged and disappointed, or we can cast off this term that has failed us and shift toward ways of thinking that can help us move toward sustainability. To do that, let's begin with examining the nature of ambition. How can we become more consciously ambitious?

AMBITION IS GOOD, BUT IT MUST BE SUSTAINABLE

Ambition is not a dirty word. It is normal to be ambitious, despite how dictionary definitions often take a negative spin, like this from Merriam-Webster: "an ardent desire for rank, fame, or power."[4] Academic research has shown that ambition can be thought of as a general disposition, meaning a character trait or way of behaving.[5] It is a part of us, even if it may manifest differently for each of us.

Ambition can be both good and bad. It can motivate us to be engaged, contribute, and accomplish great things. But it can become harmful when it's tied to external measures such as striving for awards and public accolades and results in reckless effort. Timothy Judge, a professor of management at the University of Notre Dame's Mendoza College of Business and lead author of a 2012 study, "On the Value of Aiming High: The Causes and Consequences of Ambition,"[6] was quoted in an article as saying, "I think the main takeaway is to appreciate what ambition gets you—and what it doesn't. It certainly does make people more successful in the obvious ways we define success. That's important.... However, we should not delude ourselves into thinking that success in this realm holds the key to living a happy and healthy life. Ambition is important, but so are other things—stable family relationships, enduring friendships, and so on."[7]

What this means is that ambition takes conscious management to make it sustainable, and certain ambitions and the effort put against them shouldn't overshadow those ambitions that support a happy, healthy life. I believe ambition follows a U-curve similar to the U-curve theory of pressure and performance.[8] Too little pressure and we're bored and don't perform. Too much pressure and we're overly stressed and anxious, and as a result, also don't perform. Getting the pressure just right—not too little, not too much—optimizes performance. It's the same with ambition. Too little ambition can leave us floundering and feeling stagnant. Too much ambition can take us into danger—the severe zone—leaving us in a state of hyperambition, overextension, and unhappiness. We can get negatively addicted to striving (see Figure 1.1).

For these reasons, I contend that we don't think about our ambitions enough, and I believe we can benefit from becoming

Figure 1.1. The U-curve of ambition

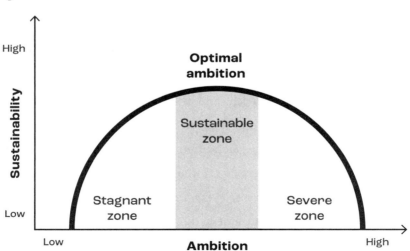

more consciously ambitious. Sustainable Ambition takes knowing ourselves, and discernment. When we strive and stretch for our ambitions, we are more likely to make those efforts sustainable if we are more conscious of the ambitions we choose at each moment in our lives, of the effort we put toward them, and of how we'll sustain ourselves. When we do so, we can take responsibility and choose what we want to be committed to and create in our lives. We can create life-work sustainability.

The term *sustainable* can have several meanings. For our purposes, it means we are motivated to put the appropriate amount of effort into our ambitions and goals across life and work and not overstrain ourselves to avoid severe exhaustion and burnout, instead preserving our well-being. We're conscious not to overextend ourselves or deplete our resources, so we can consistently pursue our ambitions in the short and long term. We do this while accepting the natural rhythms of our lives, with our level of ambition going up and down over time, depending on our personal experiences at different life stages.

When I speak of *ambition*, I think of it as a character trait (having ambition, being ambitious), but also as the aspirations and goals we hold (ambitions). (Note that I will use the words *ambition* and *goal* interchangeably—e.g., What are the ambitions or goals we have for our life and work?) These, too, are good. It is good for our well-being to have meaningful goals. Dr. Brian Little, an internationally acclaimed scholar and speaker in the field of personality and motivational psychology, in his book *Me, Myself, and Us: The Science of Personality and the Art of Well-Being*, writes, "The *sustainable* pursuit of our *core* projects shapes the quality of our lives—our health and happiness and well-being broadly defined."⁹ He notes that to positively affect our well-being, core projects (what I'd call ambitions and goals) should be self-defined and personally meaningful as well as manageable.

As I look back at my experiences as an adult, I can pinpoint a moment in college when I started to embrace such a mindset and philosophy to make the pursuit of my goals more manageable. It was when I felt overly stretched for the first time, during the last week before finals in a semester that had a heavy workload. I walked into a classroom late and found a final assignment written in big letters and centered on the whiteboard. It added to a project still due midweek for the course. In that moment, I had no margin for more. It was like the game Jenga—effort and energy extracted, and another piece of homework added to the load. I teetered.

From that moment, I became more conscious about the alignment of my ambitions with my effort. I didn't give up being ambitious or being a hard worker. Instead, I've consciously made choices over the decades to fit a range of activities into my life that honor different aspects of myself, including my work, and allow for rest and recovery. With awareness of my personality—committed, hard worker—I've also continually worked on being discerning about both my ambitions and my effort to manage my energy and create the capacity and resilience for all I want to do. This is my practice.

But I haven't always gotten it right. Just like at the start-up or the branding and design agency, work-life balance as a concept alone hasn't been what's helped me make things sustainable, especially given my tendencies. I've needed more tools to help me achieve greater fulfillment and satisfaction and maintain my well-being. Just like others, I needed and wanted to find a better way.

Often, people aren't convinced a solution exists. In this quandary, they can't see the third way—how to be ambitious and pursue goals while enjoying a sustainable life with work. For example, one of my clients shared how she always struggled to put personal activities ahead of work for fear she'd compromise her career. Another client had a genuine tension between her work and life ambitions, wanting to strive for a promotion yet also longing to slow down to have more time with her young children. A workshop participant had an aha moment in realizing that while she wanted to go after all her annual goals, it was unlikely she could do so sustainably. She painfully admitted she would need to choose.

I experience this tension myself. I have a desire to go after many ambitions at once, and I have life demands, too. Yet it doesn't have to be either-or. We can continue to hold our ambitions and make choices that allow for more sustainability. It's not easy, and it's an ongoing practice. But it can be done.

That's not the answer most of us want to hear. We interpret it as: *It's more work, effort, and time that I don't have!* We prefer to have *the answer* that tells us how to do it right and allows us to still have and do it all. We don't want to make sacrifices.

This doesn't mean we can't have ambitions for both our life and our work, or that we can't be ambitious and lead healthy, happy lives. Some may think the problem is being ambitious itself, but to be human is to be ambitious. It's a natural state, even though ambition doesn't look the same for each of us. While external factors might create friction, the solutions to help us fit it all in don't work either, because we don't make choices in alignment with our prioritized ambitions at a particular moment in our lives and we don't manage our effort.

We need to stop trying to do it all, and we shouldn't expect work-life balance; neither is sustainable. We need a better way to manage the conflicts we experience, given all we want to accomplish across our life and work, and to manage our effort in pursuit of our goals.

RIGHT AMBITION, RIGHT TIME, RIGHT EFFORT

You may be saying, "Fine. You hate the term 'work-life balance.' You've told me it's a false goal. But you think I can still find sustainability?" Yes.

The better way to sustainability is to align the right ambitions at the right time with the right effort. That is Sustainable Ambition.

The definition of *ambition* has two components: the goal or what you want to strive and stretch for (Right Ambition) and the associated amount of effort to achieve that goal (Right Effort). Through a lens of better life and work alignment, I add a third element: time (Right Time). What is it time for in your life? To get each of these components *right* takes attentiveness and adaptability—just like navigating that boat through a rough sea—to align with you and your life at this time. Doing so can help keep you in the healthy, happy, and sustainable zone and avoid the severe zone in the U-curve of ambition.

- Right Ambition has you get clear on why you're motivated by your ambitions, so they are aligned to who *you* are and what *you* want to pursue as well as to *your* metrics of success.
- Right Time has you prioritize and pace your ambitions according to what matters most to you across your life and work now.

- Right Effort calls you to discern how and when you want to expend your energy and work hard and when to replenish your energy to avoid burnout and break the overextension, overexhaustion cycle.

I have aligned my right ambitions to the right time with the right effort in some fashion over the course of my adult life.

Let's return to that class that put me over the edge in college. I remembered that experience as I considered jobs when I graduated. I had a range of career opportunities in front of me—investment banking, consulting, a real estate development company.

I weighed several factors when I evaluated my options. First, what were my ambitions? Let's be honest—my primary ambition was to land a decent-paying job so I could pay the bills and start to care for myself. Job one was to have a sufficient salary to cover all my expenses and save a little. Beyond that, I wanted foundational knowledge and learning. I also somehow had the instinct that work environment was important to me. I knew that certain egocentric, tough-driving cultures wouldn't be a good fit. I knew that power and making money weren't my primary motivators.

I had a professor tell me to pay attention to what parts of the newspaper I enjoyed reading (a good piece of advice when searching for clues on your interests). For school, I read the *Wall Street Journal* and found that I always skipped the Money & Investing section and always read the Marketplace section, which covered marketing and media. I was able to sharpen my focus when I decided between opportunities because I noticed where I put my attention.

But I also had two other ambitions: One was to live in New York City. I grew up on the West Coast and knew I'd likely land back there in my adult life. I wanted to experience New York before I got "stuck" back in the Bay Area. It was time for New York. It was also time to train for triathlons (mind you, not necessarily aligned with New York, but that didn't stop me). I was intrigued by the sport, and I knew I needed exercise to keep me sane. Why not train for triathlons? Plus, I wanted to make time for the intensity of the sport when I was young and my body could handle the impact. (Little did I know how prescient that insight was, because I endured injuries too early in my athletic career. I'm glad I prioritized my athletic focus at that time.)

Effort was also on my mind because of that class experience. I didn't want to work at an investment bank because of the misalignment of values, motivation, and interest, but also because I didn't want to give them sixty to eighty hours a week of my effort and energy, as was known to be the norm in such companies. I was open to working fifty to fifty-five hours a week, but not sixty-plus. I would work hard, but not give away all my discretionary time to enjoy New York City and train for triathlons.

I didn't know it then, but I had aligned the right ambitions to the right time with the right effort. This was sustainable for me. This choice didn't mean I never worked hard. I worked some weeknights and weekends, but not all the time, not day in and day out, week after week.

I also made this type of decision around Right Ambition, Right Time, and Right Effort when I chose the school for my master of business administration. I didn't expect to go back to school, but after two years in New York, I decided it was time to get a master's degree, because I realized the vision I had for my life and career would benefit. Not only would going back to school offer me an opportunity to further explore careers, but I thought an MBA would always be an asset. I landed at the Haas School of Business at the University of California, Berkeley, because the school aligned with my values, was a good cultural fit, and wasn't known to be a grind.

I again followed a similar logic after business school. I ultimately landed at Clorox, a consumer packaged goods company, in a brand management role. I wanted to get great foundational training that would support my career in the future and possible entrepreneurial aspirations, have a role that aligned with my strengths and motivations, and work for a company that had solid values. Plus, I wanted to work in an environment that was known for more reasonable workloads and didn't demand ridiculous hours. I still had ambitions as an amateur endurance athlete, adding running marathons to the athletic endeavor list. Clorox was a good fit on all fronts.

For me, this approach has been partly intuitive, especially early on. In this way, my values have guided me to make choices for my life and work. But that doesn't mean that I've always lived and worked in a Sustainable Ambition manner. I've lost my way. And what's brought me back to center is aligning the right ambition to the right time with the right effort.

You can too.

A PERSONALIZED METHOD TO MOTIVATE, FOCUS, AND MANAGE YOUR EFFORT

What we really struggle with when work-life balance eludes us is navigating the conflicts around everything we want and must

Table 1.1. How the Sustainable Ambition Method works

Tension	The method	Sustainable	Ambition
Navigating internal wants and external rules	Right Ambition	Motivate your effort to be personally rewarding.	It's not sustainable if the ambitions aren't yours.
Choosing ambitions across life and work, given finite time	Right Time	Focus your effort to be more realistic.	It's not sustainable if you don't prioritize what matters most now and embrace the journey.
Pursuing all we want to do despite finite effort and energy	Right Effort	Manage your effort to be more resilient.	It's not sustainable if you don't manage your effort and energy.

do, given finite time and energy, and how to pursue our goals in a way that is sustainable rather than be overly stretched to the point of severe exhaustion. That is what the practice of the Sustainable Ambition Method helps resolve.

The method helps you redefine and reclaim your ambitions by making them your own, prioritizing and pacing your pursuits, and being discerning about your effort and building resilience. It supports sustainability by motivating, focusing, and managing your effort. Table 1.1 provides a summary.

Sustainable Ambition can be found when these three elements are aligned for you: Right Ambition, Right Time, and Right Effort (see Figure 1.2).

When you live and work from a space of Sustainable Ambition, your actions are guided by self-defined, meaningful, motivating goals (Right Ambition) that are most important and right for you now (Right Time) and are aligned to your desired effort and sustained energy (Right Effort). This is the meaning, or definition, behind the method.

It sounds so simple. Wave the magic wand! But as I've said, finding sustainability isn't magic. Instead, it's a method and a

Figure 1.2. The three elements of Sustainable Ambition

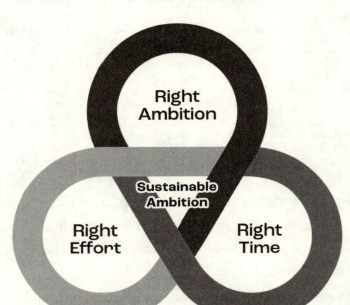

practice to help you navigate the conflicts and tensions you'll experience in your life and work along your own journey. It's also about having this mindset: Be conscious about the ambitions you choose and use self-defined success as your guide, realign toward what matters most now across life and work and take responsibility for making courageous choices, and build resilience, knowing that sustainability is a constant, personal practice.

Let's go deeper on each of the three elements, starting with Right Ambition. Right Ambition is self-defined and aligns with your personal definition of success, not society's. It is rooted in what you want, not what you should want, and is about achieving in a way that is personally rewarding to you, focusing on your own fulfillment and satisfaction.

Why do I have you start here? Because when focused here, you are in control of finding success and reducing the friction you can feel around your ambitions. You can step into a more powerful position when you shift your focus from external to internal, personal rewards and define success for yourself on your terms.

Albert-László Barabási is a network scientist, professor at Northeastern University, and author of the book *The Formula: The Universal Laws of Success*. In his research and book, Barabási studied success as measured externally, but he speaks to internal rewards as "centered on personal satisfaction and fulfillment," which, he admits, "matter a great deal."[10] I agree.

Success is actually subjective and can be personalized. Barabási writes in the book, "Private definitions of success are unique to each of us. . . . The rewards [are] internal."[11] Viewed in this way, individual success cannot be measured in external terms and through societal validation. We need to look inside to define our own success. Our ambitions need to be internally driven and what we want, not externally driven and something we feel we should do. We will be able to sustain our effort put toward goals that are meaningful and motivating to us. That will make ambitions sustainable.

Plus, research has shown that putting attention and focus on personal success linked to fulfillment, satisfaction, and happiness begets external success.[12] The opposite approach and correlation aren't necessarily true. In short, focus your effort and let yourself be guided by what is meaningful and motivating to you first, and external success is more likely to follow. Evidence also shows that activities we love can turn sour when we focus on external metrics and that a focus on external success and unproductive striving can steal time away from activities that contribute to our overall happiness, such as fostering relationships with others.[13]

Right Ambition is about you taking ownership of your ambitions and your definition of success. Make your ambition yours, not a *should-do*, by connecting to why it is meaningful and motivating to you. With this lens, the question becomes: What do *you want* to do?

Right Time considers life and work together and means choosing where you want to put your attention based on what matters most in your life and work now. It means accepting and understanding that life and work are naturally integrated and that time is finite. You can't do everything you may want to do across your life and work, in a lifetime, all at once. Plus, ambitions aren't time bound. You may have an ambition and determine it's not the right time for you to take it on, or you may find something new calling you. You may not know everything you aspire to now, or you may find that your level of ambition ebbs and flows over time, shifting where you want or need to put your energy and attention. For all these reasons, it's helpful to prioritize, pace, and plan in arcs and with horizons, determining which ambitions and goals it is time for now. It's not easy, but it's helpful to make courageous choices, letting go of doing it all now, knowing it all now, and achieving it quickly. You can instead embrace the adventure of pursuing your ambitions over time.

Right Time offers a more realistic way to look at and help you home in on where you want to put your attention, effort, and energy now across life and work. It's about finding peace in the choices and trade-offs you make. The question becomes: What is it time to do?

Right Effort is about being discerning about the level of effort you put toward your ambitions rather than treating them equally, and about how you manage your effort and energy to make your life and work sustainable. It calls you to take responsibility and puts you back in control to make your life and work integration right for you. Just like time, effort and energy are finite. You need to be judicious about where and how you optimally use your effort, figuring out what is worth the hard work and what is not, and have a plan for how you restore, protect, and support your energy and effort and build your resilience.

My friend Jenny Blake, author of *Free Time: Lose the Busywork, Love Your Business* and *Pivot: The Only Move That Matters Is Your Next One,* had this to say in our podcast interview: "One big aha that I had early on is that (with the exception of bad bosses) usually no *one* person—whether you work in a company or you work for yourself—is trying to make you feel burned out and exhausted. There's no burnout conspiracy committee that is trying to run everyone into the ground. But the nature of the beast, the nature of the times that we're living in . . . is completely unsustainable for many of us."[14]

This is why it is a constant, personal practice to achieve Right Effort and find sustainability. We have a lot thrown at us that causes conflict between all we want to do and the finite time, effort, and energy we have. It's a dance to align our effort and energy to our ambitions while we integrate life and work. The question becomes: What do you have the effort and energy to do?

I write about these as if the method is linear, yet Right Ambition, Right Time, and Right Effort interact, as you can see in Figure 1.2. These elements can also be applied on multiple levels—while looking at your life over time, when considering a single ambition or project, or when checking in and finding a way forward at a point in time. Throughout the book, I'll apply the practice with a broader view to your life and work. In Chapter 12, I share how you can bring all these elements together to apply the method to one ambition or project, as a check-in, or as a mantra to help you make choices at a particular moment.

THE CHOICE IS YOURS

When I came back to California for business school, I got together with several friends from my alma mater, the University of Virginia, who had also lived in New York City and were currently attending another business school across the Bay. As we relayed our New York experiences, they were incredulous at what I had done. "Wait, what? You went to the symphony when we were in New York? When did you do that?!" "You took a pottery class at the 92nd Street Y? Seriously?"

I smiled. "Yes, you guys. I did this when you worked your sixty-to-eighty-hour weeks!"

I made a different job choice than they did post-college. To be sure, some of these individuals can be considered more successful than me based on traditional, external measures of success. Some were already retired in their forties, having earned millions. But I've done great and achieved success on my terms. And I've appreciated my journey all along the way.

Today, I am self-employed—another personal choice—and have more flexibility in my life and work—a way to live and work that I had desired after that agency job, long before the pandemic.

For now, it works better for me to have more autonomy around when and how I work, given my natural rhythms and work preferences.

When I get tripped up around goals, I ground myself in the broad vision I have for my life, know that I've made choices for what it is time for now, live into my values, honor the contribution I want to make and how I want to give, and look to bring what I love into my work.

I continually work on my personal sustainability plan. As a hard worker, I find sustainability is a constant practice. It's why I've often struggled with the dance between ambition and exhaustion and why I sought to create flexibility for myself.

Of course, from the outside, some people might say, "You're not living Sustainable Ambition, Kathy, because you work too much." Yes, I lead a full life, and I am ambitious, but I do it with great intention and with focus. And I act consistently to build both resilience and sustainability. I can do what I do because I'm thoughtful about the choices I make for myself and because I manage my pace. I make decisions to carve out time for rest. Those rest times might not be visible to others.

Some breaks have been longer. That sabbatical I longed for when I was at the agency? It took four years between the time I longed for it and when I could take it. (I recognize it is a privilege to have been able to take such a period of time off, yet it also took commitment, planning, and sacrifice.) In 2017, I finally stepped into an eight-month sabbatical, and it was glorious. It still fills me up. All I have to do is look at the pictures from trips we took during that time; I relive the experience, and all the joy comes back to me. I took a shorter two-week creative sabbatical at the start of 2022, a time I carved out because I needed recovery time from a year of working hard and needed to feed my creative longings. I take shorter breaks, too, because we need pauses of different lengths. For example, I rely on an almost daily ten-minute meditation or short pauses throughout the day to reset myself.

But in honesty, effort is the area that I wrestle with the most. I don't always get it right. I've had times of misalignment and burnout. There were times when I either felt called to put in a lot of effort or felt the need to. And it means I have to plan, practice, and be thoughtful about it just like everybody else. Just like you.

I don't have a magical solution, and I don't promise this book will offer easy answers, because it's a challenge to navigate the conflicts and tensions across our ambitions and goals. But I have a practice that makes it all more sustainable for me. I can, at times, choose to dig in, only to realize I stretched myself too far again. But I get myself back on track when I realign my right ambitions at the right time with the right effort.

The same is possible for you too. This practice can make things easier for you just as it has for others. You can find greater fulfillment and joy across your life and work with more ease and less angst. You can have the Sustainable Ambition that is right for you.

Where do we start? We begin by challenging what we've been taught to believe about success and ambition.

Chapter 2

• • •

Reclaim Personal Success and Ambition as Your Own

People often don't believe that two seemingly incongruous words—*sustainable* and *ambition*—can go together. They think they are mutually exclusive, but I disagree. This is largely because of how we've been taught to think about what it means to succeed in life and work and what it means to pursue ambitions.

Society offers too narrow a view of these concepts. We can stand in a more powerful position and reclaim success and ambition as our own by shifting our perspective and beliefs toward more empowering definitions.

To start, it helps to remember that, as humans, it is normal to be goal-oriented and ambitious and to be driven to succeed. This is rooted in our biology and fundamentally grounded in motivations that go beyond typical external measures of success like wealth and status. Some may view the pursuit of success negatively and start to not like the word, just like *ambition*. But *success* is more nuanced than society would have us believe. Just like ambition isn't bad, striving to succeed isn't bad either. Striving can give us a sense of purpose; help us feel fulfilled; satisfy our desire for achievement, which improves our self-esteem and self-efficacy; and foster our growth and development, among other motivators. Similarly, ambition has a lot of embedded meaning in Western culture and society and is thought to be taboo. But ambition doesn't have to look the way we've been taught to see it. Part of Sustainable Ambition is pushing against such norms and challenging traditional conventions.

My hope is to shift your focus toward your personal success and to make your ambitions your own. When we do this, we take back agency, ownership, and responsibility, while at the same time giving ourselves the freedom to find more joy and ease across all we want to do in life and work.

So let's start to embrace the Sustainable Ambition Method by developing a new mindset and shifting our perspectives around success and ambition. In this chapter, I address ways we tend to think about both, given societal norms, and how we can reorient toward new, sustainable ways of thinking.

SUSTAINABLE SUCCESS IS DEFINED ON YOUR TERMS

"Who's going to be on the cover of *Time* magazine? Who's going be on the cover of *Fast Company* and *Inc.* magazine? It's Elon Musk and Steve Jobs. It's Bill Gates. These are the successful people in America. But, you know, there's how many hundreds of millions of us, and then there's billions of people elsewhere in the world. There has to be other ways of defining success, except for the not even 1 percent. The 0.0001 percent."[1]

Well said.

That quote is from an interview with my college friend and long-distance hiking guide Dominic DeMarco. Dominic and I met at the University of Virginia, and our friendship stuck when he made his way out to the Bay Area and set his sights on hiking the Pacific Crest Trail, where I joined him for a week and got introduced to backpacking. Dominic had become a thru-hiker. (A thru-hiker is someone who hikes a long-distance trail, like the Appalachian Trail or the Pacific Crest Trail, in one trip.) In his early years after college, he didn't follow the typical career path. In our podcast interview, he shared, "Like many people in their early twenties, I was a bit aimless. I didn't really know what direction I should go with my life. The traditional come out of college, get a job—that just didn't really appeal to me. I could tell I wasn't mature enough. I wasn't ready to go work a nine-to-five job. . . . It wasn't really the time or the place for that."

Dominic knew himself well enough to push against the societal norm to jump into a professional path and instead gave himself a different challenge at that stage in his life. His ambition was focused on his long-distance endeavors, which offered the opportunity to stretch himself and gain internal validation, in turn building his confidence.

While some of us at that age, like me, were concerned about setting the right, expected foundation for our careers, Dominic took what I would have thought was a riskier approach. He listened to himself and followed what called to him at that time, rather than fall into the "shoulds." He didn't worry about starting his career in the right company, earning that status symbol. Instead, he'd get different jobs, from retail to more business-oriented roles, to earn money in between his hiking quests or his cross-country bicycling trip. On these adventures, he experienced big successes, like completing the hikes at a fast pace, as well as what some might see as big failures, such as having to leave the trail because of injury or mental weariness.

Yet, over time, Dominic found his career niche and stopped taking long trips once he settled down and got married. He now runs his own successful small business, a full-service patent search firm. He has a family and a home, and continues to make time for his endurance pursuits—perhaps now just at a shorter distance. He's lived and is living a successful life on his terms.

Dominic has been a Sustainable Ambition inspiration for me over the years and has helped me see that alternative paths exist to find personal success. He made it okay to not have *the* job or to take long periods of time to do an activity you love. He's inspired me to explore entrepreneurship and consider the life of a small business owner. His choices remind me that more than one way exists to craft a life and one's work.

Dominic demonstrates, and clearly articulated, that for 99 percent of us, we need broader views of success, not just what we see glorified in the media. Not all of us will get venture capital funding, which has the long shot of making us millionaires or billionaires. (Frankly, few of us have access to such funding.) How many Elon Musks or Steve Jobses are there in the world?

How does Dominic define success? Putting a smile on your

face and focusing on what makes you happy. "It's so important to realize that there's other ways of measuring success," he said. "Do you have a career that puts a smile on your face? Do you have a home life that puts a smile on your face? Do you have hobbies that put a smile on your face? Do you have things you can talk about when you go to your neighborhood bar that you're passionate about? These are all signs of success."

We are told and taught that success is achieving fame and fortune fast and driving to be the best and busiest, all the time. But these external definitions of success don't give us what we truly want—to feel fulfilled and satisfied in our life and work while also being healthy and happy.

Unfortunately, in today's modern world, we can experience what is called "status anxiety," a term popularized and covered in Alain de Botton's book of the same name. He puts a spotlight on the phenomenon of how we worry about our perceived success in the world. Are we a "winner" or a "loser"?[2] This anxiety arises when our reality does not match our expectations and what we've been taught about success. And even when we do achieve, the positive feelings and reward are fleeting and don't lead to lasting fulfillment.

Status anxiety demonstrates the challenge with defining success based on such external measures. Looking externally can set unrealistic expectations and put us on a course to achieve goals we may not want. This can include ambitions we may not be able to reach, trapping us in a loop of disappointment between our expectation and the reality of attainment. We can experience undue consternation when we accept a narrative that we're average or don't meet an external bar.

I've certainly felt these negative emotions, criticizing myself for not having become a tech founder in Silicon Valley or reached the C-suite in a Fortune 500 company. I have to pull myself back and remind myself that those are not my ambitions. They're not what I want. I have to be grounded in what's important to me to stand confidently in my personal ambitions and not be swayed by external forces.

We benefit from normalizing a broader view of success that allows each of us to see ourselves as able to be successful in this world. Where should we look? Inward. Shifting our focus toward internal measures of success, guided by what internally motivates, fulfills, and satisfies us, is more powerful than external validation. We can't control what our efforts mean to others, but we can control what they mean to us. To be sure, sometimes we want to strive for external acknowledgment, but in other cases our well-being is more likely to be supported when we look to satisfy ourselves instead of striving for social approval.[3]

So, what if instead of chasing what society wants for us, we focus on what we want for our lives, who we are and what we value, and who we want to be and become in the world? What if we allow ourselves to live into our own fulfillment, satisfaction, and joy? This is success that is sustainable in a way that is more rewarding, realistic, and resilient.

A BROADER VIEW OF AMBITION

"And ambition—well, I couldn't find it. The dazzling quality that made me feel like my aspirations were written in the stars vanished right when I needed it to carry me. At the intersection of a physical and mental health crisis, what burst forth from me wasn't *I'm burnt out, I need help, I'm lost, I'm not holding it together anymore* but rather a confession: I'm not ambitious anymore."[4]

Rainesford Stauffer isn't the only one who has found themselves in such a state where they question if they care to be ambitious anymore, as she writes in the preceding quote from her book *All the Gold Stars: Reimagining Ambition and the Ways We Strive*. After anchoring her identity and self-worth on ambition for some time, the loss of her ambition in her late twenties was disorienting. I had the opportunity to interview Rainesford about the book for my podcast. Given her experience with ambition, she researched and wrote the book to explore ambition's roots and to ask questions about how ambition can look different in our lives. She, like me, has sought to redefine ambition. I advocate that we should reclaim what ambition means to us and think about it in a way that is more empowering and beneficial and reduces the swirl and consternation that common narratives create.

Why do so many of us feel disoriented when ambition is lost or changes? Because of what we believe ambition to be. We're taught to think ambition is about achievement that validates our identity, finding a singular career path and doggedly pursuing it without that path ever changing, doing all we want to do in life all at once and on a set time frame, and constantly striving and driving hard to achieve quickly.

But when we shift our mindset around success toward what internally motivates us, we can shift how we think about ambition too. We can stop being solely and unconsciously driven by societal norms and truly choose our ambition and make it sustainable and good.

In her book, Stauffer writes, "Will I ever strive for anything again? Will anything be worth it? Spoiler: a lot will be worth it."[5]

A lot is worth it. We can reclaim ambition and align our time and effort to make it personally right and worth it for each of us.

Ambitions Are for Life Too, Not Just Work

Societal views of ambition are limiting, often tied solely to professional endeavors and achievement. A more fulfilling and sustainable view of ambition is wide-ranging and includes life pursuits. Academic research supports this view that ambition is not specific to a context like a profession or to objects like a high salary. Ambitions can be defined across not just work but family, leisure, and more, with a desire for a variety of outcomes.[6]

Dominant societal narratives tend to promote and put value on certain types of achievement, but ambitions shouldn't come with value judgments. Ambition doesn't have just one reward or measurement. Our ambition is unlikely to look like someone else's. We aren't all wired the same, and one person's ambition is not more worthy than another's. In fact, ambition varies from person to person, from life stage to life stage, and from task to task. We can be just as ambitious about family as we are about work, and an ambition around work is not more worthy than an ambition around family.

When Stauffer conducted reporting for her book, she heard people ask themselves tough questions about what they truly valued and what they wanted to strive for that felt meaningful to them rather than pursuing what they believed they were supposed to be chasing. The outcome was that people held more expansive views of ambition compared with what we traditionally hear. It included everything from being ambitious about the desire for safety, stability, and security to nurturing relationships and community to caring for themselves and others. An added benefit of this broader view is that people's sense of self expanded, too. They didn't see themselves solely defined by their work and rather held a more holistic sense of identity.

Plus, a more expansive, holistic view of our goals benefits our well-being. The book *Wellbeing: The Five Essential Elements*, by Tom Rath and Jim Harter, is based on research Gallup conducted in more than 150 countries, representing 98 percent of the world's population. Gallup identified five universal elements of well-being that together create thriving lives and contribute to our sense of fulfillment: career, social, financial, physical, and community well-being. The authors write: "Wellbeing is about the combination of our love for what we do each day, the quality of our relationships, the security of our finances, the vibrancy of our physical health, and the pride we take in what we have contributed to our communities. Most importantly, it's about how these five elements *interact*. . . . We're not getting the most out of our lives unless we're living effectively in all five."[7] Our ambition will be more sustainable if the goals and dreams we hold for ourselves are more holistic, to honor all sides of us and contribute to our health and happiness.

This is what Stauffer found for herself. She writes in her final chapter: "Rather than landing on a single new definition of ambition, I found a stratosphere of everything I missed when I thought ambition was only one thing. I'm ambitious about being a friend. . . . I'm ambitious about imagination. . . . I'm ambitious about interdependence. . . . I noticed the more imaginative I got about my ambition, the more I felt my dreams stack up around me."[8] The more expansive she saw ambition, the more ideas she had, and her dreams grew. Ambition didn't wither; it bloomed.

Ambition Can Ebb and Flow over Time

"Is this normal?" a coaching client asked me. "Is this normal to not have the same feelings about work like I used to? To have new priorities?"

I often hear this from surprised clients, and I reassure them, "Yes, this is normal."

This is what I describe as the ebb and flow of ambition. Not only can our level of ambition go up and down as time passes, but it's also normal for what we want to change on us. It can throw us off when this happens, and I often hear the struggle people go through in such moments. We become disoriented, feel uncomfortable, and find it hard to adjust to newfound priorities and preferences. But ambition isn't a steady state, which is often what people think when they associate it with their identity. They self-define with statements like "I'm ambitious" and believe they need to operate in just one mode—*I get on a path, and I'm all-in all the time.*

Most of us grow into ourselves and our ambitions throughout our lives. We can find more ease by cultivating a mindset that delights in the journey of self-discovery, learning from our experiences, and shaping our future selves. Staying on one narrow path is like allowing ourselves to be typecast, but people generally are not one-note. When we experience a shift, we can think about how we might want to reinvent or express another side of ourselves and our identity. We can revel in wondering who or what we might become next.

Despite societal pressures to know where we're headed and to stay on track, it's unrealistic and limiting to expect ourselves to know all our likes, desires, and wants early in life or to think that we won't change. While we don't like uncertainty, because it's risky and feels threatening, we'll benefit if we can embrace ambiguity, learn to enjoy the adventure, and not be hard on ourselves if we don't reach a goal on a certain timeline or if we change course. Instead of the weight of expectations, we can welcome our evolution. In doing so, we reclaim our choice.

Making a shift doesn't mean you've failed. It means you've grown. In Oprah Winfrey's 2013 Harvard commencement address she said, "There is no such thing as failure. Failure is just life trying to move us in another direction."[9] I love this reframe.

The reality is that as we go through life, our desires, goals, and motivations change. Our values or how we weight them shifts. Early in our adult lives, we tend to think we only have work ambitions. We often don't put the ambitions we have for our personal lives, like our desire to find a partner or have a family, into the same bucket. Yet for most of us, as we age and enter different life stages, these changes lead us to reevaluate our vision for our lives and work, how we prioritize our values, how we want to contribute, and what work will satisfy us.

> The reality is that as we go through life, our desires, goals, and motivations change. Our values or how we weight them shifts.

Our ambitions shift, and they ebb and flow over time as we adjust to other life priorities.

Even so, we can often feel like we need do it all at the same time, because it seems unacceptable to allow our focus to shift toward other areas of ambition in our lives. But is that true? Can we not make choices to put life ambitions as our main focus and have that be right for us now?

Society doesn't always deem it acceptable. I read a *New York Times* article that talked about how in 1979 Patti Smith, the punk rock star who came to fame in the 1970s, was judged for stepping away from her band to settle down and have children, an example of how female artists (and many women still today) get judged and criticized if they choose to focus on motherhood and deprioritize their art or vocation as they raise children.[10]

In contrast, I love this example of the ebb and flow of ambitions from a 2005 *Time* article that featured Robin Parker, who at the time was forty-six and a former campaign organizer who had worked on presidential campaigns. She left that life in 1992 when a candidate from her party won the White House. Rather than vying for a spot in the West Wing, she instead shifted her work toward her family. She was quoted as saying: "Being out in the world became a lot less important to me. I used to worry about getting presidents elected, and I'm still an incredibly ambitious person. But what I want to succeed at now is managing my family, raising my boys, helping my husband and the community. In 10 years, when the boys are launched, who knows what I'll be doing? But for now, I have my world."[11] Her world had shifted. Her right ambition had new focus. And that was good and sustainable.

Ambition Doesn't Have to Mean Striving and Driving All the Time

For Rainesford Stauffer, constantly striving and driving became a normal mode of operating. Hard work was a refuge and a way to control her destiny. "I lit up not at accolades or accomplishments but at the acknowledgment that came with them: *Such a hard worker. Always going above and beyond.* When I faltered personally, the act of being ambitious felt like a saving grace," she writes.[12] She fell into overwork because of environmental factors but also because putting in the effort made her feel safe and the work held meaning for her. Many of us can feel the same way, and it can leave us asking, *Is it possible to be ambitious and work in a sustainable way?*

I believe so, and sustainability is crucial for our well-being. Research has shown that health consequences are associated with ambition, and ambitious people tend to experience more stress-related illnesses. So it behooves us to learn to dial in the right level of ambition and effort. Think Goldilocks here—too little and we can feel stagnant or like we are languishing, and too much has downsides for our health and happiness, like I share in Chapter 1 with the U-curve of ambition.

Plus, persistent pushing and driving can also lead to burnout. When I refer to *burnout*, I'm using it as it's more commonly known these days—to mean energy depletion or exhaustion, rather than its official definition that includes cynicism toward one's job and a decline in professional efficacy.

I've interviewed several endurance athletes as part of my Sustainable Ambition research because I see living our lives and working as endurance events that require resilience. My definition for resilience is to have the energy to continually put in the effort toward what matters to you at the moment and over time, while maintaining your well-being and operating at your best. Resilience is also the ability to manage what you juggle at one time without straining to the point of exhaustion and to sustain yourself through periods of hard work and challenge.

A consistent theme from endurance athletes is that you can't train and race pushing hard all the time. To achieve a goal, we must incorporate rest and recovery. Unbridled ambition will catch up with us. I found this to be true as I trained for marathons, using different methods to prepare for race day. I did long runs at a slower pace to put in the mileage to train my body to be on my feet and pound the pavement for a long time. I did hill repeats that were hard up, easy down to build up my strength and endurance. Other days I did speed training that included a mix of sprint and recovery that increased my foot turnover and ultimately my pace. I put in this work so that on race day I'd be prepared, and so I could, as I told myself, "Let my body take me." In my training, I was never striving and driving *all* the time. It was a constant mix of rigor and rest. Yet I also believe hard work is not bad and often required to achieve great results. My training was hard work, just not constant driving.

Humans are not machines in a factory. We aren't meant to operate at a consistent, demanding pace all the time. We are meant to operate between two states of using our energy and replenishing it to remain resilient.

• • •

Once we shift our mindset around success toward what internally motivates us, we can shift how we think about ambition, too. When thought about through the lens of self-defined success, the answers to these questions become different: What am I ambitious about that is meaningful and motivating to me? What is my level of ambition now and what are the goals I want to strive for at this time across my life and work? What matters to me such that it is worth my effort?

That's where the Sustainable Ambition Method comes in.

RIGHT MEANS RIGHT FOR YOU

Right Ambition. Right Time. Right Effort. My use of the term *right* can throw some people off. I don't mean to imply that there's a wrong way to do things. Right means that you make choices and decisions that are *right* for you. That is how to reclaim personal success and ambition as your own. *Right* means a self-defined ambition, a personal choice at this time, and a self-directed and desirable or appropriate level of effort.

It's hard to manage our ambitions and make them sustainable if we don't root them in personal meaning and motivations and in what we want now. And to do that and make right choices and decisions, we need to know ourselves. When we don't know ourselves, we turn toward external wayfinding to guide us, such as the "should" to follow a lucrative career path or the "should" to take on a side hustle or join a nonprofit board, as that is what's expected.

Sustainable Ambition calls us to step into ourselves and what we want. In technical terms, I'm asking you to step into self-authorship and to take the next step in your own development. That sounds so adult, and it is! You may not know this, but development isn't just for kids. We continue to develop and step through different stages throughout adulthood. One model of adult development is attributed to Dr. Robert Kegan. According to Kegan's model, over time adults move across different minds: operating from a socialized mind to a self-authored mind and finally to a self-transforming mind.[13]

Let me give you a high-level rundown of each. A socialized mind is one that is governed by social structures and the opinions of others. We move from being self-centered, like when we're children, and instead think about how we fit into the world. We look externally for guidance, so we are accepted by our community and experience a sense of belonging. The difference as we step into the next stage, a self-authoring mind, is that we gain perspective, shift away from social norms, and make our own decisions for ourselves regardless of our environment and the need for acceptance. Then as we step into the final stage, a self-transforming mind, we can hold multiple belief systems and can discern what is appropriate for a particular situation.

Kegan's research has shown that the majority of adults (58 percent) operate from a socialized mind, while 35 percent operate from a self-authoring mind, and less than 1 percent from a self-transforming mind.[14] So it is common for us to live from the socialized mind, looking for cues and guidance outside of ourselves and also getting caught up in doing what we think we should do.

And doing the shoulds isn't all bad when we don't know ourselves well, especially early in life. Yet, at some point for many of us, we start to reject the socialized mind and being tethered by the shoulds, longing instead to be self-authored. It becomes hard to sustain our ambition and our effort when we operate from someone else's playbook or when we no longer feel fulfilled and satisfied following someone else's agenda. It becomes time to step into who we are and what we want. I appreciate how David Brown, coauthor, with his wife, Alexandra, of the book *A Year Off: A Story about Traveling the World—and How to Make It Happen for You*, shared in our podcast interview, "There really isn't a sustainable option other than to be yourself."[15]

That's right!

TAKING STRATEGIC STEPS TO SUSTAINABILITY

What does it look like to create more sustainable success, become consciously ambitious, and build more resilience for life and work? That's the work we'll do together in the coming chapters, taking strategic steps through each part of the Sustainable Ambition Method.

In Part II, you get to know yourself better and define your four core motivations, what I call your Right Foundation, to form a base to root a Right Ambition and define success on your terms. You get introduced to some tools that can help you align and refine your ambitions to make them right for you or to uncover whether they are a have-to (an ambition externally motivated that you feel you should do) or a want-to (an ambition that is internally motivated that you feel energized to do), so you can determine if you want to keep or release that ambition. We also cover some of the emotional ups and downs you might experience on this roller coaster of life as you pursue what you want.

Building on what you uncover, in Part III we address Right Time, and you get clearer on the ambitions you hold across life and work, as well as plan how the vision for your life affects what you might pursue now, in the near term, or into the future. Importantly, we cover tools and strategies to examine the tensions across your life and work ambitions, determine the timing of your pursuits, and make informed trade-offs.

Finally, Part IV helps you manage Right Effort by being discerning and dialing in your effort, guiding you to create a sustaining plan, and introducing other concepts to build your resilience and use your effort wisely. Ultimately, it's about how you can sustain yourself when you strive and stretch in your life and work.

While I present the Sustainable Ambition Method sequentially, each element—Right Ambition, Right Time, Right Effort—has relevance on its own, and some of you may need immediate relief in certain areas. You may want more clarity around how to root your ambitions and define your own success, so jumping into Part II will be your best starting point. You may feel the immediate need to navigate tensions and conflicts and make some choices, so you might jump to the tools in Part III for more guidance. You may need relief from exhaustion and want to start putting a sustaining plan in place right away, as I share in Chapter 10. Or you may be in the midst of a decision on pursuing an ambition and could benefit from the tool I share in Chapter 12. Yes, the book is written to go through chapter by chapter, but use the book as it best serves you.

> **THE SUSTAINABLE AMBITION ASSESSMENT**
>
> If you're wondering where to start, you can find an online assessment to guide you at SustainableAmbition.com/sa-assess.

Now it's time to put yourself in charge of your right ambitions at the right time with the right effort. You can define success on your terms and bring more alignment and sustainability across your life and work.

YOUR FIRST STEP

To prepare to learn more about yourself and make *right for you* choices, first create space to do so. By doing this, you can also create a bit more ease by practicing making time for something that's important to you while also eliminating a less important task from your list.

I know some of you might be coming to this book already feeling overwhelmed. And yet I'll be asking you to carve out such space and time to better understand yourself, to build awareness of what matters and is most important to you, and to put plans in place to support sustainability. I ask you to be engaged in this work and willing to look to yourself for your answers, because one of the reasons the method works is that it is grounded in what is best for you. That is where *right* resides. The method looks to you as the guide. I don't have your answers. But the good news is that you do, and that's just where they should be. Sustainable Ambition puts the responsibility back in your hands and empowers you to make choices for yourself by putting the method into practice.

For this first step, go to your calendar and find a thirty-minute time slot each week where you can check in with yourself to get more conscious about your ambitions. You may think you don't have the time, but you do. The Stoic philosopher Seneca said, "People are frugal in guarding their personal property; but as soon as it comes to squandering time they are most wasteful of the one thing in which it is right to be stingy."[16] I'm inviting you here to be stingy. Take back some time for yourself. You might find time first thing on a morning, with your beverage of choice, before the bustle of a day starts. Perhaps you can carve out time when you're waiting for your child at their athletic practice. Or maybe it can be at the end of your Sunday, when all the activity of a weekend has quieted down and you can slow down too, to hear yourself.

If you're still finding it hard to find time to fit this in, check your calendar again and see what might be possible to take off your list. We all have lists, on and off our calendars. What is worth subtracting? Really, what could you not do without negative consequences? Eliminate it, and in its place put time for your Sustainable Ambition check-in. But be sure when doing this to communicate with whoever needs to know that you are no longer going to be doing whatever it is you were supposed to do. Let's not create a new problem that could eat up more time and energy that isn't deserved.

Also, where and when you do this work does not need to be perfect. You don't have to have special pens and paper or a candle burning—not that there's anything wrong with that. I do believe in priming yourself to do activities; I do it all the time.

But what's more important is to be present and engaged in the inquiries with yourself.

Did you do it? Great! You took your first step. You now have time carved out for the exercises and reflections to come and to check in and listen to yourself. I suggest that you start with once per week as you begin the practice. Then, consider moving your reviews to once a month or quarter to serve as a reminder to check in on how you're doing and keep the Sustainable Ambition practice alive. I share more on that later in the book.

But first, let's dive in further.

Here we go!

FREE RESOURCES

You can find free exercise worksheets and other resources to support your Sustainable Ambition journey at Sustainable Ambition.com/sa-toolkit.

Part II

Right Ambition

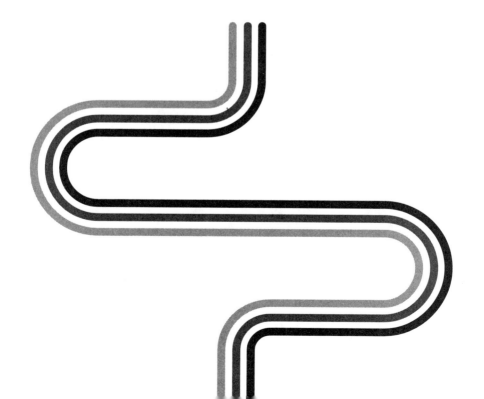

Chapter 3

Discover What Is Meaningful and Motivating to You

Eva Dienel has her priorities straight: "I like to say now I'm ambitious until three o'clock."[1]

A journalist and communications consultant, Dienel questioned the role of work in her life at a young age. After her parents divorced, her mom could find no career prospects in their small community, and while she had the opportunity to attend medical school, the nearest one was a five-hour drive away. It would have been impossible for a single parent to attend medical school and raise two small children, so Eva and her brother stayed in their hometown with their father.

Eva watched as her mom was forced to choose between her career and family and determined she didn't want to be in a similar position. "I knew I wanted to have kids, and I never wanted to have to make the choice between raising my kids and having a career. So, for the longest time, I've explored this question of what it meant to have a family and to be ambitious."

Eva searched for a solution to manage the tensions between what she described as a calling for life and a calling for her journalism profession. For guidance, she got clear on what mattered to her: place, people, and profession. This was her Right Foundation.

For place, Eva and her husband set a vision and put a plan in motion to move to his home country, Australia, where he dreamed of opening a vineyard. In such a place, they believed they could live and invest in, by working fewer hours, a close-knit community. For profession, Eva had a vision to freelance, choosing a more flexible work style, knowing that more traditional roles would not accommodate the life she wanted. Yet the timing had to be right for that step. "It took me a really long time to get to the point where I felt like I could go freelance," she said. "We had our twins in 2010, and we always had this plan that as soon as the kids got to school age, we would move to Australia. We would be basically a starving writer and a starving farmer, and that's where we are."

At the time of our interview, Eva was working twenty to twenty-five hours a week. She was motivated to design this life for herself, and she wants it for others too. In 2015, Eva started the storytelling project "The Life I Want: A Future of Work That Works for All" to bring more visibility to how the world of work is changing, and not working for most. Through the project, she continues her exploration of innovative ways to be ambitious about life and work and has interviewed people exploring alternative ways of working to live rather than living to work.

"We're here on this planet not just to work but to live," Eva said.

Many of us who want to live with Sustainable Ambition would agree. What might it feel like to make choices like Eva did? To have that level of clarity of what you'd like for your life? To know where to anchor what you want, to set a vision, and then to take action to make it a reality? Your ambition will look different. It likely won't take you to Australia. But it will be yours, and right.

To be sure, crafting a life and making such choices is not easy. But with intentionality, more sustainable decisions can be made, even if your choice is to be fully ambitious. With Right Ambition, instead of defining success based on external measures, seeking external reward, we shift to define success on our terms, rooted in what we want so it's personally rewarding.

To do so and to pursue our ambitions more sustainably, as well as more resiliently, we anchor our ambitions in what matters and is meaningful and motivating to us, rather than solely relying on external guides to shape our success. That's what Eva did for herself and her life and work—she was clear on what was important to her and made choices for more personal fulfillment and satisfaction.

Like Eva, you'll start by getting clear on what's important to you to make your ambitions your own. To do that, you first need to know yourself.

RIGHT AMBITIONS ARE YOURS

As I share in Chapter 1, Right Ambition is defined by you and aligns with your personal definition of success, not society's. It is aligned with what you want to achieve or accomplish and what is personally rewarding to you, focusing on your own fulfillment and satisfaction. Why is that important? Because you will have more energy and put in the effort when your ambitions are personally meaningful and motivating, when they really matter to you.

Yet many of us can find ourselves saying, "But I don't know what I want." If this is you, know you aren't alone, and that's okay. In this section, you'll explore how to move from being cloudy to clearer. Such broad questions (What do you want?) can sometimes feel daunting without grounding in core elements that can guide you to what matters. People I've worked with have acknowledged this—that this concept to define one's own success isn't necessarily new to them, but they get stuck without a structure to uncover where to look. That's what I'm providing here.

What's helpful in this exploration is to embrace it as a learning journey, to explore and grow into your ambitions over time. Societal pressure makes us feel as if we are always supposed to know with certainty. And yet we are constantly learning, changing, and becoming. We can't know it all, and I don't think absolute clarity is good. If we are quite certain, we just may be using external guides rather than internal ones.

Motivations can provide the roots to and drive the effort for our ambitions. Based on academic research, we can define our own success by looking to four areas that tap into our personal motivations and make our ambitions personally meaningful to us. They are the vision we have for our life and work, how we want to give and contribute, our values, and what we love to do and experience. Vision, give, values, love. We can reference these four motivators when we ask questions like these: Do I want this ambition and am

I energized by it? How meaningful and motivating is this ambition to me? Would this be fulfilling and satisfying? How can I redefine or reinterpret my ambition to make it fulfilling and satisfying?

The exploration of these four motivators becomes our Right Foundation and guides our new measurement for success, our personal reward. It's in these elements that we can ground ourselves when we feel as if we don't know what we want, are navigating tensions across our goals, or want to increase our fulfillment and satisfaction to find personal success. Does it align to your vision? Are you giving and contributing in a way that is meaningful and energizes you and aligned to how you want to be in the world? Can you step into who you are by aligning to your values or what you love?

The goal with the exploration and exercises in this chapter is for you to build a foundation that anchors your own meaningful, motivating goals and your own definition of success and success metrics. This foundation will be what you work with as you move into the remaining chapters of the book and consider your current life and work ambitions, plan what it's time for now, and determine your effort and sustaining plan. How can these be informed by your vision for your life and work, how you want to give, your values, and what you love? The foundation provides deeper insight when you experience conflict and need to make choices.

This foundational grounding will help you become more conscious and intentional to motivate your effort and support greater sustainability. While I provide some exercises for exploration, know that it's important and helpful to make time and create space to get quiet for self-reflection, which I know some of us resist. It can feel self-indulgent and self-helpy. I get it.

But self-reflection is critical for learning and allows us to create meaning of our experiences to drive future actions. It's a way to take back our agency.

It might feel weighty to start here, but this is what will help you to craft what you want. Don't worry about getting your motivations crystal clear, perfect, and final. As I continue to note, knowing yourself takes time and is part of your life's journey of becoming more yourself. What you want is what you believe to be right for you now, in this moment in time. You'll sharpen what you know as you continue to experience life and recognize *Oh, what really matters to me is this, not that. Oh, something is shifting—what's important to me now is this, instead of that.* But now is a great time to get to know yourself better, so you can make want-to choices rather than have-to choices.

THE FOUR MOTIVATORS: WHERE TO LOOK FOR MEANING AND MOTIVATION

In this section, I introduce exercises for the four motivators: the vision you have for your life and work, how you want to give and contribute, your values, and what you love to do and experience. As a reminder, you create space in your calendar at the end of Chapter 2 for this purpose. But if you don't have time for each exercise per motivator, I also offer a simpler reflection at the end of the chapter.

Motivator 1: Know Your Vision

"We don't spend enough time thinking about and crafting a life we want," said Bridget Jones, founder of Smart Sister Finance and a finance coach for women.² Bridget is a former Fortune 100 executive with expertise in finance who exceeded her goal of retiring at the age of fifty. Bridget had a vision to have financial freedom earlier than most, having lost her father at a young age and acutely feeling that life is short. She became intentional about how she wanted to live her life and proactively worked toward it. It's why when she works with clients she has them think about and get clear on their life goals: for what are they working and making and saving money?

We start here, too, because without a vision and without direction, it's hard to drive action. Ambitions and goals point and pull us in a direction and marshal our effort. Imagine taking a trip and not knowing your destination. In what direction would you move first? When we don't have a sense of what we want to shape for ourselves and our lives, it is easy to operate from the socialized mind rather than a self-authored mind. We can start to live into what others want for us and be driven by external norms rather than listening to our own desires.

That's okay for a while, but I'm calling you now to pause the should treadmill and think about your own dreams. What do you want for your life and work? What really matters to you?

Many of us miss this step. Clay Christensen, the late Harvard Business School professor, business leader, and author of *How Will You Measure Your Life?*, found that successful people often didn't define a strategy and set goals to lead fulfilling lives beyond their careers. For this reason, at the end of one of his business school strategy classes, Christensen had his students work on a strategic plan for their life that went beyond their work, including focusing on prioritizing important relationships.³ He believed his students likely wouldn't take the time after school to do so, yet they needed a vision, a road map to guide their behaviors to align with their personal fulfillment for both life and work, even if they didn't realize it.

I know it sounds big and lofty to create a vision for what you want for your life and who you want to become. Many people get overwhelmed or immediately think, *I don't know!* But the problem, often, is that we've never paused to ask ourselves what we want. So I invite you to step into this exercise with a sense of exploration, play, and wonder and to avoid getting caught up in too much detail or being overly thorough. What we're shooting for here is a general direction and a few prioritized ambitions or goals to help you plan your actions as you move forward. Plus, this is just a start, and won't be static now or in the future. As you continue living your life, I encourage you to come back to your vision and sharpen it, as it will likely evolve over time as you, your life, or your values change or shift in priority.

What I've found in crafting a vision for myself and with clients is that key broad themes come into focus. A client recently told me that he has just two lifelong ambitions—to create lasting memories with his family and to write a book on leadership principles. When I first did a vision exercise, I realized that I had just a few core, bucket list–type goals that were important to me. One was more foundational: to establish financial stability to support myself and my extended family into old age. Another was about accomplishment and creativity: to write a book (here we are!). Another was about experience, challenge, and growth: I've always wanted to live abroad, and still hold that as an ambition for the right time. One is tied to community, to invest in relationships that are important to me. And finally, I had an ambition tied to contribution: to be someone who helps people feel seen and heard so they can become who they want to be in the world, and who helps people find sustainable success on their terms.

You'll notice that, for me, these operate on different levels. Some are more macro and outcome focused, like financial stability, which are supported by activities or other goals against which I spend time, like my work. Some are more project oriented, like the book or living abroad. And still others are more about ways to be and show up in the world—the focus on community and living into how I want to contribute and give back. Your ambitions and goals can operate on different levels, too.

What's Your Vision?

To build your Right Foundation, start with your vision. The idea is to identify a few goals you hold across your life and work. Don't limit yourself, but don't think that you have to have a long list, either. The possibilities are endless, and what's most important is that they are right for you. Here are a few examples of possible goals: go back to school for a PhD, earn enough for retirement and to put my kids through college, be a parent with strong relationships with my children, or get a black belt in martial arts.

To help identify your vision, let's work through the following two exercises.

FREE RESOURCES

Get free worksheets for these exercises and others throughout the book at SustainableAmbition.com/sa-toolkit.

Exercise: The Time Traveler's Guide— a Conversation with Your Future Self

This exercise puts you in conversation with your future self, and it's one I do with almost all my clients. Such future self-reflection is used in goal-pursuit psychology to clarify what we want and what's important, increase our motivation, sustain our effort, and connect our actions today with what we want for our future.

This approach is effective for many reasons. First, as humans we have a bias toward prioritizing the present moment over future rewards. We focus only on what we want now. I invite you to expand your view to see what you want to create for yourself in the future so that it can pull and guide you forward in the present.[4] Second, we also tend to think that we will remain the same, instead of thinking we can become something more or other than who we are today. Thinking about what we want to achieve in the future makes us more ambitious. Plus, research has found that we do change over time,[5] so why not envision who we can become and put intentional focus and action toward our vision? To start to create your vision, follow these four steps:

1. *Take a trip to meet your future self.* Get a blank piece of paper or create a space to capture notes for yourself. After you read these directions, close your eyes, choose your time-traveling device, and take yourself however many years forward in time so you can visit your future self. You pick the time horizon where you'll get off and pause to have a conversation with the person you have become.

2. *Imagine your best life.* Imagine that what you've manifested for yourself is exactly what you want. You think, *This has been*

a successful life! I've loved it! I've been fulfilled and satisfied! When you sit for this conversation, what would your future self tell you about how you had lived, who you had become, and what you had experienced over the span of time you've traveled into the future? What's transpired over this period?

3. *Capture what you've learned.* Write what you heard from your future self.

4. *Summarize your life and work ambitions.* Based on what you learned from this exploration, note the most important ambitions you have for your life and work.

Exercise: Dream a Little—What's Your Possible?

Another exercise I give to most of my clients is a simple visioning exercise to dream about what's possible. If you feel as though you really don't know what you want, I encourage you to give yourself a bit of time to allow your mind to wander and ponder. Mind wandering has been shown to reach different parts of our brain when we think about the future,[6] engage parts of our brain associated with goal setting,[7] and increase creativity.[8] Also, take this time to get excited to explore. While it can feel unsettling and unnerving to not know, it can also be exhilarating to step into possibility. My mentor has asked me, "Do you know what you want?" When I've answered no, in the past, she's said with exhilaration, "Good! There are all kinds of possibilities!" I love that reframe—to step away from anxiety and worry and step into what's possible. You can do that here, too, with the following steps.

1. *Get set up.* Start with a blank piece of paper. I encourage you

to use pen and paper or a digital device that allows you to sketch and write by hand rather than write via a keyboard, to allow you to be more creative with your visioning.

2. *Consider what's possible.* Think about what's possible for you across different parts of your life and the key areas outlined by the book *Wellbeing: The Five Essential Elements*: career (or vocation), social relationships, financial health, physical health and energy (including mental and emotional health), and community.

3. *Ideate and document what you uncover.* You can take different approaches to generate and capture your ideas. One approach could be to create a storyboard with multiple rectangles that have images of key events, activities, and experiences that have happened in your life. What images might go into these rectangles that represent what you dream for yourself? Another way is to draw inspirational pictures of what might happen or to pull images from online or magazines. Or simply write a list of what comes to you. When I do a list, I often draw circles and write a headline in each. The circle approach also allows me to draw lines radiating from the circle to capture related ideas and notes for each ambition or goal.

4. *Summarize your life and work ambitions.* Based on what you learned from this exploration, note the most important ambitions you have for your life and work.

Summarize Your Vision Ambitions

If you did both exercises, combine your summarized lists into two categories: life ambitions and work ambitions. If you have more than three in each list, add a star to the top three for both life and work. We come back to these in Part III.

Motivator 2: Know What You Want to Give and Contribute

Rebecca Williams is a communications and storytelling coach who works with clients to craft bigger stories for themselves. What she has found is that when people can connect the dots, uncover their broader narrative, and identify a greater purpose, it shifts their perspective and increases their energy around what they do.

Knowing our why gives us focus and motivates our effort. In our podcast interview, Rebecca shared how this is true for her: "I'm an entrepreneur. I work for myself. If you go that route, you have to know that you're going to work harder. So how are you going to get out of bed every morning? You better know *why* you're doing what you're doing, because it's going to demand a lot from you."[9]

Our why is a powerful motivator. Research shows that we have more motivation, fulfillment, and engagement in our work when we have a clear sense of purpose.[10] We can better prioritize where we want to put our attention and focus, direct our limited time and energy,[11] and resolve conflicts and tensions to get us to act. When we align to our purpose, we can improve our well-being[12] and build resilience.[13] So much good!

Plus, purpose has been linked to success. Morten Hansen, a professor at the University of California, Berkeley, wrote *Great at Work: The Hidden Habits of Top Performers* and found, in his research, that purpose trumps passion for successful workers.

Together, they outperform and should be the goal, but if you want to lean into one over the other, look to purpose.

In today's lexicon, we often use the term *purpose* to describe our why, as I have been doing. In Hansen's book, he writes that "you have a sense of purpose when you make valuable contributions to others (individuals or organizations) or to society that you find personally meaningful and that don't harm anyone."[14] But, importantly, he also shares how purpose doesn't have to be about contributing at the societal level. It is just as worthy to contribute to organizations or to others with whom you are involved.

Building on this definition, I prefer to think about giving, contribution, and making an impact, because it makes the concept more accessible, whereas *purpose* can often feel weighty and out of reach. We don't need a razzle-dazzle purpose. Rather, giving and contribution provide an avenue to positively define success on our terms. What do you want to give or contribute in a way that is meaningful to you? Who do you want to be in the world, and what impact do you want to make around you?

For example, giving and contribution could be offering insight and clarity to help move people forward. Or bringing kindness, empathy, and joy to every encounter. Or inspiring and supporting people in being their best selves. It could be looking for ways to give and contribute in each personal encounter. Any of these can be applied to life and work.

That brings us to a key point: Remember that you can look for purpose not just at work but also in your life pursuits. To be sure, most of us (70 percent, according to a study by McKinsey[15]) want to experience purpose in our work. That's a good thing for all the benefits noted earlier. And for some of us, we may find that purpose outside of work as well or instead.

I also want to normalize that your purpose—how you want to give and contribute—may take a while to gel for you or that it might shift with a change in life experiences. That's okay. You can start with an initial articulation and hold it loosely, allowing yourself to learn and grow into what that purpose might become or allowing it to change over time.

What's Your Give and Contribute?

Understanding how you want to give and contribute can help you define your ambitions, increase your satisfaction and fulfillment by linking to them, and motivate your actions and effort by creating meaning for the work you do.

This exercise will have you identify a few ways that you enjoy giving and contributing and why each is meaningful to you.

Exercise: Your Gifts to Give and the Gains

Let's explore your gifts to give and their associated gains to unpack what you like to contribute and to create meaning behind your effort.

You might find that how you give and contribute isn't static, based on your situation or as you grow and change. It's worth returning to the exercise over time. But to start with, focus on who you are now and your current circumstances. Explore with these four steps:

1. *Identify your gifts.* Consider your strengths and what you love to do. What can you give and contribute to those around you

and organizations with which you are involved, including your work? You might pull from past feedback from others, including performance reviews or any strengths assessments you've taken.

2. *Understand what others gain.* Consider the value you can create with what you want to give and contribute. What impact can you have?

3. *Understand your personal gain.* Reflect on why it would be meaningful to you to give and contribute in the way you've identified or to add value and have the impact you've noted. Table 3.1 provides an example of what this exploration might look like.

Table 3.1. Exploring your gifts to give and the gains

Gift: What can you give and contribute?	Gain: What value does that offer or what impact does that make?	Personal gain: This is meaningful to me because...
Kindness, empathy	Have people feel seen and included.	It's important to me that people feel good about themselves and acknowledged.
Listening and sharing what I've heard	Help people and organizations understand what they might not be hearing and find clarity.	I like to help people feel seen and heard and find clarity to move forward.
Commitment to learning and ideation	Generate new ideas for individuals and organizations.	I get energized by others embracing new possibilities.
Process orientation and structure	Help people and organizations create plans that move them forward.	I like to help people make progress on what's important to them.
Connecting and caring for others	Help people feel cared for and experience great service.	I enjoy interacting with people and want them to feel acknowledged.

4. *Reflect on your life and work.* Consider how you like to give and contribute. Identify at least one way that you can apply these in your personal life and one way that you can apply them to your work life. The following are examples of reflections on how you might contribute in your life and at work.

    - Life: Be a good listener as a friend and family member, acknowledge people in everyday life through kindness and compliments, volunteer in a way to demonstrate care.
    - Work: Be a partner and sounding board in problem-solving, coach and mentor those around me, create psychological safety for people to try new things, fail, and learn.

Motivator 3: Values

I had a profound realization: *I can achieve success if I simply live according to my values.*

I paused to let that settle in when, over a decade ago, I first read about the concept of success beyond success[16] by Fred Kofman, an expert on leadership and culture and author of *Conscious Business: How to Build Value through Values*. It was the first time I recognized that a path was available to me to root success solely in who I am, a path that didn't need external societal guides. I could achieve my own success, which I can completely control, simply by living in congruence with my values. To crystallize this concept, think of someone you consider to be successful by traditional societal metrics, like a billionaire or a famous person. How could they have a feeling of success beyond external measures? They, too, could live according to their values.

For me, this was a simple and powerful concept. Ever since, I have used this as a test. Am I striving for external rewards, or have I grounded my ambitions and how I measure my success based on my values? Can I calm my anxiousness and comparison to others around achievement by shifting my focus to how I'm committed to my values? In this way, values offer a powerful way to redefine our success and claim it as our own.

Values are another way to understand what we want. They represent what's important and matters to us, guiding our choices and behaviors. In scientific terms, this is tied to what's called "identified motivation," a goal that is meaningful to us and expresses our values and aligns to who we are. Values also motivate our action and effort. Academic studies have shown that aligning our goals with our values leads to more satisfaction, higher persistence, and more goal attainment.[17]

Value fulfillment theory, developed by Dr. Valerie Tiberius, a philosophy professor at the University of Minnesota, supports the concept of values being aligned to our success. In her book *What Do You Want Out of Life?*, she writes, "The value fulfillment theory says that to live well is to succeed in terms of our own values."[18] What's also powerful through Tiberius's lens is that values create less friction. She notes, "Values are goals that are high up in our hierarchy and ones we are not internally conflicted about."[19] As such, they are a good foundation to help us make choices and prioritize how we use our time and effort across stages of our life and work. We can reduce some tension (not all!) by rooting our ambitions in our values.

Conflict may still arise when goals rooted in values are in competition with each other or shift on us unexpectedly. As I share in Chapter 2, the weighting and importance of values can change over time. In my interview with Dr. Art Markman, professor of psychology, human dimensions of organizations, and marketing at the University of Texas at Austin, he emphasized the importance of getting clear on what we value in the moment and focusing on what we care about, not what external systems and others have told us to care about. Why? Because, he said, "The closer I can get to engaging in activities that allow me to express those values, the more that I am going to feel in a sustainable way that I am succeeding at the work that I'm doing."[20]

What doesn't feel like success? Dr. Markman went on to say, "I think when people begin to feel like they are putting in a lot of effort and not succeeding, it is often because the accumulation of the work that they're doing feels like a mismatch to some of [their] values."

Simply, values alignment matters. Rooting our ambitions in our values can help ensure we're aligned to our personal success and acting and behaving consistently with what matters to us.

What Are Your Values?

It's time to learn what you value across your life and work. First, you'll identify your values, and second, you'll define each value to articulate how it uniquely shows up in your life or work. We may share a similar value like creativity, but how we want to express creativity may be different (e.g., writing, painting, dancing). This detail will serve you well as you move forward into the next parts of the book and determine what to prioritize in your life and work arc and in your sustaining plan.

At the end, you will have identified three to five values across both life and work (this could result in ten total, not that you have to be so precise) and have defined what these mean for you.

Exercise: Your Highlight Reel

It's a common coaching practice to uncover values through highlighting key events in a person's life and work—what I call a "highlight reel." This approach is rooted in self-reflection because it's a way for us to excavate our experiences and evaluate them to create understanding and meaning.

In this exercise, you will explore "highlight experiences" to find out which resonated with you and which didn't, to inform what you value. I suggest you do this exercise through both a life and a work lens. You are likely to find that you have values that cross between both domains, but you may also find that you have values that apply in one area and not the other. Uncover your values with these steps:

1. *Identify your highlight experiences—the dramatic highs and lows over the course of your life.* Consider your life and work experiences thus far and think of the positive, dramatic highlights, experiences that you found rewarding and where you felt alive, powerful, or joyful. Write those across the top of the page in chronological order from left to right, putting your life experiences at the top and work experiences below. For life, these could include anything from a creative experience, a travel experience, or starting a family (with more specificity than I note here). For work, these could include anything from a successful project, being on stage at an

event, or coaching employees. Then think about the negative, dramatic lows across your life and work, experiences you found draining or where you might have been frustrated or angry. Write those at the bottom of the page, with life experiences at the top and work experiences below. Across the range, note at least three experiences for both life and work, or more as you desire.

The Highlight Reel Timeline

Dramatic Highs
Life _____
Work _____

Dramatic Lows
Life _____
Work _____

2. *Reflect to uncover your values.* Consider the positive experiences you identified. What made you feel alive, powerful, or joyful in those moments? What values were honored? Conversely, look at the negative experiences. What made you feel drained, frustrated, or angry in those moments? What values were violated? As you do this exercise, it may be helpful to reference a list of values. You can find a list at SustainableAmbition.com/sa-toolkit.

3. *Summarize your top values.* Create a list of up to five values for both life and work. If you have more, capture them, but don't feel the need to have a long list. While it's helpful to prioritize values, you also don't have to feel pressured

to narrow them down if you have multiple values that are important to you.

4. *Make your values clear.* For each value you noted, go deeper to determine why the value is important and how it shows up in your life by answering the following prompts.

    - I am someone who appreciates . . .
    - What this value looks like in my life is . . .
    - This is important to me because . . .

See Table 3.2 for an example.

Motivator 4: Know What You Love

Mike Trigg worked for twenty-five years in Silicon Valley as a founder, executive, and investor in dozens of venture-funded technology start-ups. He knew the trials and tribulations of start-up life, and after a few failures, he learned to focus on the joy of his job, not the outcome of an exit to earn millions.

"As I did start-ups later in my career, I was doing it because I loved that part of the process," he said in our podcast interview. "I wasn't so focused on the outcome, because I knew from experience that the outcome is very, very hard to realize. If you're only doing it for the outcome, chances are you're going to be upset and disappointed."[21]

What Mike was attuned to is what science calls "intrinsic motivators" and what I call "knowing what you love." Intrinsic motivators are internally derived benefits and come from the experience itself.

Table 3.2. Value detail examples

Value	Value for life, work, or both	I am someone who appreciates ...	What this value looks like in my life is ...	This is important to me because ...
Financial stability	Life	Feeling secure around my financial well-being	Saving regularly, being thoughtful about my purchases, investing	I want to lower my stress around finances, be able to support my family, be able to fund retirement.
Variety and complexity	Work	Being able to work across multiple topics and dig into complexity	Working on multiple different types of projects at one time	I'm more engaged when I get to work on more than one thing and avoid boredom.
Growth and learning	Both	Always being on a growth curve and learning new concepts I can apply to my life and work	Taking classes, reading fiction and nonfiction, listening to webinars, attending talks, going to museums	I want to better myself, and I get a lot of personal satisfaction and joy from learning.

These are activities that you enjoy and satisfy you or merit putting in the effort to succeed, such as learning new topics, building skills, or mastering a competency. Like Mike, you'd do it for the experience itself, not the outcome.

Loving what you do and enjoying the process of working on the goal are key to boosting your motivation, fueling your effort, and sustaining your pursuit. Dr. Ayelet Fishbach, a professor at the University of Chicago Booth School of Business and an expert on motivation and decision-making, in her book *Get It Done,* writes, "Intrinsic motivation is the best predictor of engagement in just about everything. . . . When we set goals that are intrinsically motivating or apply strategies that increase intrinsic motivation, we have a better chance at success."[22]

This sounds obvious: *Motivate myself by doing activities I enjoy and love.* Of course. Yet, when we make decisions, we often don't prioritize these factors. Instead, we prioritize and make decisions based on extrinsic rewards, like with work and choosing a job based on titles, salaries, and a promotion. Interestingly, research shows that focusing on these extrinsic rewards actually lowers interest in the work.[23] Perhaps this is why at some point, extrinsic rewards can stop motivating us. Plus, it's been found that those who set intrinsic over extrinsic goals are happier and experience more satisfaction.[24]

> Loving what you do and enjoying the process of working on the goal are key to boosting your motivation, fueling your effort, and sustaining your pursuit.

A final point: Don't think that leaning into intrinsic motivators means what we work on should solely be about enjoyment. Research by Barry Schwartz, the professor and psychologist known for his work on the paradox of choice, and Amy Wrzesniewski, an organizational psychologist at the Wharton School of the University of Pennsylvania, shows that doing work you love is not all about pleasure; that we will do unpleasant activities, as long as they serve working toward something we want to master or achieving a level of excellence.[25] For example, practicing athletic or musical drills is not much fun but is often done to become a better athlete or musician. Schwartz and Wrzesniewski also state that what's more important is the association between the activity and the outcome rather than the outcome itself. So don't just focus on what makes you happy and activities that are enjoyable. Think about where you eagerly put in effort, what you want to practice, and where you want to excel. Is the activity serving a meaningful goal worth the effort?

This is all to say success on your terms can also be rooted in intrinsic motivators and focusing on doing what you love in service to a meaningful goal. We are more likely to experience personal success, satisfaction, and sustainability if we link our ambitions and goals to what we love.

So let's start to uncover what you love, while also becoming aware of what you don't.

What Do You Love?

We learn what we love, and what we don't, by doing and testing, not just through thinking. *Do I like chocolate or caramel ice cream? Let me think about it.* No. You have to taste them and see what your taste buds tell you. We can uncover what energizes us and drains us when we reflect on our behaviors and consider how we feel after we act.

Exercise: Your Love-and-Loathe List

In this exercise, you'll rely on self-reflection to uncover meaning from your recent past experiences. It's not difficult to identify what we love and loathe; it simply takes paying attention and being intentional in our observations.

At the end, you will have a list of activities you love—those that are energizing, light you up, leverage your strengths, or put you into a flow state when you are effortlessly and intently focused—and, importantly, also activities you loathe—those that drain you, sour your mood, don't leverage your strengths, and that you struggle to have energy to do. By the end of this exercise, target having at least three to five love and three to five loathe activities on your list that span life and work domains. You can capture more as suits you. These lists reveal activities you can add to your days to increase your fulfillment and satisfaction and those to avoid or reduce so they don't deplete you. Start here:

1. *Consider the past week.* Pull out your calendar from the last week and go day by day through your activities. Reflect and consider when you were energized, excited, felt your best, or felt focused and in the zone. Capture these moments on your love list and put each into the life or work category, as appropriate. Consider also when you were drained and not energized. Put these on your loathe list and under either life or work. Summarize those activities that most pull you toward them (love) and those that you push away (loathe). See Table 3.3 for an example.

2. *Pause to reflect.* Take a moment to look at the full lists. What do you notice for yourself when you consider both lists? What might you want to add or move toward, and what would you want to avoid or move away from? What's become clear to you having done this exercise?

3. *Bonus: Review your calendar for the past three, six, or twelve months.* You can repeat the same exercise for a longer time frame to gain more insight, uncover seasonal impacts, and see deeper patterns. It doesn't take as long as you might think to quickly scan your weeks across the quarter or year.

Table 3.3. A love-and-loathe list

Activities	Love	Loathe
Life	• Being physically active • Being outside in nature • Anything that helps me learn, like listening to podcasts, reading a book, or taking a class • Getting immersed in a novel • Bonding time with my partner and friends • Personal, one-on-one time with my kids • Attending my kids' activities, like sporting events or a dance recital	• Cooking dinner during the week • Cleaning the house • Running errands in traffic • Picking up after the family • Commuting to my job in a car • Paying bills and checking my finances
Work	• Listening to clients and helping them unlock an insight and move forward • Ideating with colleagues • Getting the best ideas on the table with my team • Having a seat at the table and a voice in decisions • Mentoring and coaching employees • Quiet thinking time • Problem-solving • Working on creative ideas • Working with my hands	• Administrative work • Constant back-to-back meetings with no time to think • Unproductive, unnecessary meetings • Constantly being on the road • Set times I have to be at work • Not having autonomy in how I do my work • Not being able to connect with people and build relationships in person on a regular basis

THE FOUNDATION TO MAKE CONSCIOUS CHOICES

You've now done the work to create the foundation to define your Right Ambitions and step into self-authorship. Amazing! My hope is that you also know yourself better, are clearer about and more conscious of what you want, and as such, are better armed to make courageous choices rooted in what's important to you. With this foundation, you can also shift your focus from external to internal rewards, finding success in what is personally meaningful and motivating to you.

Your Right Foundation includes:

- Your vision: You identified three or more priorities for your life and your work that you'll hold loosely and take as a guide as you start to plan your life and work arcs in Part III. These represent your desires for your life and who you want to become. At the end of your life, you would be fulfilled and say, "Now that's a life well lived."

- Your give-and-contribute list: This is a short list of how you like to give and contribute across your life and work to inform and help identify ambitions and goals, to guide who you want to be and become, and to motivate your effort.

- Your values: You identified your top five or so values for life and work, with details outlined so you know what to honor and how to prioritize activities and actions to find fulfillment and satisfaction.

- Your love-and-loathe list: This list guides you in what to add or avoid in your days and activities to optimize your satisfaction, enjoyment, and energy.

> **FOUR MOTIVATORS REFLECTION EXERCISE**
>
> Didn't have time for the individual four motivators exercises? I want to offer a shorter reflection exercise to generate inspiration for your Right Foundation. Spend thirty minutes to an hour with these questions.

- *Vision:* At the end of your life, what would you have needed to experience and who would you have needed to have been to say, "This has been a well-lived, successful life! I've loved it! I've been fulfilled and satisfied!" What would you regret or be disappointed to have not done or been?

- *Give:* What are your gifts and strengths? How do you like to contribute to others and to your vocation or work? What would you like to contribute and offer to those around you and to your world?

- *Values:* What is important and matters to you most in your life and in your work? What are adjectives that would describe how you want to be and show up in the world?

- *Love:* What activities do you enjoy, and which energize and excite you the most? When do you feel you're at your best or operating with effortless focus?

I can imagine you might have skipped some of the exercises, because they require time and space for proper reflection. I understand and encourage you to take breaks as needed—this is key to Sustainable Ambition. I offer the simpler four motivators reflection questions if you didn't have time for all the exercises now. These exercises will be available for you to complete and come back to when you can. My hope is the learning process becomes your foundation to claim your ambitions and success as your own and to make your life with work sustainable.

As you move forward in the book, you'll use your Right Foundation to choose self-defined, meaningful, motivating goals that are right for you now; make choices across life and work; and inform your sustaining plan.

With this foundation complete, most importantly, you will now know yourself better and have the foundation to refer to as part of your practice of creating Sustainable Ambition for yourself. When you continue to step into being more conscious about your ambitions and being self-authored, this foundation can guide you toward personal motivation and reward.

Let's move into the next chapter and start to put this newfound knowledge into practice.

Chapter 4
• • •

Make Your Ambitions Yours

In 2023, I saw a revival of *Merrily We Roll Along* in New York City. I didn't know anything about the play before I saw it, so it surprised me to find the themes of success and ambition central to the plot—themes that have plagued us since long before the play's creation. The play itself was originally written in 1934, chronicling American society from World War I to the Great Depression. The musical adaptation, written with songs by Stephen Sondheim and George Furth, first played on Broadway in 1981.

The show is told in reverse chronological order, perhaps as a reminder that we can't see the dangers and consequences of unconscious choices ahead of time but only in hindsight. It opens at the home of Franklin Shepard, where a party is in progress celebrating the premiere of his latest film. Frank, a talented songwriter who started his career creating musicals, abandoned his dreams and his creative partner, Charley Kringas, to pursue making and producing movies in Hollywood. Mary Flynn, a dear friend of Frank and Charley's from their young adult days, is visiting. Instead of being in awe of Frank's accomplishments, she's anything but impressed and is disgusted by the scene in front of her and disappointed by what he has prioritized over the years.

The friends quarrel, and Mary storms out, leaving Frank distraught too. At that moment, he's forlorn in viewing what's become of his life. How did he get here?

At the end of the play, you see what their lives were like at the start of their friendship and what choices they had in front of them. The friends—Frank, Charley, and Mary—are optimistic and excited about the possibilities that lie ahead for what they can create and who they can become.

How did I get here? I imagine Frank thought at that party at the start of the play, looking back at his life and journey. He just rolled along, perhaps in the end not so merrily, chasing external success and devoting all his time and attention to building his career while losing sight of his friends, family, and dreams.

Watching the play reminded me of what I often hear from people—that they just put their head down, pursued and achieved what was in front of them, and never paused to consider what they really wanted or to make conscious choices that connected to what motivated them. Just like Frank, despite external success, they, too, wonder how they got here. They may realize they no longer want what they achieved or question if they ever wanted it at all. They also realize that they are no longer merrily rolling along. Because when we focus only on external guides, we can lose ourselves and lose sight of what truly matters to us.

My intent with Right Ambition is to help you find your connection to your goals, to find your motivation and energy behind them. To not just merrily roll along and go with it, but to become more conscious and connect to where you are putting your time and effort. You can make your ambitions sustainable and successful by making them yours.

In this chapter, you learn how to test whether an ambition is yours and how to link your ambitions to find your motivation. What I mean by linking is to use your Right Foundation to identify your motivation behind a pursuit. How does a goal connect or link to one of your four motivators? Linking can be especially helpful when we work with what we think are external ambitions by seeing how or if we can connect them to what motivates us. Along these lines, linking helps us find our motivation for our have-tos and, in turn, hopefully helps us find some peace in putting effort toward what we think are shoulds. Because, let's be real—it's unrealistic to think we will always be ardently committed to all we are pursuing, but we can align to our motivators to find the energy for them. Finally, linking can help when opportunities pop up (I'm all for serendipity!), and we wonder if the opportunity is something we want to pursue. We may or may not find a connection to what motivates us, and in that, we have the information to decide what action we want to take next.

> You can make your ambitions sustainable and successful by making them yours.

The exercises I offer here do as intended for many people: help them find their motivation and create meaning behind their goals. My coaching clients and workshop participants have found that the exercises have helped them get unstuck, find direction, get more clarity, and recommit.

The final thing you'll do is create your own success metrics for your ambitions, a critical way to create your personal reward and define success on your terms. Eva Dienel, from the previous chapter, who was ambitious until three o'clock, championed this idea of personal success metrics, saying, "When I quit my job, I said I want to run as many miles a week as I work. I want to spend more nights camping outside. Those were going to be my measures of success for my life."[1]

My hope is to provide you with a road map to take responsibility and claim ambition and success as your own, perhaps shifting where you are putting your attention. Let's make sure you are putting your effort against the right ambitions for you now.

ARE YOUR AMBITIONS YOURS?

When I went to college, I had already started to question my ambitions: Did I want to be a University of Virginia guide? Or was I pursuing that ambition simply because it was what was respected and admired? University guides had a chance to live on the Lawn at the school, which is considered an honor (this was the university Thomas Jefferson designed with students' rooms on the Lawn next to pavilions for teaching). Did I want to give tours of the university so that I could possibly live on the Lawn? Did I like public speaking, and was the possible reward important to me? Was it a want-to or have-to? If I had had my Right Foundation, my motivators, to reference—my vision, give, values, love—it would have been easier to know. We'll get to that next.

But first, one way to determine whether your ambitions are a have-to or a want-to is to consider if they are externally or internally motivated and then to consider your energy. To do so, I created a Know It's Yours Map, a 2 × 2 matrix with the corresponding axes Ambition (Internal/External) and Energy (High/Low) for plotting your ambitions (see Figure 4.1). I've explained why it's important to understand where our goal motivation resides—internal and personally motivated or external and extrinsically motivated. The reason I point you toward energy for the second axis is because where we put our energy and effort is further confirmation of whether we are personally motivated. How we *feel*—our sense of energy—is a clue.[2]

The map provides a quick method to get a sense of what you might want to do when you experience tension, conflict, or uncertainty about pursuing a goal.

Figure 4.1. Know It's Yours Map

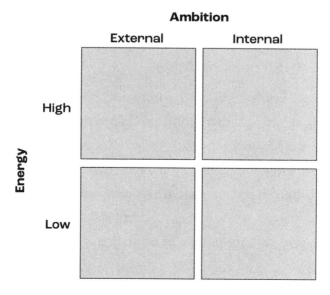

Exercise: Know If It's Yours

Let's explore mapping an ambition or goal of your own. Is the ambition self-defined and meaningful—a want-to, not a have-to? At the end, you'll have greater clarity around how you want to move forward with your ambition, what you might need to further explore and consider, and the next action you'll take. Follow these steps:

1. *Identify one ambition you want to map.* Choose an ambition or goal you identified as part of your vision exercise in the prior chapter. Or consider one that gives you angst rather than energy, that you feel tension around, or that feels unsustainable.

2. *Determine if it is an internal or external ambition.* Check your ambition against your Right Foundation and see how it aligns to your motivators. How meaningful and motivating is this ambition to you? If it feels highly meaningful and motivating, it leans toward the right side of the map and is internal. If it doesn't feel very meaningful and motivating, then it may be external.

3. *Check your energy.* Tap into your bodily awareness and insight around this ambition. How much energy do you naturally have for it now? Are you drawn to it and energized by it? How much energy are you putting into it? Map your ambition to the appropriate quadrant according to whether your energy is low or high. Figure 4.2 shows an example of mapping an internal ambition that you have low energy for.

4. *Reflect on the mapping.* Note where your ambition lands on the map and how it aligns to which quadrant: Confirm,

Figure 4.2. Low energy for an internal ambition

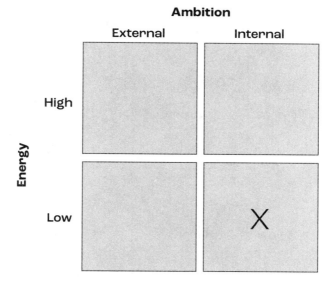

Question, Link, or Resolve (see Figure 4.3). Based on where it lands, you can consider what step to take next.

- *Confirm* your intention. It's likely a Right Ambition, given that it is internally driven and you have high energy for it.

- *Question* the ambition for further understanding. It may be an internal ambition, but your energy is low—why? It could be that it's just not the right time for the ambition, because you don't have the energy for it now. It could also be that you haven't fully linked the ambition to your Right Foundation to motivate your energy and make the ambition yours, which you can explore in the next exercise. Or you may be experiencing fear, or limiting beliefs are diminishing your energy and sabotaging your desire to go for it. Tread carefully here!

Figure 4.3. Quadrants to determine your next action

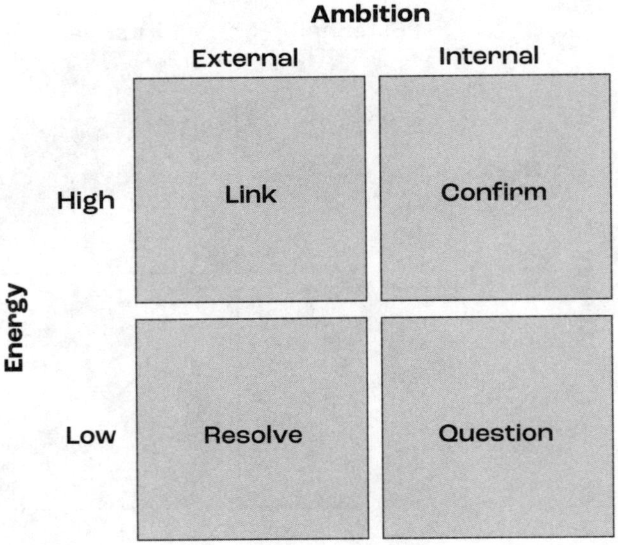

	Ambition	
	External	Internal
High (Energy)	Link	Confirm
Low	Resolve	Question

- *Link* the ambition to your motivators to create more meaning. You have energy, but it seems as though it's an external ambition. Can you make it yours and make it more satisfying and fulfilling by linking it to your Right Foundation?

- *Resolve* how you want to proceed. It may not be a Right Ambition, given that it is externally driven and low energy. Consider the additional strategies I share after step 5.

5. *Determine your action.* Choose what's next based on your personal reflection. This isn't formulaic, so use your best judgment to guide what decision makes most sense for you now. The next exercise can help further confirm your

intention, support your questioning and understanding, and link the ambition to your motivators.

Ambitions and goals that we need to resolve—those that fall into the bottom left quadrant in the mapping (external/low energy)—tend to create the most friction for us. Too often, many of our ambitions or simple to-dos fall here. What do we do with such ambitions or tasks?

The main objective is to shift our mindset around them to reduce the frustration we may hold. How can we come to peace with these ambitions and to-dos, or how can we minimize their impact on our energy and time?

We can start by considering whether it is truly an ambition or simply a to-do that must be managed. Not everything on our to-do list rises to the level of a major ambition. By making this mental shift, perhaps we can reduce our attachment to how much effort we might put into an activity. Remember, too, we often have shoulds we must do. We won't love everything we are asked to do at work or in our personal lives. This is a reality we have to accept.

Yet I get it—these can still eat up our energy and time and take away from the other pursuits that truly matter to us. I go deeper into strategies for prioritizing where we put our effort in Part III. For now, beyond eliminating such ambitions or to-dos, here are four strategies to consider: (1) limit how much effort you put into it; (2) outsource, delegate, or get help with it; (3) do your best to link it to your Right Foundation to motivate your effort—connect it to your vision, give, or values—and think about how it might support other ambitions and values you hold; and (4) link it to something you love to do to make it more enjoyable.

EVALUATE AND LINK AN AMBITION

As I shared earlier, it would have been easier for me to decide if I wanted to be a guide in college if I'd had my Right Foundation to help me in that evaluation. I could have considered whether it would help me pursue my vision for my life. Would it have aligned with how I like to give and contribute or with a value I held? And would it have connected to an activity I love? I would have realized, with much less struggle and wasted energy, that it wasn't a fit and that I preferred to pursue being on the yearbook committee, as that aligned better to my Right Foundation. This simple alignment exercise would have cut short my deliberation and saved my energy for more important endeavors.

Our Right Foundation can also help us find more meaning and motivation in our ambitions and goals, especially in those that we may think are externally driven. The following exercise helps us dig deeper to make the connections to create more fulfillment and satisfaction. Can we link the ambition or goal to at least one of our foundational elements to make the goal matter to us and shift it toward being a Right Ambition? You can apply this to life goals, like raising kids or caring for parents, or work goals, like finding more meaning in your current job. It's not wrong to have externally driven goals per se, yet linking can help us experience greater fulfillment and satisfaction in them and make them more sustainable when they are aligned to who we are or who we want to become. On the flip side, you may find that such linking doesn't result in any connection or meaning. Perhaps you can't identify why it matters to you. In that case, the ambition isn't yours and you may want to make a different decision.

This exploration doesn't have to take a lot of time, but reflection can help you get unstuck, find direction, or recommit to your goal, as I've found with clients and workshop participants. It can offer new perspective and direction. It can be validating, inspiring, and energizing.

Exercise: Make It Meaningful and Motivating

This exercise builds on the previous one to help you go deeper in understanding your ambition and can further help you confirm your intention, support your questioning and understanding, and determine how to proceed.

You'll link an ambition to your Right Foundation to see how it connects to your motivators: Does the ambition align to your vision? Are you giving and contributing in a way that energizes you? Does the ambition align to your values or what you love to do? Use the following steps to rate and evaluate an ambition and determine how you want to proceed based on your reflection.

1. *Identify the ambition or goal.* Work from the ambition or goal you mapped in the previous exercise. Alternatively, if you come back to this exercise in a nonlinear fashion, consider a current ambition or goal that you are curious about, or pick one that gives you angst rather than energy, that you feel tension around, or that feels unsustainable.

2. *Rate the ambition or goal.* Assess how much you agree with this statement: "I want this ambition or goal." Rate on a scale of 1 to 5: 5 = strongly agree, 4 = agree, 3 = neither agree nor disagree, 2 = disagree, 1 = strongly disagree.

3. *Evaluate the ambition or goal.* Reflect on and write how

the ambition or goal connects, or doesn't, to your Right Foundation using these prompts across vision, give, values, and love.

- Vision: How does this ambition or goal connect to the vision you have for yourself?
- Give: How does this ambition or goal allow you to give or contribute?
- Values: What is important to you about this ambition or goal? What value does it serve?
- Love: How does this ambition or goal allow you to do something that you love?

4. *Rewrite your ambition or goal.* Rearticulate your meaningful, motivating goal based on what you learned in your evaluation. If it's a Right Ambition, make it clear to help energize you and spur you into action.

5. *Rate the ambition or goal again.* Assess how much you agree with this statement: "I want this ambition or goal." Rate on a scale of 1 to 5: 5 = strongly agree, 4 = agree, 3 = neither agree nor disagree, 2 = disagree, 1 = strongly disagree. Did the rating shift up or down for you, or did it remain the same? What does that mean for you?

6. *Determine your next actions steps.* Complete these final reflections. What do you need to further explore or consider, if anything, to determine next steps? What actions will you take next? Table 4.1 provides an example.

Table 4.1. Example of linking an ambition to your Right Foundation

	Ambition: writing a book	Ambition: exercise
Starting rating:	5	4
Vision: How does this ambition or goal connect to the vision you have for yourself? • If you were to step out to the end of the year and be your future self, what might they share with you about this goal and how it relates to what they want for you? • What will you think about this goal at the end of this year? Ten years from now?	• It supports a body of work that is my own.	• I grew up an athlete, so I view myself that way. • I want to continue to be healthy and strong as I grow older to remain active. • I want to have the energy to do the things I want to do throughout life.
Give: How does this ambition or goal allow you to give or contribute? • What are you committed to around this goal? • What impact do you want to have? • What do you want to give? What will they gain? What gifts will you use?	• I want to help people feel less angst and more joy and ease around their life and work. • I want to help people find more clarity of what they want around their work with less anxiety and more adventure. • My purpose is to help people succeed on their terms. • I do this through offering synthesized research and tools.	• Staying healthy allows me to have energy to support family and friends and do my service work.
Values: What is important to you about this ambition or goal? What value does it serve? • What matters to you about this? • How will this be rewarding to you?	• This is important to me because I want to have a voice in the world. • I value and am someone who appreciates creative production and growth and learning. • It will be rewarding to have created something of value.	• I value vitality—being healthy and feeling physically strong.

continued

Love: How does this ambition or goal allow you to do something that you love? • What makes it satisfying to you? • What makes it enjoyable to you? • What makes it worth the effort?	• I love being strategic, thinking, finding patterns, and developing structures to help solve a problem. • I love being in conversation with people to learn.	• I love to move my body and be in nature.
Rewritten goal:	I want to write a book as part of my body of work to feed my desire for creativity and to add value and help people succeed on their terms.	I am committed to staying healthy and strong to support all I want to do in life.
Ending rating:	5	5
Further explore and consider:	Determine the right timing to take this on.	I need structure. What classes and support will help me?
Next steps:	Research support resources	Research classes

FREE RESOURCES

Get free worksheets for this exercise and others throughout the book at SustainableAmbition.com/sa-toolkit.

DEFINE YOUR PERSONAL SUCCESS METRIC

"Choose the right yardstick." That's what Clay Christensen, the Harvard Business School professor, wrote about the importance of personal metrics in closing his well-known *Harvard Business Review* article on the topic of life success. He wrote, "This is my final recommendation: Think about the metric by which your life will be judged, and make a resolution to live every day so that in the end, your life will be judged a success."[3]

Define your own success, define your own metrics. That's what I say. Recall the metrics that Eva Dienel created for herself—she wanted to run a certain number of miles in a week and camp a certain number of nights a year. That was success on her terms. We can't control how the external world will evaluate our ambitions or goals. What we can control is what our ambitions or goals mean and how they please us.

I practice this regularly, as it is easy to get pulled into measuring ourselves against external metrics. As humans, we naturally look to external evaluation because it, too, is a motivator that confirms our competence, supports self-efficacy, measures our goal progress and performance, and ties our effort to our desired outcomes.

But external measurement can turn sour. We can lose motivation when it starts to overshadow intrinsic motivations and when we believe our efforts are tied just to external rewards, turning an activity we love into something we loathe.[4] In contrast, we are more committed to our goals when we set the targets ourselves rather than rely on such external metrics.[5]

One way I practice taking back control is to remind myself to focus on what is personally rewarding. I root my goal in my Right Foundation and look to my personal success metrics that are meaningful and motivating, so they mute the negative effect. I'll admit—it happens over and over. For example, I'm often asked about the size of my podcast audience or if I make money off it. At first, I feel a sting, a sense of judgment and evaluation, and think, *I know. It's not a big, syndicated show. I may be wasting my time and energy with it.* But upon quick reflection, I can move myself forward with a more positive stance and answer, "No, not directly, but it's an asset that pays personal and professional dividends." I go on to share all the ways it is rewarding to me—how it pays out according to my metrics such as in my personal learning and how the insights apply to my business and coaching—and why it's well worth my effort for others and myself. I can also get swept up in the comparison game when I look at my number of LinkedIn post "likes" or when people share the number of subscribers on their newsletter lists. Here I shift my attention to what matters to me instead—building new connections with partners and feeling like I'm part of a community of like-minded people.

The external forces around us are strong. So continually, I practice stepping into what is important to me and remind myself of my personal rewards. How can I feel successful, satisfied, and fulfilled on my own terms? This is where I can be more grounded and find genuine personal happiness, especially when it's connected to my Right Foundation.

Let's wrap up making your ambitions yours with this final exercise to define your personal success metrics, leveraging what you've learned about yourself through your Right Foundation and what you've learned about the ambition or goal you've been exploring.

Exercise: Your Success, Your Success Metrics

Here, you'll do a short self-reflection exercise to create a personal, meaningful, motivating success metric based on the insights you've gained creating your Right Foundation. To make them more motivating, write your success metrics to be actionable and easy to measure. For example: Learn at least one new insight from each podcast conversation. Create your metrics with these four steps:

1. *Identify the ambition or goal.* Work from the last ambition or goal you mapped, as long as it is a Right Ambition. Alternatively, if you found in the last exercise that the goal isn't a Right Ambition, or if you come back to this exercise in a nonlinear fashion, consider a current ambition or goal that you believe is a Right Ambition for you and do the prior Make It Meaningful and Motivating exercise before proceeding to the next step.

2. *Reflect on what personal success means to you.* Considering what you learned in the previous linking exercise, define what personal success looks like for you around this ambition or goal. Answer the prompt, "My personal reward looks like . . ." Refer to your Right Foundation if needed.

3. *Create your metric.* Define your personal success metric by answering the prompt, "I'll measure my success by . . ." See Table 4.2 for an example.

4. *Revisit as needed.* As you move forward in pursuing your ambition or goal, come back to your personal definition of success and your success metric to claim your own success and personal reward and to help quiet any noise from external influences.

WHAT TO DO IF YOUR AMBITIONS ARE NOT YOURS

In this chapter, you've explored an ambition you identified as part of your vision exercise, or one that gives you angst rather than energy, that you feel tension around, or that feels unsustainable.

Table 4.2. Example of a completed success metric

Ambition or goal	Personal success: My personal reward looks like . . .	Personal success metric: I'll measure my success by . . .
Maintain the *Sustainable Ambition* podcast	Supporting guests in their goals. Offering listeners helpful insights. Enjoying meeting new people, interviewing, being in conversation, and learning from others.	Featuring guests in other mediums. Tracking whether listeners connect with guests' content or business. Tracking listener response. Tracking at least one new lesson from each interview, feedback on my interviewing technique, and enjoyment of conversations.
Build community and connection with family and friends	Feeling like I've deepened my connection and relationship with others and learned about who they are.	Spending dedicated time at least two times a month with family or friends where I challenge myself to be fully present during the experience.
Build consulting business	Contributing a new insight or helping a client move forward in each interaction, engagement, or assignment.	Listening deeply to strive to add valuable insight in every meeting and interaction. Creating a "make progress plan" or "carrying this forward plan" with every final deliverable.
Maintain coaching practice	Helping my clients feel seen, heard, and supported in achieving their personal success by finding more clarity in the moment to move forward.	Coaching so each client has an aha moment and helping them create an action plan to move them forward around their growth agenda.

In doing this work to make your ambitions yours, you may have found confirmation of your motivation and meaning behind it and found more clarity and commitment. For example, with an ambition that emerged from your vision work, my hope would be that you are more grounded in how that is a Right Ambition for you.

But for those ambitions and goals you explored where you were already experiencing tension, you may have either become grounded or unmoored. You may have been able to link an externally derived goal for more meaning and to motivate yourself, or you might now be wondering what to do if you found that you don't want the ambition, that it is a have-to that you want to put down.

It can be hard to cut your losses or shift away from something you don't want anymore. How hard likely depends on the scale of the ambition or goal. Giving up my ambition to run a marathon is different than giving up my ambition to live abroad or have resources to care for my family. Giving up starting a venture-backed start-up could be different than giving up having a family or another child. Walking away from an ambition to become a doctor could be different than walking away from learning how to play the guitar. But it all depends on you—what's important to you and what your emotional attachments are to these goals.

What's real is coming to terms with giving something up and giving yourself permission to feel what you feel. On the positive side, you may experience relief and jubilation. *Yes! I give myself permission to move on from this goal!* You may experience a newfound freedom and feel unshackled from expectations.

Or you may experience grief stepping away from an ambition. What's key is to be patient, compassionate, and caring with yourself as you come to terms with an important goal ending. You may need time and space to process this shift and could find comfort talking with friends and family who are empathetic and good listeners. You may want to seek professional help to support you through the experience. Slowly but surely, with active attention and space, you'll find you can move forward.

You may also have to have conversations where you make your decision known to others who were enrolled in your pursuit of that ambition: people like your parents, your spouse, a boss, or possibly friends. These aren't easy but are necessary to bring people along with you and to get their support and alignment, especially with a partner or, potentially, other family members (think kids who are affected or parents who may have paid for your education).

Finally, it's not uncommon to feel like you wasted your time pursuing an ambition. Yet you can think about the sunk-cost fallacy and accept that you can't change the past (that's the sunk cost), but you can choose how you move forward knowing that you are better off moving on from the goal. What's helpful is to give yourself grace, understand that you made the best decision you could at the time, and know that you can take forward all that you've learned to date and apply those lessons in the future.

> Be patient, compassionate, and caring with yourself as you come to terms with an important goal ending.

A final reassurance around releasing a goal is to remember that ambitions have more likelihood of being sustainable and successful by making them your own.

• • •

When it comes to claiming your ambition and success, remember that your Right Foundation and these tools are practices you can revisit to help ground you and find clarity as you move forward. Taking time to be more conscious about your choices can help you avoid just merrily rolling along. Instead you may think, *Oh yes, this is why I want to do that. I'm in!* Or you may think, *Oh no. This isn't what I want to do after all. I'm out!* Both are great responses—if they are *right* for you.

A final word—I want to acknowledge that this work and navigating our ambitions in general can bring up a range of emotions, as we've just explored. Before we move on to Part III and determining what's a priority now for your life and work, let's dive further into navigating our emotions around our ambitions.

Chapter 5

● ● ●

Navigate the Ups and Downs of Ambition

Sonya Thomas was over her ambitions. In a workshop I was leading, asking her to think about her ambition for the next five to ten years of her life was a hard no. "I can't do that, Kathy. I already went after my ambitions, and it's left me spiraling."

Sonya had performed well at her private high school in Alabama. She'd excelled in college too and landed a solid job as she entered adult life. She continued the trajectory, attending a top business school and establishing a successful career in marketing, earning good income and enjoying the work. But years in, as she looked at the next rung in the company and saw what could be next for her, that also became a hard no. She had put a lot of effort into her ambitions and had succeeded. But here she stood—unhappy, disillusioned, and lost. "If this isn't what I want to do after all, what now?" she asked.

Up to this point, Sonya had been ambitious. But after this experience, she was over her ambitions. She felt they had steered her wrong, landing her in a place that didn't deliver what many of us seek—to be satisfied and feel fulfilled in both life and work. But what would it look like to not be ambitious? Sonya was a striver. Ambition was part of her identity. If she wasn't ambitious, who was she?

Sonya certainly isn't the only one to have this experience, or the only one to have such feelings about ambition. Emotions can run high as we navigate what we pursue in our lives. Coming out of the COVID-19 pandemic, Amil Niazi wrote in *The Cut*, "2022 may be the year my ambition truly dies, and to that I say, 'Good riddance, bitch.'"[1] I heard a similar level of frustration in a client call, mid-pandemic, with a mid-career woman who exclaimed that she wasn't sure what she wanted for her life and how work should and could fit in. She longed for a way to remain ambitious and stay engaged with work yet make it all a bit more sustainable.

My goal with helping you develop a Right Foundation and create Right Ambitions is to help you get more comfortable with your ambitions by rooting them and your success in what is meaningful and motivating to you. The hope in doing so is that it will reduce high degrees of misalignment and future frustration.

But emotions are unlikely to go away completely (we are human, after all), and you'll likely still feel tensions even when you have heartfelt, genuine ambitions that you choose and pursue. I face this myself, and I see it with my clients and workshop participants, so I want to prepare you for similar feelings, which could already be surfacing for you.

You may, at times, encounter friction or resistance in the form of tensions with want-tos and have-tos, making comparisons, having doubts and lacking confidence, overstretching yourself, and experiencing disappointment. In this chapter, I address the most common niggling voices and offer some tips to help you quiet and move past them. These voices fall into three areas: (1) where right ambitions meet realities and responsibilities, (2) right-size ambitions, and (3) keep ambitions in the healthy and happy zone.

I also want to be honest and direct here: Dealing with your emotions around ambition can take personal work. While I am a coach, I'm not a psychologist or psychotherapist. So I don't want to overpromise or overstep in what I can deliver in this chapter. While I want to offer some insight into how to navigate your emotions around these topics, I also want to be realistic and acknowledge that unpacking your internal wiring can take additional time with professionals or on your own. External pressures get embedded in us early and over time, and therefore, it takes time to rewire our mindsets and behaviors to be more productive and empowering. This is also why I want to reiterate that Sustainable Ambition is a practice that needs repetition. It doesn't mean anything is wrong with you. You're simply human and learning to navigate this life, along with everyone else.

WHERE RIGHT AMBITIONS MEET REALITIES AND RESPONSIBILITIES

It's a reality—we need to operate in a world with existing structures, and we need to consider other people, including those we care about. In navigating our ambitions over time, it's not uncommon to find ourselves feeling off track, experiencing tension between what we want and what society wants of us, and needing to balance what we want with personal responsibilities.

Did I Really Want This?

Like Sonya, people can find themselves in the unnerving situation where they set their course to pursue ambitions with the best of intentions, put in years of hard work, and wake up one day realizing that they aren't satisfied or fulfilled. They become disillusioned and unsure of what to do next.

Three intersecting factors can help explain why we can find ourselves in this position: our growth through the adult stages of development; learning more about ourselves over time; and the changes that we, our lives, and our environments go through, which all affect what satisfies and fulfills us.

With adult stages of development, remember it is natural early on to use external cues to guide us. So it should be expected that many of us will find ourselves ready to step into the next stage of self-authorship, where we'll want to lay claim to our futures and make different choices. When a person makes this transition, they often either beat themselves up, believing they followed the wrong path, or they blame their ambitions and society for where they stand. I don't think either point of view serves us well or provides a positive, empowering narrative.

Instead, I'd point us to trust ourselves and give ourselves the benefit of the doubt that we made the best decisions we could with the information and self-knowledge we had at the time. We can also accept that we used external guides to inform such decisions—and that's okay, and normal—rather than be frustrated or annoyed by such societal structures. Perhaps it's healthier to say, with a shrug, *That's just me being human and using social cues to guide me.*

On this journey, it's also helpful to acknowledge and embrace how we have learned more about ourselves as we've grown and changed over time, that we've had experiences that have given us information about what truly satisfies and fulfills us, and that we are wise to now embrace these insights to adjust as we step into what's next for us. These lessons and insights further fuel our growth. Thus, as we step into new ventures, we should expect that we'll continue to evolve and need to adapt accordingly.

Our lives and environments change too, shifting perhaps our vision or our values. Just because this happens doesn't mean our past was wrong; it was simply a stage in our journey. People often think they wasted their time on a pursuit. I know I've thought this. Yet we learn about ourselves by doing. We make the best choice we can in the moment. We take steps forward. We learn. We adjust. We move forward again.

Our time is rarely wasted. Where I'd point you instead is toward three reflection questions: (1) What did you learn? (2) What are you curious about now? (3) What story do you want to tell yourself?

What did you learn? As I've said before, we won't know with certainty if we will like or want something until we try it. We can do all the due diligence we want, but until we put ourselves fully into a situation to test it, it is hard to know for certain. This learning is critical to help us in our evolving journeys. So, when you find yourself disillusioned or recognize that you don't want something after all, ask yourself what you've learned from the experience and what it means about the way forward.

What are you curious about now? It's natural to feel unmoored when we realize the path we are on is no longer what we want. I like to point people toward asking what they are curious about to inform their exploration of what might be next. It's my favorite prompt, rather than "What are you passionate about?" Ugh. Many of us aren't *passionate* about anything. It sets too high a bar. But curious? Yes. I suggest that you simply start to observe what catches your attention now. This can begin to frame what you experiment with next.

What story do you want to tell yourself? The stories we tell about our lives can shape our perspective, how we feel, our well-being, and how we live going forward. Crafting our personal, powerful stories is rooted in a concept called "narrative identity," which has us connect the dots between who we are and what we've experienced in our lives. We can choose to tell ourselves empowering or disempowering stories. More positive stories can increase our *self-efficacy*,[2] our belief that we can be successful and achieve goals. So instead of being angry with ourselves for past choices and directions, we can shape our narratives to move us forward positively and powerfully.

We don't have to play the victim to our ambitions; nor does ambition have to be the evil force in our stories. What's more helpful is to keep our ambitions in a space where they support our well-being and ability to flourish. There's a greater likelihood of this if we align our ambitions to our Right Foundation the best we can and embrace our learning and growth journey.

How Do I Navigate My Wants with the Realities of the External World?

This is a question that I've wrestled with many times, and one that is fundamental to Sustainable Ambition. How do we allow ourselves to have more agency, to step into a self-authored mind, and yet thrive given societal constructs and systems and the reality that external success is rooted in social rewards? We want to be self-directed and feel empowered to be who we want to be in the world, yet in doing so, we must operate within its expectations and constraints. These tensions between what is expected and our personal desires can leave us feeling limited, alienated, and powerless.

Despite these constraints, remember, we do have choice in the matter. We are not solely subject to our external world. To navigate, look for congruence between the external world and who you are and your Right Foundation to connect to your internal motivation. I did this early on when I considered job roles at the start of my career. I didn't go into investment banking, because I gleaned that the culture was not for me. I wouldn't fit in. Now, I could get upset and think that that environment should change to allow someone like me to fit into the culture. Yet we can't expect every corner of the world to change to accommodate each individual. That's unrealistic. Instead, what I did was look for industries, companies, and jobs that better aligned with my values and my personality.

In this search for congruence, you may feel as though you don't belong anywhere. In this case, I'd encourage you to remain committed to your search. This is a vast world, with many communities. Continue to know yourself better, be curious, and explore other possible options that might be a good fit for you to find your belonging.

When it comes to feelings of success, here, too, we have a choice. Yes, we can feel dissonance between what's required to succeed and what feels authentic to us. We might resent that to reach a goal we have to do activities or fit into external structures that don't align with who we are. The choice becomes: do the work to achieve external success if it's what you desire, perhaps ideally finding innovative ways to accomplish the goal that align with who you are, or define success on your own terms.

Our external world influences but doesn't dictate our path. However, I acknowledge that some of you are likely to experience biases that prohibit you from pursuing and succeeding in your chosen ambitions. Such circumstances go beyond what I cover in the book, but they are real. And, often, courageous, strong people fight and drive for change and to accomplish their goals despite such barriers.

How Do I Balance My Wants with My Responsibilities?

Are Right Ambitions a luxury? Like how pursuing a passion for our work can be considered a luxury?

Some people may feel conflicted about postponing their dreams because of responsibilities—earning to provide for their family, saving for retirement, or caring for children. But Right Ambitions aren't in conflict with these choices. Rather, my hope is we can find more peace by aligning these choices with our motivations and finding congruence between our effort and ourselves.

I once interviewed a senior leader who had just become an

empty nester and was in the midst of a career transition. He shared how he had held his corporate job until his daughters had completed college. He valued providing for his children's education so that they felt prepared and ready to enter adulthood. His job was sufficiently satisfying, but he put off another ambition, starting a business, until after they graduated and were able to support themselves. He didn't want to have the uncertainty around his income during those core financial years. Now that he was past that stage, he felt more confident to work toward this new ambition and take some risks.

This example demonstrates how we can find alignment between our responsibilities and our wants. This leader found alignment between his vision for who he wanted to be as a father and his value to care for his family. We can follow a similar strategy to create meaning and motivation by linking our responsibilities to our vision, how we want to give and contribute, or our values. Or if these responsibilities are difficult to link in that way, we can add a bit of love to increase our intrinsic motivation.

Being in alignment with our motivations doesn't have to be at odds with being responsible. Create the link to why it matters to you.

RIGHT-SIZE AMBITIONS

We often judge the size of our ambitions, influenced by both external and internal forces. We may wonder if our ambitions are big enough. While society suggests ambitions are meant to be big and bold, they can start small and grow over time. We may question if we're playing it safe, holding ourselves back and acting small. Or perhaps our desires swing too far the other way, reaching for too much and wading into unhealthy ambition.

Are My Ambitions Big Enough?

At times, we can judge our ambitions or compare them to others' ambitions, creating unnecessary pressure and anxiety. We may wonder if our ambitions are too small to be worthy of our effort. But ambitions come in all shapes and sizes, and they can look different for each of us. Ambitions don't have to be grandiose to make them meaningful and motivating. Evaluating the size of our ambitions can keep us from pursuing activities that delight us, fuel our growth, and contribute to our resilience.

Look to yourself to right-size your ambitions. When I trained for my first marathon, my goal was simple: complete the race. I wasn't striving to make the Olympics, but that didn't diminish the goal's importance to me. If I had fixated on comparison or my ability to achieve a certain time, I might never have signed up or trained for the event. What's important with any ambition, regardless of scale, is ensuring it's a goal you genuinely want, that it's the right time for you to pursue it, and that you have the energy for it—that it aligns with your Right Ambition, Right Time, and Right Effort.

What's more, ambitions can start small and grow over time. With the right circumstances or inspiration, our ambition can ignite and expand. For example, we might not have been interested in traditional schoolwork, but find an outside interest highly motivating. Or we're comfortable operating at our current level, but then develop our skills, gain confidence, and realize we're able to step into more responsibility. For me with the marathon, I ran the race, completed it, and surprised myself by running a time that qualified me for the Boston Marathon. Wow! That was totally unexpected. I now had a new ambition to pursue.

This idea of growing ambition aligned with similar guidance I had heard from Ruth Gotian, author of *The Success Factor*. Based on Ruth's decades of research interviewing some of the most successful people of our generation (based on external measures), including Nobel laureates, astronauts, and Olympic champions, she acknowledged that we will likely raise the bar on our ambitions as we increase in mastery. She gave an example in our interview: "Look at all the scientists—when they start out doing research, they don't think they're going to get the Nobel [Prize]. When somebody first starts in a sport, they don't think they're going to be an Olympian. But as you get closer and closer, that becomes the new goal—first to be an Olympian, then to be a medalist, then to be a gold medalist, then to be world champion, then to whatever it is. So, the goals change, especially as you get closer to it."[3]

This mindset frees you to embrace small ambitions that are right for you and discover how they grow and flourish over time.

Am I Playing Small?

While you may find your ambitions growing as you gain confidence and self-efficacy, on the flip side, self-doubt and limiting beliefs can also hold you back. You may unintentionally not reach for more. Let's explore five strategies for when you find yourself wondering, *Am I playing small?*: (1) get curious, (2) challenge timing assumptions, (3) reach for the next aspiration, (4) embrace being uncomfortable, and (5) find your believers, advisors, and instructors.

A good starting point is to recognize and challenge our limiting beliefs, what Gay Hendricks calls the Upper Limit Problem in *The Big Leap*. Hendricks explains that we often get in our own way of achieving happiness and success, because of three core limiting beliefs: fear of failure, fear of being alone, and fear of outshining others. These fears can lead us to sabotage ourselves from pursuing what we want or stretching for our desired outcomes.[4] How can we remove these self-imposed boundaries?

Get curious. If you're worried you are limiting yourself, get curious about why that might be. Consider an ambition that is self-defined and has meaning for you, yet your energy for it is low. Is your energy low because of a limiting belief or your mindset? *I can't do that. I don't deserve that.* Ask yourself: Is fear holding me back? Why am I resisting moving forward?

Or is your energy low because of a capability challenge, where you can build your skills and self-efficacy around this ambition? When we feel it's within our capabilities to accomplish our goals, we tend to have more energy for them and feel they are worthy of our effort.[5]

Or is your energy low because perhaps you don't want the ambition after all? It's worth testing the ambition's level of meaning and motivation for you. Do you still want it? Are you committed to this goal? How determined are you? I loved the mantra that Katie Ceccarini, executive coach and founder of Endurance Management Coaching, shared in our podcast interview to get past limiting beliefs: "Make it matter, and when it matters, you make it happen."[6] Truth! Link to your motivators, and you're more likely to find your drive.

Ultimately, don't automatically ascribe low energy to truth. It's worth checking if a limiting belief is creating self-doubt and affecting your perceived capability to achieve the goal, in turn reducing your desire and energy to pursue it.

Challenge timing assumptions. You may also start to have doubts if you aren't making progress as fast as you might like. It's helpful to recognize that many goals take longer to accomplish than we realize. As Dorie Clark writes in her book *The Long Game*, we should check our expectations on speed to success. One of her tips is to do due diligence to confirm how long it has taken others to achieve similar goals. We often find that our time expectations are out of whack.[7]

One method to ease the pain around your progress and the timing of the outcomes is to revisit your Right Foundation. For example, one of my workshop participants, after years of questioning the pursuit of an ambition, found that her foundation helped combat her self-doubt. Linking it to her motivators reminded her why the ambition mattered and helped her recognize the progress she'd actually made toward what she wanted for herself.

Reach for the next aspiration. Recall what I shared previously about how our ambitions grow over time. We may not think we can reach a goal because it's not yet within our frame of ambition. We simply can't see it for ourselves. To not play small, consider the next level of aspiration you want to reach from where you stand today. For example, you don't need to go from running a 5K race to training for the Olympics. Such an expectation sounds silly, right? But after running a 5K, perhaps your next aspiration might be running the 5K at a faster time or running a 10K. With each step and success along our journey, our ambitions can grow as we experience positive progress.[8]

Embrace being uncomfortable. While you can gain the confidence to move forward, I also want to advocate for challenging yourself to get comfortable with being uncomfortable. If we never get uncomfortable, we're likely playing it too safe. Yes, we can feel negative emotions when we stretch beyond our comfort zone—that's why we call it our comfort zone! But ambitions call us to step out. When we're growing and trying something new, we're likely to get nervous. Many actors say they'd be concerned if they stopped getting nervous before a performance, as it would be a sign that they didn't care anymore or weren't on their game. It comes back to the U-curve theory of pressure and performance[9]—to do our best, we will feel stretched. The key is finding that sweet spot of optimal challenge without feeling overwhelmed, overly anxious, or excessively stressed.

Find your believers, advisors, and instructors. To move forward in the uncomfortable zone, seek encouragement from mentors, a coach, or those who believe in you. We can often reach greater heights when we believe we can achieve more, and that spark is often ignited by those who see more in and for us than we see for ourselves. They can motivate us to step into what's possible. If you're breaking out from your traditional path or don't feel supported by those closest to you, identify people who share your ambition, who can offer insight and guidance and encourage you to endure. That's what I did in writing this book. I was lucky to have a coach and be part of a community who believed in me, offered counsel, and pulled me forward to completion.

Are My Ambitions Too Big?

Who's to say if we're overreaching with our ambitions? I say go for it if you want to dream big, assuming those big ambitions are truly yours. The only reason to consider answering yes to the question "Are my ambitions too big?" is if pursuing them is causing friction for you or those around you.

First, we want to avoid when ambition goes bad—when we strive to the point where we neglect other important aspects of our life that keep us in the healthy and happy zone. We must guard against putting too much pressure on ourselves to achieve our ambitions such that we unwittingly give up other goals that matter to us. In essence, we give up Sustainable Ambition.

Just like we can be overly ambitious in pushing ourselves toward our aspirations, we can also overstretch, pushing beyond our capabilities and resulting in unproductive stress. Or we may experience negative health consequences when we lack confidence in our abilities to achieve the ambition. For example, people can get depressed when working on demanding projects where they feel incapable.[10] In this situation, I suggest making a big ambition smaller, lowering the level of aspiration to gain confidence and then build up to greater ambitions. Or consider getting outside help and expertise to help you make progress. Dreaming big is right, not wrong, but be realistic about where you stand and what it might take to fulfill your longer-term goals.

Another factor that causes friction is when big ambitions turn into big expectations, both of ourselves and for our desired outcomes. In this case, an expectation is considered a guaranteed outcome as opposed to a probabilistic one. We can become frustrated and disappointed when our expectations aren't met and when we don't get the outcomes we want.

The trick is to keep our expectations around goal attainment realistic. Having high expectations of ourselves isn't necessarily bad, because it motivates us to higher performance. But we want to stretch in the right zone so that the goals we set for ourselves are attainable, given our capabilities and growth opportunity now.

Big ambitions can also turn into wanting a lot. I believe in Sustainable Ambition being a no-judgment zone, so I hesitate to go here. But unsustainable wanting based on societal norms of consumerism or keeping up with others can cause unwanted pain. Despite what Gordon Gekko of the 1987 movie *Wall Street* said, greed is not good. It can lead to grasping or driving too hard and shift us into unhealthy ambition. It's helpful to ask, *What is enough to fulfill and satisfy me in this life?* But we each need to answer that for ourselves.

Letting go of excessive wanting can also create more ease. Research has shown that once our basic needs are met, more income, wealth, or possessions are not correlated with lifelong happiness.[11] Getting clearer on what is enough can help us feel content with what we have.

I'll admit, this isn't easy to do. As I've shared, we are influenced by societal norms to want and have. Another concept of this is called "mimetic desire," which French philosopher René Girard defined as desires shaped by those around us rather than being personally derived.[12] And yet, with Sustainable Ambition, I call you to step into self-authorship, to shape your own identity, choose your own ambitions, and find success by creating fulfillment and satisfaction for yourself.

A final way to counter wanting too much is a practice that some Stoic philosophers, like Seneca, called "voluntary discomfort."[13] Seneca wrote, "Set aside a certain number of days, during which you shall be content with the scantiest and cheapest fare, with coarse and rough dress, saying to yourself the while: 'Is this the condition that I feared?'"[14] The idea is to intentionally experience discomfort and train ourselves to realize we don't have to satisfy our every want. Just learning about this concept called me to challenge myself to be more contented with and grateful for what I do have.

KEEP AMBITIONS IN THE HEALTHY AND HAPPY ZONE

As I note at the start of the book, ambition isn't good or bad. It takes getting it just right. That's what I mean by keeping our ambitions in the healthy and happy zone. We humans can drive too hard, be addicted to achievement, and kick ourselves when we don't accomplish what we set out to do. How can we create a bit more ease by being more consciously ambitious?

Are My Ambitions Taking Me into the Severe Zone?

How can you know when your ambition is helping versus hindering you? It comes back to the U-curve of ambition. Think about it as finding that optimal zone for you—dialing it in to get it just right. You want to have Right Ambitions that positively motivate you. But sometimes we roll along and chase goals only to look up at some point and realize we aren't happy.

The shift from the healthy, happy, sustainable zone to the dangerous, severe zone often happens when we drive too hard. Our emotions and energy offer clues when this happens. Are we motivated and energetic? Or are we miserable and grinding? When exploring this, look from two angles: a single ambition view and a full life and work ambition view.

But first, I'm assuming you are working with Right Ambitions. If not, revisit the prior chapter and link your ambitions to your Right Foundation. You're more likely to fall into the severe zone if you put time and energy into ambitions that aren't connected to your personal motivations.

When you look at a single ambition, notice your energy. Does the goal energize or drain you? Is the ambition motivating your effort? Is it helping you achieve what you want? If you're rooted in a Right Ambition and you feel positive energy, you're likely in good shape.

But be careful here, too, and don't assume pursuing an ambition will always be fun and games. Recall the research I shared from Barry Schwartz and Amy Wrzesniewski—to go after our ambitions and goals or be in flow doesn't always *feel good*. Let me tell you—I experienced moments in this book-writing process that were painful. Yet you now hold this book. I kept going. How did I do it? I went back to my Right Foundation and found my motivation to persevere.

Pushing forward isn't always the right solution, though. Even with a Right Ambition, feeling lots of negative energy might signal it's time to pause and get curious. You might have shifted from working in a flow state into a grinding state. If so, it's time for a break and likely more sustaining activities.

When you take a high-level view across your full life and work ambitions, here, too, it's helpful to gauge how you feel. Are you energized or not? Are you putting time and attention against only certain ambitions and ignoring others? Are you too singularly focused around ambition pursuit and achievement at the expense of what truly matters to you? You can stay out of the severe zone and in the healthier and happier sustainable zone when you don't neglect key elements that fuel your well-being, such as investing in relationships and keeping yourself sustained.

Must I Achieve More?

Achievement orientation has upsides and downsides. Just like ambition, achievement isn't inherently bad. Many of us, myself included, value accomplishment, stretching ourselves, and striving for excellence. Plus, achievement builds self-efficacy and confidence.

But achievement can turn sour. Society conditions us to seek rewards attached to accomplishment, which can lead to fixating on performing to external standards. In turn, we can link our identity to constant achievement and hunt for external validation and acknowledgment to fuel our sense of self-worth. This can lead us to feel constant pressure to do more, creating added stress. We can develop perfectionist tendencies that can drive us to work too hard, possibly leading to burnout, and be self-critical when we don't meet expectations and goals.

So the short answer to the question *Must I achieve more?* is no, or not necessarily. You can try several strategies that align to the pillars of Sustainable Ambition to help manage the downsides of overachievement.

A place to start is to untangle your identity from achievement and reduce your attachment to it. One way is to anchor in your Right Ambitions and set challenging yet realistic goals with your own success metrics. You can also build a healthy sense of self-worth that isn't tied solely to goal success and constant accomplishment. For example, you can build a stronger sense of self through affirmation and acknowledgment of your personal character strengths. What do you appreciate about yourself as you are and for who you are as opposed to what you do or achieve?

Consider, too, giving yourself permission to create more ease around achievement. I cover Right Time and Right Effort in more detail in upcoming parts of the book, so here I'll simply note that we can't do it all or achieve it all at once, and we need to manage our energy and not overextend ourselves, as energy is finite, just like time. Only you will know your capacity, as it's based on all your demands. You will benefit from monitoring it to know your limits around how much you want to and can achieve at a particular moment in time.

To help manage our effort, we can work on our perfectionist tendencies and embrace self-compassion. When working on a particular goal, check in with yourself to see if you've reached an acceptable level of accomplishment rather than driving endlessly for perfection. And instead of chastising yourself when things don't go well, choose to be kind to yourself to manage setbacks and move forward. Self-compassion can also help you let go of the need for perfection and instead embrace your own definitions of success.

For some of us, managing our achievement tendencies to stay out of the ambition severe zone is a lifelong practice. Relieving the pressure to achieve isn't easy and takes awareness and practice, like everything with Sustainable Ambition.

What If I Don't Achieve What I Wanted?

It happens—you put in the effort and don't get the outcome you wanted or the external reward you were seeking. You worked hard on a presentation but didn't receive a positive response. You were in line for a promotion but didn't get acknowledged this cycle or didn't get the big role. You trained but didn't hit your goal time.

To be sure, not achieving can be disappointing and frustrating. Honestly, you may need a moment to allow yourself to feel what you need to feel. And it can be helpful to remember that such circumstances are learning opportunities, despite them feeling as though they are failures.

Your Right Foundation can serve you well in these moments too. Despite the external outcome, you can find success by identifying what was personally rewarding. For example, how did this action move you one step closer to your vision? How did your work and effort honor what you want to give or your values? What did you love about the process? This is also where your personal success metrics can be handy. How did you do based on those metrics?

I love how Jack Hsueh, an ultramarathoner who has run races like the Tahoe Rim Trail 100-mile race and the Western States 100, thinks of such moments when he doesn't experience his desired outcome, despite his extensive preparation. Jack has trained for big, audacious goals like the Tor des Géants, a 330-kilometer race through the Italian Alps, a course that took him six days to complete while only sleeping five hours. The training required trade-offs and sacrifices, made not only by himself but also by his family.

When things don't go quite as planned out on the race trail, Jack has a healthy perspective: "I no longer define success based on whether or not I finish. There's probably a time that I did, and there was certainly a time that I felt like I had to finish at all costs.... There are people that have done that, and they wear it as a badge of honor.... But that's not really a healthy perspective. I now define success around other many accomplishments along the way and along the training process.... Finishing is just a bonus."[15]

Jack finds success because he values the effort he puts in—being disciplined and committed to his preparation—and appreciates the enjoyable moments in his training journey, like taking in the pure beauty of the outdoors, which is one of the reasons he runs.

All is not lost when you don't reach your intended outcome. Shift from a mindset of failure to one of personal contentment and learning to create meaning. What story do you want to tell yourself? Another reframe is to lean into the theory of possible selves, seeing new versions of who you could become from here. In doing so, you can view the situation as an opportunity for redirection and growth.

A final strategy is to let go of expectations around outcomes and step into acceptance. When you do, you can more easily come to terms with what is. Actor Michael J. Fox, who lives with Parkinson's disease, said, "My happiness grows in direct proportion to my acceptance, and in inverse proportion to my expectations."[16] That sounds about right. We can find more peace when we embrace our reality.

• • •

At the end of Part II, you now have your Right Foundation to ground your Right Ambitions; claim your meaningful, motivating goals to step into self-authorship; and define your personal success and success metrics. With this foundation, you can also shift your focus from external to internal rewards and find success in what is personally meaningful and motivating to you.

My hope is that you now know yourself better and are more conscious of what you want and, in being so, are better armed to make courageous choices rooted in what's important to you now. That's what we explore in Part III, "Right Time," starting with embracing both life and work ambitions.

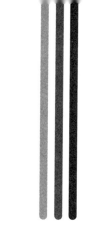

Part III

Right Time

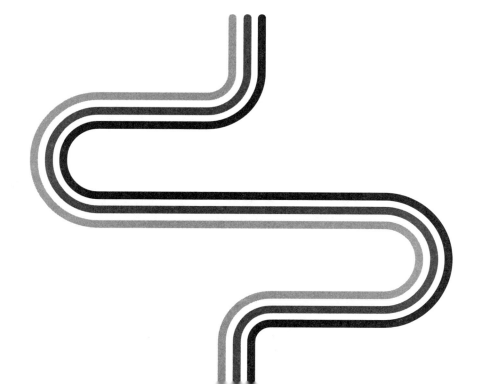

Chapter 6

• • •

Define Your Life and Work Ambitions Now

Every evening when Christine Bader came home from work and opened the front door, she'd find her husband on the sofa reading to their young twins. Today was different. Today her twins were reading to their father. *When did that happen?* she thought.[1]

Christine had it all and was doing it all. The author of *Evolution of a Corporate Idealist: When Girl Meets Oil*, she had established herself as a force in the sustainability world, landing her a role in her dream job. She had purpose in her work, leading the Social Responsibility group at Amazon, where she could make a significant impact. Plus, she and her husband were raising their two children. Based on all external measures of success, Christine had done well. But that evening, she realized she was missing out on parts of her life. She hadn't expected it, but when she saw her kids reading, her ambitions shifted.

Even those of us, like Christine, who consciously, merrily roll along and live the life we believed we wanted can be confounded when our ambitions shift. Despite doing our best to shoot for work-life balance, the concept too often fails to deliver the desired outcomes. We long for more. Or we reach a crossroads and question if the trade-offs we've been making are still worth it.

As I discuss in Chapter 2, our ambitions across life and work evolve and ebb and flow as we change. This is natural. Yet most of us are surprised when we hit such an inflection point and then often ignore that gnawing restlessness in the pit of our stomachs telling us something is off. Society tells us to get on a path and just keep going and doesn't offer easy, safe ways and scripts to explore what might be next. Plus, we humans don't like change, and we resist discomfort. It can be an unsettling time as we recognize that adjustments are required and as we accept that what we've pursued is no longer the path we want to stay on.

Societal norms also can make us feel trapped, as if we can't choose. Sometimes we can't (many of us *have* to work and *have* to care for our families), but we can choose where to invest our time and energy, even if it means being fiercely focused.

Remember—ambition doesn't have to be about doing it all, or about achieving quickly. What if we allowed ourselves to make courageous choices about what matters most to us now? What if we allowed ourselves to change course and not be tied to a set path? What if we allowed our ambitions to ebb and flow over time and chose to set our own pace?

Right Time considers your life and work together. Choose

where you want to put your attention, effort, and energy based on what's personally important and matters most in your life and work now. It asks: What is it time to do?

Right Time also calls us to put life ambitions on equal footing with work ambitions. Yes, you are allowed life ambitions! Our life ambitions contribute to our happiness just as much as work ambitions, if not more so. I've found this to be true; pursuing personal ambitions alongside professional ones throughout my adult life has fueled me and given me energy for all I do.

In this part of the book, with this lens, we explore the evolution of our life and work ambitions and how to navigate competing ambitions, helping determine where to focus our time and attention. The purpose is to clarify which ambitions to prioritize now and how to sequence others for the future. This offers a more realistic and sustainable way to manage all we want to do across a lifetime.

> Choose where you want to put your attention, effort, and energy based on what's personally important and matters most in your life and work now.

Navigating our ambitions over time and embracing change as a continual practice can be unnerving. Yet change can be reframed around having freedom and personal agency to choose differently, and around adventure when met with curiosity. If we don't adjust as our circumstances evolve, we, too, might find ourselves asking, *How did I get here?* We have a choice: Stay on a path that no longer suits us, or embrace change and do the work to align with the life we want to create and who we want to become now. Instead of resisting and meeting change with fear, we can step into the excitement of exploring new possibilities.

That's what Christine Bader did. She quit her job at Amazon, and the family moved to Indonesia to live abroad for a year. When they returned to the United States, they moved to a small town in Oregon and started to reshape their lives with a new vision. Christine is just as ambitious as she was when she had her professional titles at big companies, but now she has crafted her life in a way that more holistically meets all the ambitions she holds for herself and her family. She's found fulfillment rooting herself in her local community and making an impact there. She teaches at a local university; participates in her town's diversity, equity, and inclusion advisory committee; and is coaching a girls rugby club. As she wrote in a blog post, "That's more than enough. I feel like I am living the life I want."[2] Christine demonstrates how our ambitions can ebb and flow over time and that ambition doesn't have to look a certain way. We can hold broader views of ambition that personally serve us best to create the lives we want for ourselves and to achieve the outcomes we seek.

WHAT'S IMPORTANT IN YOUR LIFE NOW?

"I started to feel a little crazy," Clarence So said.[3]

No amount of ibuprofen could control the constant pain he was experiencing, which affected his sleep, his thinking, and his ability to bring his best game to work.

Clarence was ambitious about his career. He was driven and excelling in his role at Salesforce, an early-stage start-up at the time. He gave his best hours to the job, working weekends, flying around the world, and relentlessly grinding to help grow the company. Little did he know that, after four years, the negative impact on his body had accumulated.

While Clarence's brain wanted him to keep driving and pursue his career aspirations, the debilitating pain he was experiencing demanded his immediate attention. Working with the right doctors, he learned he had a rare, chronic autoimmune disorder that didn't fully express itself until he was at the height of his career at age thirty-three.

"Sometimes your body just forces you to focus on your body and not anything else," he said. "My diagnosis was chronic. There was no guarantee I would get better. In fact, my doctors suggested I should expect to get worse until I became fully disabled."

Clarence went on disability leave, with no idea how long it might be before he could go back to work, if he could. While his body experienced pain, it was also emotionally painful to give up a job he enjoyed, with no expectation that he'd be able to return.

"It was a difficult shift around my identity, my ambition and ego," Clarence said. "Aside from the physical pain, there was a mental adjustment around believing I had control over my path in life. Up until then, I believed I could achieve whatever I set my mind out to achieve. If my mind says this is what I want, it means this is what we're doing. But it turns out, that's not always true. . . . There's a lot out of your control, and allowing that to be true for me was hard."

With the proper diagnosis, Clarence was able to get access to new treatments and immunotherapy clinical trials at the University of California, San Francisco. The new drugs worked—Clarence was a super responder—and within months the pain subsided. He was able to get back to his life, including to his work at Salesforce, where he spent another twenty years.

The drugs aren't the only thing that made a difference for Clarence. He also gained a clear intention to prioritize his health. Since he was sixteen, Clarence has set annual intentions to guide his daily pursuits and actions. What changed with managing a chronic health issue was the prioritization of that list. Health had never been on the list prior to 2003. Since then, it's always been at the top of the list. Work is still a priority for him, but health comes first.

"Before my disability leave, I thought my first job was to serve my employer and career ambitions," he said. "After my disability leave, I realized my first job, on any given day, was to take care of my health. Every morning, I self-evaluate what my body is willing to give. Some days, my body says I can do it all. On other days, my body has less to give. I want to give my wife and kids the best version of me. There are days where I can't afford to give my best hours to my career."

That meant that Clarence couldn't reliably put as much effort into his work relative to his peers. He had to make trade-offs.

"Certainly, I don't feel like I've squandered my life. It just didn't go the direction I anticipated pre-2003," he said. "Turns out, there's a lot to life beyond creating unicorn start-ups and high-flying tech companies."

So true. Clarence's experience with novel immunotherapies led him to purpose-centered work that pursues health-care advancements in precision medicine. He received generous support from Salesforce's CEO, Marc Benioff, along with philanthropic funding and access to strategic partnerships. Today, Clarence focuses on his own projects and advises companies committed to a double bottom line, balancing social impact with financial impact.

Most of us will (hopefully) never experience a chronic disease that forces us to reenvision our career aspirations, like Clarence. But other life events can serve as a catalyst for a similar reorientation. Getting married, raising a family, and caring for elderly parents are common life-changing events that prompt reevaluation of our priorities. Clarence experienced all of the above with his wife, two young kids, and parents. Shifting an ambition and career focus can be difficult to accept and can affect our identity. What Clarence learned was there's a lot out of our control. He's also embraced the benefits.

"As my ego has taken a back seat to the rest of me, I've become happier and found more purpose serving something bigger than my own personal career ambitions," he said. "If forced to choose, would I rather be somebody or do something? As I move into the second half of my life, it's easier to choose the latter."

For Clarence, his health crisis made it abundantly clear what was important in his life now and shaped how he framed his ambitions across both life and work. I invite you to get clearer and more intentional about what you want for your life too.

Exercise: Your Life Ambitions

What ambitions do you have for your life? Here you'll reflect on your Right Foundation to identify and build on the goals that are important to you and that you can take into the next chapter to further home in on your focus. Don't think your list has to be perfect or long—just create one that feels right enough for you at this point, and know that you can always come back to modify and refine it.

1. *Identify your life ambitions.* Refer to your Right Foundation. Review the ambitions you identified in your vision. List those first. Then consider whether you want to add anything as you reflect on the other elements, starting with your values. Which values are a priority for you now, and what are the ambitions you hold related to those values? Then think about what you want to give and what you love—what do those suggest for your life ambitions?

   To prompt further ideation, consider ambitions or goals across the four nonwork dimensions identified by the book *Wellbeing: The Five Essential Elements*: social relationships, finances, physical health and energy (including mental and emotional health), and community.

   Some example life ambitions include:
   - Having a strong, supportive, long-lasting relationship
   - Raising resilient, independent, caring children
   - Fostering a strong friendship community
   - Helping my parents enjoy happy golden years
   - Saving enough for retirement
   - Being physically and mentally strong and healthy for as long as possible
   - Being a mentor or volunteer at an organization
   - Visiting every national park
   - Climbing Mt. Kilimanjaro

- Living abroad
- Getting a PhD
- Learning a language
- Learning to dance or play a musical instrument
- Writing a fiction book

2. *Right Ambition check.* Reconfirm if the ambitions you list align with your Right Foundation. Are they Right Ambitions when you consider whether they link to at least one of your motivators? Can you make them Right Ambitions? Do you want to take any off the list because it is a should or a have-to? See Table 6.1 for an example.

3. *What's most important now?* Reflect on your final list and put a star next to up to three meaningful, motivating life ambitions or goals that are most important to you now. We come back to this in the next chapter.

Table 6.1. Example of a completed Right Ambition check

Life ambition	Right Ambition alignment			
	Vision	Give	Values	Love
Have a strong, supportive, long-lasting relationship	X	X	X	X
Raise resilient, independent, caring children	X	X	X	X
Help my parents enjoy happy golden years		X	X	
Be physically and mentally strong and healthy for as long as possible	X		X	X
Live abroad	X		X	X
Learn a language	X		X	X
Write a fiction book			X	X

WHAT'S IMPORTANT IN YOUR WORK NOW?

Mara Yale had excelled all her life in the traditional ways. She went to Brown University for college and played varsity hockey. She attended Scripps Institution of Oceanography at the University of California, San Diego, for a PhD in geophysics. She navigated job changes, ultimately landing at a company in Boston as a software engineer and manager, where she worked for almost two decades. During this time, she made a personal decision to have two children on her own. She got promoted while on both maternity leaves and was able to return on a flexible basis until she ramped back up to full time, working for a boss who valued her contributions.[4]

Over time, Mara was able to resiliently manage and navigate her life changes with her work while dealing with major challenges, like her second child having a stroke at birth and the death of her mother. But it was changes at work that made her rethink her professional ambitions. Ironically, being ambitious was the catalyst. Mara felt she had outgrown her longtime manager and asked to work for someone new, driven by her desire to continue to stretch and grow. This seemingly minor change in management changed everything.

Mara's new boss was toxic. Despite being the same person who had excelled for over a decade, Mara found herself experiencing levels of stress that eventually forced her to take leave. She was burned out and physically ill. During her time away, Mara minimized what was happening to her and the coaching she received on stress management, saying, "I'm getting paid really well to learn how to manage my stress." But the impact of a toxic boss went beyond ordinary workplace stress; it couldn't be resolved with training. Instead, a pattern formed—Mara returned to work, got burned out again because of the environment, and then needed to take leave once more.

Mara wondered how she could break the cycle and leave her employer for good. It had been a great place to work for so long. She was torn between the extrinsic rewards of a lucrative job that supported her family and the need to support her well-being. But the pattern couldn't continue.

The good news was that during this difficult period Mara was in action, testing future work options. She took a class on teaching geometry. She studied Feldenkrais, an approach to learning through movement that she was using herself as part of her healing practice. Mara didn't know that these actions would become the basis for her next career move, but at some point, she had enough experiments and money in the bank to feel comfortable leaving her job on her terms and starting to craft her work in a new way that would better support her and her life at this stage. Mara is still ambitious. Her work ambitions just look different now.

Like for Mara, a job event or change is one of the top triggers for rethinking our work ambitions. Sometimes it's not as severe as what Mara experienced; we may simply feel called to do something new, though I realize that navigating this is anything but simple. We may have gotten overextended for a time and want to dial down our ambition in order to recharge. Or we may find ourselves on a career path or in a role in which we are highly engaged—the work is meaningful and motivating—and we want to identify new ways to stretch or strive. In any of these situations, we want to get clear on our work ambitions and goals.

Exercise: Your Work Ambitions

What are your work ambitions? Create a list of meaningful, motivating work ambitions or goals. This list may be narrower than or not as long as your life ambitions list, and it can include both short- and long-term work and career ambitions. Again, don't think that you have to get this fully complete or right. You can always come back to it and refine it as ambitions become clearer over time. Create your list following these steps:

1. *Identify your work ambitions.* Refer to your Right Foundation. Review the ambitions you identified in your vision. List those that are work related. Then consider whether you want to add anything as you reflect on the other elements, starting with your values. Which values are a priority for you now, and what are the ambitions you hold related to those values? Think about what you want to give and what you love. What do those suggest for your work ambitions?

    Some example work ambitions include:

    - Getting promoted to the next level
    - Becoming an expert in a field or topic
    - Starting a company
    - Being self-employed
    - Having a role that is sufficiently challenging yet offers the flexibility and level of work that allows me to sustainably be there for my family
    - Helping build innovative products that improve people's lives

- Being an advisor to purpose-driven organizations
- Succeeding at an important work project
- Earning enough to contribute sufficiently to retirement
- Working with people I enjoy from my past professional lives
- Becoming a professional speaker
- Writing a book

2. *Right Ambition check.* Reconfirm whether your ambitions and goals align with your Right Foundation. Are they Right Ambitions when you consider whether they link to at least one of your motivations? Can you make them Right Ambitions? Do you want to take anything off the list because it is a should or a have-to? See Table 6.2 for an example.

3. *What's most important now.* Reflect on your final list and put a star next to up to three meaningful, motivating work ambitions or goals (if you have that many) that are most important to you now. We come back to this in the next chapter.

Table 6.2. Example of a completed Right Ambition check

Work ambition	Right Ambition alignment			
	Vision	Give	Values	Love
Start a company		X	X	
Be an advisor to purpose-driven organizations	X	X	X	X
Earn enough to contribute sufficiently to retirement	X	X	X	
Become a professional speaker			X	X
Write a book	X	X	X	X

• • •

Did you attempt the Your Work Ambitions exercise and struggle to find focus? That may be because you are at a work inflection point. Perhaps you aren't fully satisfied with your current work path or think you need to make a bigger change. Those circumstances are what I address in the remainder of this chapter.

OPTIMIZE YOUR WORK AMBITIONS

In his early thirties, Doug Milliken started to experience periods of heightened anxiety. He was on a career trajectory he thought he wanted. He had been successful up to that point, steadily progressing and getting promoted. But his anxiety was trying to tell him something.[5]

To investigate and diagnose what was going on, Doug did a simple exercise to identify when he was and was not energized at work (similar to what I have you do in the Love and Loathe exercise in Chapter 3). At the end of a week, he looked at his lists of what he loved, what he hated, and what was neutral. In that moment, he had an epiphany—and then a panic attack. The evidence suggested that the path he was on to become a general manager of a business unit would have him doing activities he loathed and didn't think he was good at. Doug realized what the anxiety had been trying to tell him, which led to the panic. *I'm on the wrong path? Yikes, what am I going to do!*

Like many in this situation, he felt unmoored. Luckily, a wise friend suggested that he write his own job description and ask his boss if he might be able to add value in a new role. That's exactly what Doug did, and it put him on a trajectory of a decades-long, fulfilling, and satisfying career. It was one that he skipped off to every day, to do work he loved and that he was good at in an organization that valued his contributions. To create this, Doug had paused to understand himself better and how he best liked to contribute and add value; then he acted to optimize his role and find congruence.

If you, too, are in an uncomfortable state of not being fully satisfied and wondering how you can optimize your work to be more motivating, do as Doug did: Pause, check in, and do a quick self-assessment before taking further action. To optimize, Doug wanted to align his personal nature—how he thinks and who he is—with the nature of the work. In the language I've been using in the book, I see this as aligning to your work values and what you love to do, along with your strengths.

One way to do an assessment and identify how you can optimize and find more satisfaction in your work is to consider if your job or career is meaningful and motivating to you. Does it link to one of your motivators in your Right Foundation? If the answer is yes, next check your energy level—is it low or high? Your energy level can give you a clue as to what to explore next, because there isn't one right answer. If your energy level is low, you may be exhausted and need time to restore and recover. Or is your energy low because you are bored and ready for your next challenge? Or does your low energy point to a possible shift in your ambitions?

If your answer was no and your work is lacking meaning and motivation, revisit what we explore in Chapter 4 to see if you can link your current work to your Right Foundation. Social constructs can lead to having high expectations for our work and its role in our lives. Before making major changes, pause to consider what purpose work serves for you at this stage in your life and determine if you can find more satisfaction and fulfillment by connecting to your motivators. Can you align your work to your vision for your life? Can you identify a way to give and contribute that ignites your motivation? Can you link a value or something you love to what you do now?

Recall how linking to our purpose can increase our motivation and engagement at work. Similarly, a study found that doing things we love at work just 20 percent of the time in a week can increase our feelings of engagement and well-being.[6] We don't need to love our work all the time, but linking to something we enjoy increases our ability to stay committed to our goals. So look to dial up your love while also dialing down the loathe.

> We don't need to love our work all the time, but linking to something we enjoy increases our ability to stay committed to our goals.

Another area Doug focused on was being in an organization that valued what he had to offer. You may not always have a choice, but if you can, try to work within organizations where you find both value appreciation and values alignment. I learned to make this a must-have for me as I joined organizations throughout my career and considered it when making choices as I switched jobs. You are more likely to feel like you can contribute in a meaningful way and like you belong when you are in a place that creates less friction with who you naturally are.

A change may be required if linking to your motivations doesn't recommit you to your current path. If these strategies aren't enough to increase your satisfaction and fulfillment from your work, you might be ready for a more significant shift and in a position to explore a new path.

EXPLORE A NEW WORK AMBITION

Exploring a career change in depth is a topic for another book, but I want to provide some guidance to help you take initial steps. I also offer additional resources on my website and recommended reading in the Resources section at the end of the book. For now, I point you to three questions to consider as you explore a new work ambition:

1. What do your current actions tell you?
2. What's your next ambition?
3. What are possible avenues to explore?

These aren't simple questions; nor are the answers always quick or easy to uncover. You will likely need to make time and space to reflect, explore, and allow ideas to take form over time. This exploration often calls us to develop a deeper understanding of ourselves and what we want now, to act without being certain, and to learn and evolve as we take steps forward.

What Do Your Current Actions Tell You?

Recall the adage that actions speak louder than words. Our actions often demonstrate our true commitment to and preference for what we are seeking to pursue. We may think and say we want something, but our behaviors and actions can tell us otherwise.

Start to unpack what might be next for you by exploring your current actions and activities to see what's drawing your attention now. Consider what's trending down and what's trending up. Create a list for each, exploring the work actions and activities that are still satisfying for you and those that are not.

In one column, start with the trending down list and note activities where you are naturally *not* putting time and effort or feel less inclined to do so. What are you less drawn to now? Then consider the strengths, interests, and skills you feel you may be open to letting go of or leaving behind as you step into what's next.

In the other column, do the opposite. Note where you are drawn to invest your time and effort. Start with the activities that are trending up: those that most draw your interest now, including new topics, ideas, and activities that you are curious to learn more about or are interested in learning or mastering. Next, capture the strengths, interests, and skills you would like to carry forward with you into whatever you might do next.

Pause to reflect on what you've uncovered, and write a short statement to summarize what you want to move from and what you want to move to. See Table 6.3 for an example.

What's Your Next Ambition?

As noted previously, you might realize your energy is low because you have plateaued, grown bored, and are ready for a new challenge or aspiration. Consider: How do you want to stretch yourself next? How do you want to grow or what do you want to learn or master next? Or what might you want to strive for next?

Table 6.3. Example of what's trending down and trending up

Trending down	Trending up
• Technology that doesn't address a meaningful user need • Fast-paced, unpredictable environment • Managing up and playing politics	• Social impact work • Nonprofit management • Collective team building
Letting go	**Carrying forward**
• Industry-specific experience • Traditional corporate role	• Marketing • Research • Communications • Storytelling • Creative development
Moving from	**Moving to**
• Marketing leadership within a specific industry	• Marketing leadership for nonprofits

What Are Possible Avenues to Explore?

When it comes to career moves, I subscribe to what Herminia Ibarra champions in her book *Working Identity*, in which she states that changing careers is like stepping into a new identity. And to do that, you have to try on options, get immersed in them, and see if they fit you. For this reason, when people make big career moves, I prefer to be honest in declaring that such shifts often take time. We should step into making a change knowing that it's a journey that requires taking action, as Ibarra articulates in one of her strategies: "Act your way into a new way of thinking and being. You cannot discover yourself by introspection."[7]

Considering the preceding two questions and explorations around actions and ambition, brainstorm three different avenues and areas you are curious to explore as possible career paths.

Then for each, identify one way you can test it and take action to learn more. With this approach, you can experience each path and determine which resonates most strongly with you. Again, this won't necessarily be a quick exercise. It may require multiple experiments.

When you prepare to test each option, consider noting what you want to test, how you'll test it, any assumptions you want to understand, and what lessons to capture as you execute your plan. When I say *testing*, such activities might include networking or conducting informational interviews with people in the area you are exploring, attending events on topics of interest, taking classes to expand your skills, or doing a consulting assignment to test a new space. If you don't have time to test them all at once, start with the avenue that most appeals to you. Then, decide whether you can execute small, quick tests in the other areas to determine if one drops out or is still of less interest than your primary path.

• • •

Coming out of this chapter, my hope is you more deeply understand and are clear about your current life and work ambitions and that you give yourself permission to expand the range of your ambitions. From here, we'll explore how to converge these ambitions by considering timing: What is the right time to pursue each? How do you prioritize them considering your life vision? What is it time for now, near, and next? Let's learn more about how to plan in arcs and pace your ambitions.

Chapter 7

• • •

Plan in Arcs, Pacing Your Ambitions

"You can't have it all at once," said Dr. Sahar Yousef. "You have to really think about what needs to get done. And that has two components: one is desire or motivation, but it's also about timeliness.... This is how I view my life. It's how I run my kitchen. It's how I run my career. And it's absolutely how I manage my to-dos every single day."[1]

Sahar is a cognitive neuroscientist and faculty member at the University of California, Berkeley's Haas School of Business. She has followed a method that uses a future self-orientation to help her prioritize life and work decisions on a day-to-day basis. "What will my future self thank me for? It's a question I like to ask myself daily, monthly, annually. I'm constantly thinking about Sahar in the future, and I'm doing my best to honor her wishes.

So I'm here almost in a way as a present puppet to serve my future self. And I think a lot about what I will regret *not* doing."

When she finished college, Sahar considered multiple paths she could take for her career. Yet she realized she didn't need to—and couldn't—do everything all at once. What she could do was plan her ambitions and desires for her life over time horizons. And that's exactly what she did.

"I knew that my future self, Sahar at ninety years old, would have said, 'Tsk, tsk, tsk, girl. You were positioned correctly. You had an opportunity, you had the interest, you could have done it. And guess what's going to be harder at forty-five? Sure, you can start a business because you have examples of that in your life. You see that. What you don't see—people busting their butts in labs doing menial labor or PhDs in pursuit of mastery.' And I'm so grateful I picked that path. I don't think I could do what I did at twenty-five today."

To navigate tensions around what to do now, we often have to make trade-offs and choose between things we want, not just eschew shoulds. In making such choices, Sahar made a distinction between thinking about needs versus desires in terms of avoiding regret. "The reason I use the word *need* is about that future self-positioning. Again, I think about: *What do I need to do today? What do I need to accomplish in this year in front of me to make sure that my future self isn't going to look back and go, Sahar, what were you thinking?* That's what I mean by need. It's almost as if I'm creating a life and systems around avoiding regrets." And yet Sahar doesn't believe in regret if she has sought out information and made the best decision at the time for her future self.

Part of this requires managing our ambitions and desires so

they don't become problematic, and we don't grasp for too much at the same time.

"I think desire alone can lead people to unsustainable ambition, or rather to reckless ambition," she said. "I have lots of desires. I wanted to travel the world when I was younger. But I was stuck in a lab at twenty-six years old, working on research that I also loved. If I kept fanning the flame for both desires, then I'd be bummed out all the time. You have to assess all the desires, assess the needs, thinking about your future self. What needs to occur today that cannot occur or will occur with less fidelity, with less ease next year, five years from now, ten years from now?

"And then once you've decided it, just take a deep breath and accept it and just focus now. It's done. Don't keep running the wheels in the background saying, 'Oh, but what if, but what if?' I think that's also a form of reckless ambition."

Just as Sahar did, we can make our life with work more sustainable if we make courageous choices about what matters most now and plan our ambitions across periods of time, or arcs. In 1921, author Ray Cummings wrote, "Time is what keeps everything from happening at once."[2] We don't want to create a traffic jam with our ambitions, trying to squeeze everything we want to do into the same time highway. It's better to consciously choose rather than feel constant tension, have others choose for us, or experience burnout.

Is this easy? No. We want to have it all, and we want it all now. Is it fair that we have to choose? Perhaps not.

And to be sure, should our societal systems be more supportive of the realities of life and work demands? Yes. Do most of us not have a choice about needing to work? Yes.

With all that said, I don't want to discourage you from dreaming big. I hope you dream big! But the reality is we operate within the constraints of our finite time and energy. If you choose to pursue big goals or many at once, I suggest that you be thoughtful about the support structures you have in place around you and your sustaining plan, which we cover in Part IV. So if that's your choice (and it is *your* choice), plan accordingly to keep yourself sustained and your ambitions in the healthy and happy zone rather than in the severe zone.

You have the power to make choices for yourself. My hope is that you do so with eyes wide open—that you do so consciously. That you do so considering life and work together, knowing what matters most to you in the present, and factoring in your life stage and desired pace to inform decisions about allocating your time, attention, and effort now. Adopting this strategy will allow you to sustain your ambition over time, not just today but into the future, and allow you to make space for those things in your life that will fulfill and satisfy you.

Now let's get clear on what it is time for now.

PLAN IN ARCS AND WITH HORIZONS

Ambitions aren't time bound. What's helpful is to pace your ambitions by planning in arcs and with time horizons, determining which ambitions it is time for now, soon, and later. We often do this naturally. *I'll change jobs soon. I'll settle down with a partner and have children later. I'll travel when I retire.* That's a way of planning in arcs and deciding where to focus your effort and energy now and what you'll put off until later. But when you do this with more intentionality, you can ease the conflicts and tensions that crop up across your life and work ambitions and find more peace with the trade-offs you're making at the moment.

As part of this, it's helpful to think about your current life stage and be realistic about it. As I share in Chapter 3, it's normal for our priorities to shift as we enter different phases of life and work. What we wanted and what fulfilled us in the past may differ at present because we and our lives have evolved. Planning in arcs can help us have more compassion about these shifts and permission to redefine what matters most for us at this moment.

Another reason to plan in arcs is to embrace how your level of ambition can ebb and flow over time and to align it better with the pace you want to operate at now. Some of us define ourselves by our drive, thinking it only has one gear. But we can experience times when we want to pursue goals more intensely and other times when we want to dial it back. I think we're better served when we give ourselves this freedom without letting it be a judgment of our character. In many instances, we also misinterpret our drive—it's not that our ambition has waned; rather it's that our ambition is redirected to another area of our life, such as recovery and rejuvenation or a life goal that fuels us.

At this point I can look back at my life and see my arcs more clearly, even while having been conscious of the choices I made at the time. It's similar to an artist's creative periods, like Picasso's Blue and Rose periods or Georgia O'Keeffe's time in New York when she first uncovered her abstract style, and later in New Mexico when she furthered that approach in connection with nature. For me, my twenties were my discovery and athletic period or arc. My thirties and early forties were when I established my life and work, having married my husband and invested more time in building our life together and my career.

I've also had arcs with my work. I knew early on that I wanted to get foundational training before I stepped into an entrepreneurial venture, which is exactly the path I took. I sequenced my experiences in that regard. In my mid-to-late forties and early fifties, I entered yet another arc, focused on caring for older parents and investing time in creative and service work. My ambitions have shifted and grown over time for both my life and my work, and I've adjusted my path accordingly.

PACE YOURSELF

"Thirty under Thirty." "Forty under Forty." Ugh. I hate these lists. Well, that may be too harsh of a statement. I don't mind celebrating people who accomplish great things at a young age, but I don't like the expectations such headlines create and the pressure they breed.

We don't need to rush to the top and achieve quickly to be successful. We are not all on the same time schedule, and rushing can create its own issues. Frankly, rushing isn't sustainable.

I worked with Geoff Tanner, currently CEO of Simply Good Foods, at a time in his career when he was racing toward the top. He had been clear on his ambition to be a CEO from a young age. Yet, once he got to the C-suite (but not in the top role), he learned an important lesson from his mentors, which became his favorite career advice: "Widen your tolerances, and be patient with your career."[3] We can all benefit from being more patient; I know I can. And Geoff did at that stage, valuing the time he had to learn as a member of an executive team before stepping into the role he always had his eye on. But societal pressure doesn't make this easy.

While being patient, we can feel as if we're falling behind, because we don't think we're gaining traction. It often takes more time than we realize to achieve the results we seek. We can take the pressure off and enjoy the journey more if we remember that, with many of our ambitions, we need to play the long game, as consultant Dorie Clark espouses in her book of the same name.

Beyond speed, consider how hard you want to be driving now. It's best to align your current ambitions with your desired pace. Are you ready to be in a hard-driving period? Or do your life stage and goals better match a moderate intensity or measured pace?

Thus, an important part of planning in arcs and horizons is to learn to pace your ambitions—and to do so in a way that is right for you. Consider the natural rhythms of your life and factor that into your plans. So instead of feeling time pressure around your ambitions—"I haven't achieved this yet. I'm behind!" or, "I can't do that now. I should have taken more risks when I was younger. It's too late!"—you can learn to keep your eyes on your own arcs. You can eschew societal expectations and comparing yourself to others to make choices that are right for you now.

Narratives around time vary. You constantly hear, "Things take time—be patient," "It's never the right time—carpe diem, seize the day!," "Life is short, and life is long." All are true. What's also true is time is finite, and it's challenging to do it all at once. To step into sustainability is to accept these truths and contradictions.

But I get it—it can feel uncomfortable to put important desires off, to trust that you can come back to them later. Life, indeed, can be short. Next, let's navigate these tensions as you start to build your arcs.

MAP YOUR ARCS

What is it time for now and what can wait for future horizons? Getting clear on what's important at this moment in your life will inform how you answer that question and map your arcs.

To plan your current arc, you'll think about what matters most now across life and work, what's important given your stage in life, and at what pace you want to be operating. I have you consider life first, since your work fits into the vessel of your life. You may still choose to prioritize your work ambitions in this arc, but you can do so consciously with intention and know what it means for other choices you'll need to make across your goals and in your life.

The planning tool we'll use is the Horizon Map. It serves as a vision and an intention that can pull you forward and will be a tool you can come back to and adjust over time as you, your life, and your work change. Your map doesn't need to be too detailed or firm. Plan at a high level and hold it loosely. This isn't an exact science. It is meant to serve as a guide to help you decide how you want to pace your ambitions across different time horizons and where to focus your attention and energy at this moment, in turn creating more ease and reducing friction.

My coaching clients and workshop participants have found that this exercise achieves its purpose—helping them be honest with themselves, gain perspective and clarity, and then direct their effort moving forward. It's not uncommon for people to be surprised when creating their map. In seeing all their ambitions laid out in front of them, they often realize they're trying to do too much and need to make choices and prioritize. Or they notice how life and work ambitions intersect and recognize that they want more space for their personal goals. In response, they may choose to keep their world small and focus on what they currently deem most important.

> **PLAN IN ARCS WITH DIFFERENT TIME HORIZONS**
>
> Planning in arcs to pace your ambitions and goals is a flexible concept. You can use it to plan across longer time frames, like five-year cycles, or decade to decade if you are a long-term planner. Or you can use it to plan your goals for a shorter time frame, such as year over year across a three-year horizon. You can also use it for a year and plan quarterly or monthly to pace and sustain yourself.

Exercise: Create Your Horizon Map

You identify your current life and work ambitions in Chapter 6, as well as future ambitions as part of the vision exercise in Chapter 3. The Horizon Map exercise is where you'll bring together your present ambitions and your future vision of what you want for your life and work as you build your arcs.

You play with time in this exercise. Sounds supernatural, right? But time is a standard construct we use to manage and navigate our lives. To help you make choices, we'll explore three time dimensions—past, present, and future.

Contrary to what you might think, looking back can help you look forward and think about what you want to shape for the future. These time periods aren't disconnected, and in fact, we use similar parts of our brain to both remember what happened in the past and think of what's to come. In this exercise, you'll ask what your past says about what it might be time for now. Then, you'll look at the present to identify your current priorities. Finally, you'll call on your future self, as Sahar Yousef did, to help fight present bias and keep yourself from only prioritizing what would be satisfying now versus what you should invest in for the future. Ambitious people tend to prioritize short-term rewards over long-term goals. Bringing your future self into the reflection can help you make choices you won't regret and consider the consequences of the decisions you make today.

At the end of the exercise, you'll have a working Horizon Map, with prioritized ambitions across life and work that you can continue to shape over time. Let's get started.

1. *Confirm your long-term vision.* Refer to your Right Foundation and capture your long-term vision ambitions across your life and work to help inform how you'll map your arcs across the Now, Near, and Next categories. Table 7.1 shows an example.

2. *Confirm your ambitions and goals.* Gather the current life and work ambitions you identified in Chapter 6.

3. *Determine your time horizons.* Choose the time horizons against which you'd like to plan. As noted in the callout, this exercise is flexible. You can do a three-year horizon (so Now is this year, Near is next year, and Next is two years out) or

Table 7.1. Setting your long-term vision and time horizons

	Now	Near	Next	Long-term vision
Time	1 year	5 years	10+ years	20+ years
Life				• Family cared for • Strong community • Live abroad and in other US locations • Travel • Still strong and exercising, vitality
Lower priority				
Work				• Earn more and work less • Still engaged in work but fewer hours • Still coach • Volunteer and more service-centered work • Continual learning
Lower priority				

a five-year horizon (Now is this year, Near is the next two years, and Next is the following two years). You can also plan much further out like Sahar—for example, in five-year arcs (Now is the next five years, Near is the following five years, and Next is five years after that). Pick which horizon you think will work best for you and note it on the map. You can also mix it up, as shown in Table 7.1.

4. *Map your life ambitions to the arcs.* Reflecting on what matters most to you now across life and work, your current life stage, and your desired pace, map your current life ambitions in the Life row of the Now column. What is this period of time for? You can consider putting your highest priorities in the top line and note lower priorities in the second line. Then look at the other life ambitions on your vision exercise and determine if and how you'd map those to future arcs, putting them in either Near or Next. As you do this, you might identify other ambitions and goals you want to include. Add as you'd like. Table 7.2 gives an example.

5. *Map your work ambitions.* Now do the same with your work ambitions. Based on what matters most now and where your ambition is currently leaning—more life, work, or equally split—map your current work ambitions in the Work row of the Now column. Consider putting your highest priorities in the top line and note lower priorities in the second line. Then look back to your other work ambitions and determine how you'd map those to future arcs, putting them in either Near or Next. Again, you may identify new ambitions and goals as you complete this. Add as you'd like. See Table 7.3 for an example.

6. *Courageously choose.* To finalize the placement of your ambitions and goals across the time horizons of Now, Near, and Next, review the map and determine if any life and work ambitions need shifting as you view them together. If you're uncertain about what fits where, consider these time dimension prompts:

Table 7.2. Mapping life ambitions to arcs

	Now	Near	Next	Long-term vision
Time	1 year	5 years	10+ years	20+ years
Life	• Attend activities to avoid stagnation • Prioritize health care • Connect with parents and extended family	• Foster community • Redo backyard • Travel one time a year • Spend one month living and working from another US location • Reprioritize athleticism • Care for parents	• Take second sabbatical • Live abroad and in other US locations • Care for parents • Travel with friends	• Family cared for • Strong community • Live abroad and in other US locations • Travel • Still strong and exercising, vitality
Lower priority	• Care for parents • Foster personal community • Foster work community			
Work				• Earn more and work less • Still engaged in work but fewer hours • Still coach • Volunteer and more service-centered work • Continual learning
Lower priority				

Table 7.3. Mapping work ambitions to arcs

	Now	Near	Next	Long-term vision
Time	1 year	5 years	10+ years	20+ years
Life	• Attend activities to avoid stagnation • Prioritize health care • Connect with parents and extended family	• Foster community • Redo backyard • Travel one time a year • Spend one month living and working from another US location • Reprioritize athleticism • Care for parents	• Take second sabbatical • Live abroad and in other US locations • Care for parents • Travel with friends	• Family cared for • Strong community • Live abroad and in other US locations • Travel • Still strong and exercising, vitality
Lower priority	• Care for parents • Foster personal community • Foster work community			
Work	• Write first book • Test speaking and facilitating • Solidify consulting practice	• Strengthen consulting discipline, sell work with my own IP • Establish platform and personal business with a mix of work streams • Explore or write second book • Explore getting master's or PhD	• Still consult and coach, but fewer hours and flexible • Volunteer and more service-centered work	• Earn more and work less • Still engaged in work but fewer hours • Still coach • Volunteer and more service-centered work • Continual learning
Lower priority	• Coach training		• Continual learning	

- Past: What does your past suggest you should prioritize now? For example: Prioritize well-being and vitality actions to remain healthy, strong, and energetic.
- Present—life: What might you prioritize based on what's important now in your life and based on your life stage? For example: Spend time with and be available for my children before they go to college.
- Present—work: What's important based on the role and requirements of your work now? For example: Develop technology skills to remain relevant.
- Future: Step into your future self at the end of the time horizon you've chosen for your arcs. What does your future self want you to prioritize now? What will they think about this choice in five years? For example: I will wish I had invested time with and cared for my parents and older extended family.

7. *Pause to reflect.* Sit with your current mapping. What did you notice while doing this exercise? What final insights do you want to note? Based on what you've mapped so far, what does it mean in terms of structures and support you might need to make things sustainable across your life and work as you plan for Right Effort in Part IV?

At this point, your Horizon Map should include in its current arc the ambitions that are right for you at this time. These are, ideally, self-defined, meaningful, motivating goals for which you have the energy now. If you question any of these ambitions, return to Chapter 4 and use the exercises there to reconfirm if each ambition is a have-to or a want-to. Remember that rooting your ambitions in your Right Foundation will help keep you on the right path.

Also, a reminder that the Horizon Map isn't meant to be precise or static. Like any prioritization exercise, you can revisit it, as needed, to adjust for life and work changes and determine if your prioritization still feels right given current circumstances. I suggest you review your map at least annually to track progress. Note that for further-out time horizons, the map serves only as a rough guide. It's unlikely you can predict that you'll meet a milestone in a particular year, so don't get too attached to set time frames and specifics.

You may have made other observations from this exercise, like realizing that you want to pull ambitions forward rather than waiting for a later arc and that they require earlier planning and investment. Or you may have noticed how life and work ambitions intersect and recognize that you want more space for your life ambitions. Or you may find that you want to reinterpret some ambitions to make them feasible despite current realities. It's also possible that by simply putting ambitions and goals on the map, you can quiet any disappointment you may feel about missing out on them in the present.

After completing your Horizon Map, you may still struggle with making choices. Tensions might remain, like wanting to do too much or needing to dial down your level of ambition. We cover how to navigate these challenges in Chapter 8.

For now, remember that just because some of your goals might be off on the horizon doesn't mean you can't still dream big and keep them alive.

NURTURE YOUR AMBITIONS

When placing ambitions in your arcs, you likely pushed some to the horizon. Doing so can bring up a range of emotions. It can be hard to put an ambition or goal on the back burner. After all, it was on your list for a reason, so, understandably, you could become sad or resistant to making such a choice. And while life can be long, we're given no guarantees, which I know sounds morbid. Sorry! So it can feel uncomfortable to put important desires off and trust you can come back to them later.

One strategy to manage this is to keep an ambition alive by finding small ways to nurture and explore it while focusing on other prioritized goals. I still encourage you to pace yourself, but if you don't want to put an ambition off, see what actions you can take to move it forward.

Don't forget that future ambitions and goals may include multiple steps to achieve the desired outcome, extending the timeline. Break these larger goals into smaller milestones to map on your Horizon Map as well.

Another factor to consider is that ambitions can take time to form, grow, and take shape. Or they may sneakily shift unexpectedly, even when you think you're being conscious about your choices. Thus, it's helpful to explore what you want for your future sooner than you think. I encourage you, as part of your Sustainable Ambition practices, to make it a habit to continuously explore your curiosities, always learn, and regularly experiment, in turn planting seeds to inform your future goals. As I noted previously, those of us who are ambitious can become too focused on the present and forget to invest in and seed our future.

Consider Mara Yale's story from Chapter 6. When she stepped

away from her corporate job, she gave herself a year to find her footing. She didn't know how she would use her Feldenkrais training, but now Feldenkrais, the seed she planted, is part of her portfolio career, which consists of four different types of work.

So challenge yourself—how can you keep an ambition alive? What are you curious about or what do you want to learn or experiment with now? How can you test an ambition to see if it's one you might want to pursue in the future?

IT'S NEVER TOO LATE

When we create our arcs, some of us might think it's too late to pursue an ambition. For example, I might tell myself I can no longer live abroad; I've missed my window. But I don't accept that outcome. Would you?

Taking more risks is one of the repeated wisdoms I've heard from people I've interviewed on the podcast when I ask about the advice they'd give their younger selves. My friend Mike Murgatroyd in our podcast interview built on that with the idea to take *good* risks as part of creating an extraordinary life.[4] Using the constructs from the book, what qualified as a good risk to Mike was an action that aligns with your Right Foundation. Good risk pushes you to step into what you want for yourself and your life. These insights combined with the idea of playing the long game made me realize that risk is not just for the young. I would encourage us all to take *good* risks, always. This builds on the concept of nurturing ambitions and planting seeds, but I share it here as encouragement to accept that it's never too late to pursue an ambition that inspires you. If you've had a dream that's been dormant, pull it out and dust it off. Could this be the time for that ambition?

It's also worth maintaining dedication and perseverance in your work as you age, if you are still motivated and aspire to achieve your goals. Not all of us realize our ambitions quickly. Some of us require time to come into our own. Revisiting Albert-László Barabási's book *The Formula: The Universal Laws of Success*, he argues that age is not a limiter to performance as many would have us believe.[5] Rather, his research indicates that people can achieve desired results if they remain committed and continue to produce. The lesson is: Rather than abandon your goals, be consistent and persistent with your work.

Returning to Mara Yale's story again—she's now in her fifties and still ambitious, and she desires to continue to be sustainably so. She never wants to set a retirement date and rather wants to build her life with work, so she can pursue her professional capacity for another twenty years and still adjust to her life circumstances. She doesn't know exactly how it will all play out, but she's not restricting herself or worrying yet about how things might change as her kids go off to college. Instead, she's open to how her work might evolve and embraces the concept of planning in arcs and allowing ambitions to develop over time.

> It's never too late to build your life and work in a way that works for you. Muster the courage to go after your ambitions.

It's never too late to build your life and work in a way that works for you. Muster the courage to go after your ambitions.

Some of us may take more time to figure out where we want to fully invest our effort, to fully commit ourselves, or for the spark to show up and connections to align. Your time can be now.

• • •

In this chapter, I encourage you to make courageous choices for what it is time for now. And I also suggest that you nurture some ambitions and realize that it doesn't have to be too late. Have I exacerbated the friction you may be feeling around all you want to do? See, it's a challenge to navigate our ambitions and these conflicts. Let's move into exploring the most common tensions and how we can better approach these choices.

Chapter 8

• • •

Navigate the Tensions across Ambitions

Deciding what it's time for now isn't always easy. Did you feel nervous, frustrated, or apprehensive when you made those choices and mapped your arcs? Such decisions can be uncomfortable, causing internal turmoil, especially in your current arc.

After all, we can feel called and inspired to do a lot. You may be like one of my workshop participants who, in doing the Horizon Map from Chapter 7, said, "My one-lane road map turned into a four-lane highway!" You may feel tension when choosing between life and work ambitions, wanting to protect your time and energy for activities and priorities in your personal life. You may feel pulled between a real desire to step back and a desire to lean in. Or you may feel the natural undercurrents of the ebb and flow of ambition or a need to coordinate your goals with a partner. It's hard to make these trade-offs. So what do we do?

Here, I want to tackle these challenges and the internal conflict that can be present when we navigate these choices and provide some ideas and ways to think about how to prioritize. I cover five areas: (1) when we can't choose when, (2) when we want to do too much, (3) protect what's important in your life, (4) make room for life and Right Ambitions, and (5) navigate the ebbs and flows of ambitions.

My hope is that this guidance helps you make decisions with more clarity and peace. And remember, as circumstances change, you can always make different decisions in the future as they do.

WHEN WE CAN'T CHOOSE WHEN

You may find that you resist eliminating any ambitions and goals. If that's the case, one strategy is to first coordinate your ambitions to reduce tension. Another place to start is to unpack why you feel tension in making the decision to unlock insight to help you move forward. We explore both here.

First, Coordinate Your Ambitions

Before eliminating an ambition or goal, consider if you can resolve tension by better coordinating them instead. In my interview with Dr. Ayelet Fishbach, the motivation researcher, she illustrated this concept using the analogy of a food buffet. When we eat from a buffet, it's ideal to put food on our plate that goes well together—that is coordinated, if you will.[1] Imagine eating a meal of escargot with sardines, artichokes, and ice cream. That likely wouldn't be digested well; nor would our ambitions and goals if they were equally misaligned. So we need to think about not only how much we put on our life and work buffet plates but also whether what we put on goes well together. That's one way to reduce conflict.

Motivation research also points us to create a goal system, identifying our main goals and how others connect to them. We want to maximize goal attainment and look for and create positive connections while minimizing negative impacts. The desired outcome is to align our goals as best as possible to reduce friction. An additional strategy of a goal system is goal stacking—identifying initial goals that will support long-term ones, as I explain in Chapter 7. This phases goals across arcs—what needs to come first to help you gain momentum and confidence and then what might come next in support of your long-term aspirations?

Another benefit of better syncing our goals is to help reduce time pressure. One research study found that people who believed their goals conflicted not only felt more stressed and anxious but also felt short on time.[2] If we pause to think about this, we can imagine how this can be so. The internal friction we feel when our goals clash can generate time tension by creating a pressure-filled experience of running from one event to the next rather than seeing how our activities work together to move us toward a common, desired outcome.

But after applying this strategy of better coordination, we may still need to, at times, make trade-offs and simply prioritize some ambitions and goals and postpone others. We *don't* have to do it all. And if we are experiencing a lot of tension around a goal, it may make sense to let it go, even if for the time being.

Explore the Tension and Trade-Offs

A simple approach to better understand the conflict you're feeling around an ambition is to explore the tension and trade-offs, considering the reward you'd gain through its pursuit or the reward you'd forgo. Doing so can help you uncover what might be causing the consternation, so you can identify if a better way exists to coordinate your goals or choose another path forward.

Ask yourself these questions:

- What pulls me toward this ambition? What pushes me away from this ambition?
- What tension exists? What is the trade-off if I don't pursue the ambition? What is the trade-off if I do?
- What are my observations from these reflections?
- What are the implications of these observations? Do I want to choose to continue with this ambition or goal? Can I better coordinate it, or will I need to compromise?

For example, here's what the exploration of my ambition to live abroad looked like:

- What are the pull and push?
    - Pull: I want to experience a new culture, learn a language, and play hooky in another country. It will contribute to my learning and growth, which I value.
    - Push: Can I take time away for an extended period or afford to do so? I need to work, and I don't have a visa or overseas job. Plus, I'm caring for my parents, which is also important to me.

- What are the tension and trade-off?
    - Tension: It's a life dream, yet it never seems to be the right time, or the opportunity hasn't presented itself and landed. I've never made it a priority to try and pull it off. I assume it needs to happen later.
    - Trade-off: I may never have the experience. I could throw off my career and may not be here for familial needs.
- What are my observations?
    - I'll be disappointed if I don't live abroad. It is a life vision ambition.
    - I need to create a proactive plan to make it a reality.
- What are the implications?
    - I will continue to have this goal on my Horizon Map, and I will continue to delay it for at least twenty-four or more months. I want to compromise and reinterpret the goal in the short term to make it a possibility by designing a similar type of experience.

WHEN WE WANT TO DO TOO MUCH

How can we navigate when we have competing Right Ambitions and are drawn to do a lot? After coordinating, we can choose or compromise. Christina Wallace did both.

Christina and her husband were deliberate about having children and thoughtful about the family life they wanted to create. In our interview, she shared: "We were both on the older side. We could have easily chosen not to have kids and had continued on with our very big lives, but we wanted kids. We were making this choice."³

At this life inflection point, Christina had to decide her next career move. She had held demanding, always-on jobs as the founder of start-ups, which she loved. Now, she knew she needed to do something different to create the family experience she and her husband imagined. As Christina had her first child, she stepped into a new role as a professor at her alma mater, Harvard Business School. It was a great fit to accommodate this stage. But Christina learned that compromising and choices didn't stop with work. She had to consider life activities, too. She couldn't fit everything into her schedule, even if she valued it.

Christina has been a singer and musician throughout her life. When she moved to Boston, she explored joining a choir, adding into the mix an activity she'd find energizing. But in her exploration, she realized the time demands didn't add up. Between rehearsal times and her husband's schedule as a public servant, two nights out of the week they'd be single parenting—not what they had envisioned. And then she considered other demands across choir, her role as a professor, and other ambitions, like her new book. "And I start doing the math. I'm literally getting back to the 110 percent capacity that I had prior to kids, and that's not what I want."

Christina knew the answer wasn't for her to just work harder. She didn't want that for herself at this stage in life. Instead, she was ready to make a courageous choice. "And so it was a really hard decision, but I put choirs on the back burner for a little while. I put a number of things on the back burner while I said, right now, my portfolio has a lot of time dedicated to my kids, and that's okay. That's what this chapter of life requires. It's not forever."

In Christina's case, she compromised on her job and made choices around her personal goals while embracing the concepts of arcs and pacing to keep her life and work sustainable. "What I'm hoping, and I'm literally telling myself this over and over, is that having it all doesn't mean having it all at the same time, allowing myself seasons and giving myself the permission to ebb and flow what all those things are. And just because I put something on the back burner doesn't mean it can't come back. It very well may come back. And if it doesn't come back, it might be because I no longer want it."

Sometimes what is needed is prioritization and focusing our effort. It's okay to make our life and world smaller in scope for the moment to make it more manageable and sustainable.

To follow Christina as a role model, we can think about two dimensions in making similar choices—urgency and energy. Related to time, consider: How urgent is it to pursue an ambition or goal? Related to motivation, consider: How much energy do you naturally have for or are you putting into an ambition or goal now? These together, if you think of a 2 × 2 matrix, reveal several strategies to choose and compromise: prioritize; reinterpret, coordinate, or link; nurture or postpone; or let it go (see Figure 8.1).

> It's okay to make our life and world smaller in scope for the moment to make it more manageable and sustainable.

- *Prioritize.* The easiest strategy is to prioritize and commit to an ambition for which there is high urgency and motivation to do it now. Or it could be an ambition that is central to who you want to become now.

Figure 8.1. Possible choose and compromise strategies

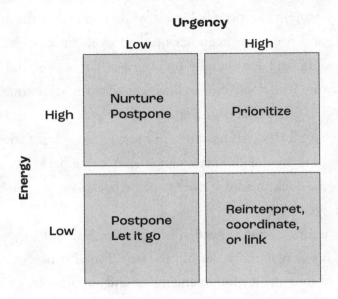

- *Reinterpret, coordinate, or link.* We can adjust our ambitions and goals when they are urgent, but our energy is low. We can reinterpret them in a way that delivers the same outcome but requires less effort and energy. We can better coordinate with our other goals to create energy efficiency. Or we can link an ambition to our Right Foundation to increase our motivation and energy.

- *Nurture.* You may have an ambition for which you are highly motivated, but it's not urgent to pursue now. If you have competing goals, you could renegotiate how much you put toward the ambition and take some action that requires less energy. That way, you continue to nurture your interest and make progress but use less time or effort.

- *Postpone.* The situation could be that you can't carve out time or energy for an ambition that you're drawn to but isn't urgent; other ambitions are a higher priority. In this case, you can compromise and choose to postpone the less urgent ambition and put it on the back burner for now.

- *Let it go.* You may have ambitions that are low urgency and for which you have low energy. Some of these may be at the end of their life, where more effort won't yield significant results; you are at a point of diminishing returns. In these cases, it may be time to simply let it go with acceptance and self-compassion to ease the potential pain of the decision.

How can we know which of these strategies to take with our ambitions? Pausing to reflect on the urgency and our energy can help.

Consider what trade-offs you want to make. What is it time to do? Where will you choose or compromise to create more ease for yourself? Whatever you decide, make a conscious decision that's right for you now.

FREE RESOURCE

To explore further, you can find a free exercise, the Present Priorities Matrix, at SustainableAmbition.com/sa-toolkit.

PROTECT WHAT'S IMPORTANT IN YOUR LIFE

I've advocated that we prioritize life ambitions on a level with work ambitions. This isn't easy to do. Some have asked me how they can protect what's important in their lives and get clear on nonnegotiables: priorities that must come first, where you are unwilling to make trade-offs. What do you *not want* to compromise for your ambition?

One way to think about this is to get clear on what you put on your calendar first. Where do you protect your time and energy for what matters most to you? In First Lady Michelle Obama's podcast interview with her good friend Valerie Jarrett, they both talked about how they prioritized either caring for themselves or making time for their family all through their working lives. Mrs. Obama described it as putting herself on her calendar first before anything else.[4]

Clarence So, who I introduce in Chapter 6, follows a similar strategy based on his priorities and to manage his life with a chronic autoimmune disorder. Every day, he aligns his calendar based on his priority intentions and what is required to manage his health. For example, if his back is bothering him, he'll put back exercises on his calendar first. Clarence is deliberate in aligning where he spends his time with his priorities.

When you think about your own calendar and your life non-negotiables—those things you want to prioritize and won't compromise on—what would you want to put on your calendar first? Is it time with your children, your partner, or a friend? Is it time to exercise or be in nature each day? Is it a ten-minute meditation in the morning and evening? Or take it beyond the calendar and consider what priorities or practices you won't budge on—that must be firm. Would it be no phones at the dinner table or no work on vacations? You can consider putting in place structures to help support you in keeping these firm commitments. The obvious one is to actually block your calendar by putting your priorities on it, or you could sign up for a class or commit to an action with a friend for accountability.

On the flip side, it's also helpful to understand where you can allow yourself some leeway around your nonnegotiables, so you can reduce friction and frustration when things don't go as planned. Around the areas you want to be firm, where might you be willing to flex? You might find that you want to continue to be firm on a particular commitment, but you may also find that you can give yourself some freedom to add ease when needed.

> **FREE RESOURCE**
>
> To explore further, you can find a free exercise, Be Firm and Flex Your Life Nonnegotiables, at SustainableAmbition.com/sa-toolkit.

MAKE ROOM FOR LIFE AND RIGHT AMBITIONS

My friend Evette Davis built her successful public affairs firm in a challenging environment called "San Francisco politics." She negotiated difficult years and situations, but that didn't stop her from exploring her ambition to become an author. She told me when her first book launched, and several times since, "All I want to do is write my books." Her creative ambition has called to her for some time. But since that event and the Great Recession, her business has boomed, mainly because of her business development savvy.

Evette has nurtured her creative ambition while raising a daughter, caring for aging parents, and running and growing her business. Each of these ambitions has ebbed and flowed over her different life stages. She has had to postpone several books while managing work and life emergencies, but she's figured out how to carve out space for her writing and continues to publish books when she has time. Evette has never wavered. Instead, she's remained committed to her ambition and has nurtured her talent, because it's a calling that sustains her.

To many, Evette's story may sound unbelievable. They also have life or Right Ambitions that they want to prioritize and not give up. Yet people commonly find that high-urgency, low-energy activities use a disproportionate amount of their time and energy.

I heard this often in my workshops. For example, one participant acknowledged this with clarity and frustration: "I found that for my life ambitions I have high energy but less urgency, whereas my work ambitions are high urgency with less energy. So I always end up prioritizing those over what I want to do." Another responded to that reflection with "And here is where resentment lies." Yep.

When do we get to prioritize our life ambitions? When do we decide that they are urgent? How can we move from resentment to more personal reward by carving out time and energy for the life and Right Ambitions that matter to us? How can we be more like Evette?

One approach is to leverage the choose and compromise strategies from earlier in this chapter.

- Simply choose one life or Right Ambition that you will prioritize. Easy to say, but perhaps it can and should be that easy.

- Step into that choice with excitement, not worry, knowing that adding such an ambition to your priority list can increase your energy level as opposed to drain it.
- Take the nurture approach and determine a small action you can take to keep the ambition alive for you at this time.
- Consider reinterpreting the ambition to have it deliver your desired outcome yet align with the level of effort and energy you can put toward it now.

Another way we can create more ease around how we focus our energy is to better align where we spend our time with where we wish we spent our time. Despite having more discretionary time than in the past, most of us—80 percent, in fact, according to analysis of research from a Gallup Organization survey—feel we can't fit in all we want or need to accomplish each day, which can negatively affect our health, happiness, and productivity.[5] We can combat our sense of time pressure by examining where we invest our hours and how we'd like it to shift. That's what you can do in the next exercise.

Exercise: Where Time and Wish Time

We can often feel time pressure, yet we have more agency around this feeling than we realize.[6] The friction exists partly in our minds because of the gap between where we put our time and how that feels and where we wish we put our time and how that might feel. This exercise has you explore both realms and points you to consider your Right Foundation to identify what might be causing the friction between your have-tos and your want-tos. In this exploration, you might uncover that you don't spend time on your Right Ambitions. Or you may learn that your priorities have shifted, and you no longer wish to spend your time the same way. This exercise can help you confirm if you are putting your time and energy into what matters most to you right now.

For the exercise, do this:

- Pull out your calendar and look at the previous week to note where you spent your time. Capture where you typically spent your time in high-level categories, such as work, shuttling kids, specific hobbies (e.g., creative writing, playing an instrument, woodworking), exercise, and so forth.
- Think about how you wish you had spent your time. To guide you, revisit the ambitions and goals you have in your current arc. If you'd like, also revisit your Right Foundation to consider your vision for your life, how you want to give, your values, and what you love.
- Step back, reflect, and note your observations. What do you notice? What insights do you have? Do you spend your time putting effort into your prioritized Right Ambitions? Or do you spend more time on have-tos? What changes might you want to make in how you use your time to create more life and work fulfillment and ease?
- Note what actions you want to take based on your observations. Can you put in place a new structure to support where you want to shift to align better with your wish time? (See Table 8.2 for an example.)

Table 8.2. Where time and wish time example

Where time	Wish time
• Consulting work • Travel for work • Coaching • On computer too much • At home a lot	• Creative work • On computer less • Outside of home more • Careful about too much work travel • More adventures away with my partner
Observations: Get out more to enjoy activities in the world given so much at-home work. Pace work travel and turn projects down. Proactively schedule creative projects and breaks.	
Actions: Start a small creative project. Schedule desired activities. Combine those with other goals like my community ambition. Check in on work level before I commit. Put more downtime on the calendar.	

NAVIGATE THE EBBS AND FLOWS OF AMBITIONS

The changing and pacing of our ambitions can be full of friction. How do you know if your ambitions have truly shifted? How do you allow yourself to, at times, dial down your ambition? How do you navigate the pacing of ambitions with a partner? Let's explore these tensions now.

How to Know If Your Ambitions Have Truly Shifted

We can hit moments in our life when our energy for an ambition or goal changes, and it can be distressing. Do we stay the course or is something deeper going on? You may wonder, *Is this just a short-term setback and I just need to pause and restore myself after a demanding period?* If you're exhausted, time and space alone may resolve how you feel.

Or you may wonder, *Is my ambition truly shifting? Do I not want this anymore?* To answer these questions, first reflect on whether a significant life or work event has occurred that is causing you to rethink your ambitions. Also consider whether you've entered a new life stage that is making you rethink what you want.

A way to further unpack and understand if you are at a moment of shifting ambitions is to return to your Right Foundation and explore if your motivations have changed. Perhaps a chapter is closing, and you are being called to something new. Is a new vision for your life, work, or who you want to be taking shape? Do you want to give or contribute in a new way? Are you being drawn toward something new that you love? You might be at a point where you are ready to move on from a goal, even if you haven't fully realized it, and longing to grow and challenge yourself in a new way.

Go back to your values, too. As I share in Chapter 3, we often reprioritize our values as we step into new life stages or periods. A worthy exercise is to see how you might prioritize your values now and determine whether that evaluation shifts where you want to focus your effort. I've experienced this myself, for example, when I recognized that right now I'm prioritizing my value of creative production over my value for vitality and health. I'm not ignoring vitality and health completely, but a disproportionate amount of my effort is being put against creative ambitions. I've learned to accept this and not make myself feel wrong for the focus. I'm simply called to do this work in this period of my life.

Don't be startled if ambitions shift or ebb and flow on you again after you experience one round of changes. Consider yourself forewarned! You may not be ambitious now, but you might be in the future, or you might find yourself being ambitious about a surprising new direction.

It's Okay to Dial It Down at Times

Jacinda Ardern became one of the youngest prime ministers of New Zealand, at age thirty-seven, and was recognized for her outstanding leadership in crisis situations and her handling of the COVID-19 pandemic. She also had her first child early in her first term in office, so she juggled many roles.

Ardern had won reelection twice, and at the end of 2022, before the summer season in the southern hemisphere, declared plans to run for a third term. At the beginning of 2023, just three months later, she made another announcement. She shocked people by stating she was stepping down from her role. What happened?

Some criticized her, suggesting she couldn't handle the job. But she wasn't leaving because the job was hard. She had been doing the hard job. What she said was "I am human" and "We give all that we can, for as long as we can, and then it's time."[7]

Jacinda Ardern made a courageous choice for herself, her family, and her country, and in doing so took control of her life and work. She knew to ask, "What is it time for?" and, in answering that question, stepped into her next life and work arc.

Being prime minister had been the right ambition at the right time when she first stepped into the role, and she was able to give it the right effort. While it might still have been a right ambition for her, her energy had been depleted, putting the timing into question. She said that she had tried to build up her reserves and resilience in the summer but hadn't been able to do it as she had planned. Plus, she believed it was time for her to step back and let someone else lead.

Ardern demonstrates that it's okay to step away from the big job—one of the biggest—and make room for other ambitions, such as those for life. Doing so doesn't mean you can't still be ambitious about your work; it just may look different. Ardern hasn't stepped away from her career. Instead, she's accepted fellowships and appointments in areas for which she holds passion and interest, among other activities.

I loved her closing lines from her announcement: "I hope in return I leave behind a belief that you can be kind, but strong. Empathetic, but decisive. Optimistic, but focused. That you can be your own kind of leader—one that knows when it's time to go."[8] I see this as a rallying cry to be a leader of your life and to make choices that are right for you now.

You may be in a similar position where you need or want to step back to allow room for other ambitions in your life. Making such a decision is yet another conflict-filled moment. We can feel torn between multiple important ambitions. And yet this is a time when we need to give ourselves permission to make the choice that's right for us.

What makes such decisions even more difficult is that it seems inappropriate in our society to ask, *Am I ambitious right now or not? Do I want to step back or keep pushing?* This is especially true for women with children, in particular those who have young ones at home. Is it okay for them to not be as professionally ambitious as their younger selves while they raise their children? Is it okay for them to take an "ambition step back" in the short term? While they want more sustainability in their lives, they also know it won't feel great or look great to take a back seat—it challenges their nature and societal norms. Culturally, we confound potential with pace. Yet the idea of a direct, fast path to the top is unrealistic for most of us. We often need to be willing to modulate our ambitions to accommodate life.

Despite society acknowledging how hard Americans work today and sabbaticals becoming more common, it doesn't seem acceptable for people to take career sabbaticals. A sabbatical can be seen as stepping off the fast track, and many people fear future employers may view it negatively. In the end, dialing it down never feels right to us or the employer market.

This was true for Clarence So, too. Despite having a significant improvement in his physical health after his initial diagnosis, his emotionally difficult identity issue was something he learned to manage over time. Relative to his peers, Clarence couldn't reliably put as much effort into his work. While he saw his peers continue to drive and accomplish, some noted he was compromising on his career. Occasionally, stinging comments would be made, like "Wow, you're squandering a lot of great career opportunities. What's up?" Sharing details about his chronic health limitations felt like a complicated topic, and so his typical response was to quietly demur, "Sorry, it's not right for me." Then his feelings of FOMO and loss of relevance would inflict narcissistic injury.

Instead of suffering from these pressures, my wish is that we embrace and normalize what Anne-Marie Slaughter espoused in her book *Unfinished Business: Women, Men, Work, Family* about allowing for off- and on-ramps around our career. When your ambition is waning, you could take the off-ramp and then have the opportunity later to take the on-ramp back into your career. By adopting this model, we could reduce the worry and nervousness attached to making decisions to dial down our ambition when we need to.

Until societal norms change, in these moments of tension, we can look to the strategies I shared when we want to do too much. We can simply choose to prioritize one ambition over another and in doing so postpone the other or give it up. We can also choose to keep our focus and our lives smaller to make it all more manageable.

But the more likely scenario is to reinterpret your work ambition for better life alignment, as Jacinda Ardern did. Work realignment can include renegotiating your current role, transitioning to a new position within your company, seeking a new job with a new organization, or stepping into self-employment. Many today are choosing the latter, when traditional work environments fail to offer suitable life-work structures.

The other strategy I suggest is nurturing ambitions during times you may take an off-ramp. Pressing pause can be temporary, and I don't believe that our potential is diminished if we adapt to our life or our work ambition ebbs and flows over time. But what we should do instead to buttress against negative perceptions is foster our potential at the same time we're dialing back our ambition. Consider where you can invest in your potential, building skills and positioning yourself for the on-ramp.

An added benefit of this approach is bolstering your identity. Often, stepping back affects how we view ourselves, as I share in the example of Sonya Thomas in Chapter 5. Sonya attached her sense of self to her ambition. If she wasn't the hard-driving, high-achieving Sonya, who was she? I commonly hear this from coaching clients, podcast guests, and friends who have shifted their ambitions—they don't know how to ground their identities as they make changes. So investing in your potential is also investing in your identity. How can you explore a new skill or interest to expand how you see yourself? Who do you want to be now, in this new space and given where you are focusing your time?

Along these lines, we should acknowledge that we are multidimensional and claim our full identity, including our role as a parent, if that is a focus for us at this time. Karyn Flynn, one of my podcast guests, shared in our conversation how it took her a long time to see her role as a mother on par with her professional responsibilities—not that it changed how much she loved her children. But now she defines success for herself by prioritizing being a mother and has made choices accordingly. "I was very clear that being able to be around for my kids before they headed off to college was really important," she said. "And going forward, being able to be available to them emotionally and physically in terms of time to do things or meet their needs is really important to me. I'm very candid and nonnegotiable about that."[9]

Acceptance is also powerful. We can spend a lot of time and energy fretting about our decisions and choices. Yet we can find more peace and save the energy churn by stepping into acceptance. This is an area I practice regularly, and it does take repetition. Perhaps the better way is to find more joy in the choices we make for ourselves, as Oliver Burkeman encourages in his well-regarded book *Four Thousand Weeks: Time Management for Mortals*.[10]

Ambition over one's lifetime ebbs and flows. At times, we are going to go for it, and at other times we'll choose to dial it back to prioritize another part of our lives or for rest and rejuvenation. Let this be acceptable for yourself.

Navigate Ambitions with a Partner

Nine months before we got married, my husband-to-be quit his well-paying, secure corporate job after ten years. What was next for him? He stepped into a new job at a cabinet shop to explore his passion for woodworking, curious to know if it should become his career. His salary became less than 25 percent of what he used to earn, which had an impact on our finances and my ambitions.

At the time, he didn't discuss his decision with me. Yet it had major implications for how we were going to live our life together. We should have talked about it.

But we did talk about it after he took the job and revisited the decision as he stayed in it for the first three years of our marriage. Since that time, we've gotten better, but not perfect, at discussing the ebb and flow of our work and personal ambitions. When either of us is at an inflection point in our career, we check in and make work decisions together, keeping in mind our finances and the life we want to create together. We've had moments where we've had to take turns, if you will, with our job choices. I've stayed in a job to have stability and health care while he's been self-employed, and now he does the same while I've stepped out on my own.

These tensions exist when you're in a relationship, and you may need to make decisions between one person's career or the other's. What's most important here—and I've heard this counsel from others—is to bring the important people in your life into your decision-making process and make choices considering the life vision you, together, hold and being wise about your finances. You shouldn't make these decisions in a vacuum; instead, involve and, if you must, negotiate with your partner and family members, since they are affected by your choices. It's better to have transparent, direct conversations and not skirt any issues.

When we make such decisions on careers or on who does what in our households, it's helpful to know ourselves and make choices with everyone's personal ambitions and motivators in mind. As I've noted, and perhaps you've experienced, these types of choices can affect our identity and how we see and think about ourselves.

My podcast guest Bethanie Baynes experienced this herself as she became the primary earner for her family while her husband focused on his music career and stepped into being the primary caregiver for their children. Bethanie is a leader on the topic of breadwinning women and champions having these difficult conversations with our partners and other important people around us. When making decisions about roles and responsibilities for a household, she suggested asking your partner questions like these: Does that match with your goals? Does that match with your identity and self-worth? If not, talk through why that is. Are those things that you can unwind and adjust and rebuild? Are those things that you're just making assumptions about? From there, you can then make decisions with more insight and, once decided, align on the expectations around those roles and responsibilities you're shaping for your family.

We can reduce the frustration or unease we may feel when we make such life choices with partners if we invest the time to have challenging conversations and get clear and comfortable in the decisions we make together.

•••

As you leave this chapter, you still may feel resistance and tension when you make decisions on what it is time to do. Allow yourself to be aware of and acknowledge how you're feeling. Then get curious and explore what that resistance and tension are trying to tell you. What do you want instead? You have a choice on how you want to move forward. And remember—you can change your mind. Nothing is static. Nothing is locked in. If you aren't fulfilled or satisfied, change your context. But time and energy are finite, so it's time to focus on what matters most to you now.

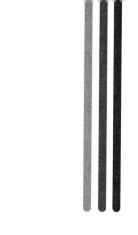

Part IV

Right Effort

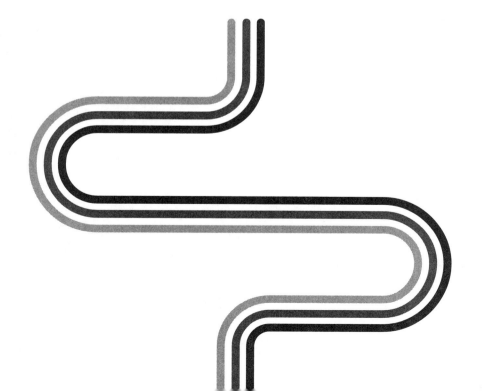

Chapter 9

• • •

Prioritize Your Effort

I sat at the dining table with the ceiling light beaming down on me as if I were on a performance stage in the spotlight—the light mirroring my level of intense focus on my work. I paused for a moment and looked out the window at the dark night sky on the third night in a row working past midnight and thought, *Do I want to work this hard?* Was it worth it to work way past normal hours, beyond what was already a twelve-hour day, and give up personal time and sleep to do so? My answer was yes—because I saw an opportunity to demonstrate my value to my boss's boss. I consciously made the trade-off.

At the time, I was a director of brand strategy at the branding and design agency, and I was working on a last-minute assignment that offered the opportunity to work with the agency's chief strategy officer. He knew me well, but we had never worked directly together on a client project.

My choice to put in that effort directly resulted in my promotion to vice president of brand strategy. The effort led to the reward I sought, and more. In this case, it was an external reward, yet the intrinsic and personal reward for me was my individual achievement, growth, and learning, which I value, and the opportunity to lead.

In this circumstance, I was deliberate in investing my energy in an ambition, but we often go on autopilot with our effort and make these trade-offs unconsciously. We don't think about whether the effort we put in is worth it or if the payoff is there. I do this myself at times, being a hard worker with perfectionist tendencies and natural drive, always eager to check items off my list. So I need to intervene and catch myself so that I prioritize my effort.

I love this quote from Henry David Thoreau: "It is not enough to be industrious. . . . What are you industrious about?"[1] It highlights the idea of not being pulled along by the noise of a random list of to-dos. Intentionality is implied. What do you want to be industrious about? What are your priorities and where do you want to put your attention and your effort?

Right Effort asks us to be discerning about the level of effort we put against our ambitions—not to treat them equally—and about how we manage our effort and energy to make our life and work sustainable. Yes, we want our ambitions to be meaningful, motivating, and right for us at this time—to motivate and focus our effort. And we want them to be manageable. That takes managing the effort put into our pursuits to protect our well-being and building resilience for life-work sustainability. The question you can ask is this: What do I have the effort and energy to do?

AMBITIONS AREN'T CREATED EQUAL

While we typically associate being ambitious with a willingness to put in hard work, we rarely explore how much effort we should actually invest in our ambitions. We dive right into all we want to do with the same intensity—we're all in, all the time. At least, that's my inclination.

What's important to realize is that our ambitions and goals aren't created equal. How much effort and energy we want or need to invest in each one will vary. To help you better align your ambitions with your right effort, let's examine the following three questions:

1. How good do you want to be?
2. What is worth the hard work?
3. How much effort is desired and required?

How Good Do You Want to Be?

That question stared me in the face in big, bold font as I turned the page of the book *It's Not How Good You Are, It's How Good You Want to Be*, by Paul Arden. It caught my attention and made me pause and wonder if I was being conscious of and deliberate with my answer: *How good did I want to be? Had I always been clear on my answer to that question across my ambitions and goals? Had I been willing to commit to an answer?*

> What's important to realize is that our ambitions and goals aren't created equal.

The book spread that contains the question, which I call "The

Napoleon Page," shows pictures of different people associated with a level of aspiration—quite good, good, very good, the best in your field, the best in the world.[2] Napoleon represents the best in the world, of course (his ambition and aspiration were clear, no matter his ultimate demise and how he may serve as a cautionary tale of unhealthy striving).

I discuss this illustration not to suggest that we should always strive to be the best. On the contrary, the image for me brings into focus the idea of dialing in our ambitions with the appropriate amount of effort aligned to our level of aspiration. What are we motivated to be good at and at what level? To be sure, the terms from "quite good" to "the best in the world" aren't the only way to measure ambition when it comes to our personal success metrics, but the visual nonetheless makes the point.

The concept anchored around this key question also gave me permission to accept that in many areas of my life I operate in the "good" territory, and that's just fine. It raised my awareness that *I* can define my own ambitions and level of aspiration against a goal—how good did I want to be?—and it made me realize that my ambitions didn't all have to be at the same level; nor did the effort.

Let me give a simple example. We eat dinner every night for sustenance. What is your goal around that meal? Do you want to make a gourmet meal that would impress your guests and require lots of planning, prep, and cooking time? Do you want to cook a quick yet healthy and nutritious meal for your family that needs to be ready and on the table within an hour? Or is it one of those weeknights when you are on your own and want dinner to be quick and simple, yet healthy—a meal you can prepare in just fifteen minutes? Dinner can be accomplished, but each of these has a different aspiration and desired outcome and requires a different degree of effort.

In this example, each of these scenarios exists for us; I know they do for me. The circumstances dictate the ambition and the associated effort. And yet it takes me being clear about my right ambition at the right time with the right effort to be fulfilled and satisfied with each. Dinner does not have to be "very good" each night. For many nights, "quite good" and "good" are satisfyingly sufficient.

How many of us consciously think about how good we want to be—our level of aspiration? There's no right answer to how good. We need to define that for each goal. We already deploy this strategy more often than we might realize. I'll again use running a marathon as an example. For those who take on such a goal, we likely aren't striving to win the race. Our goal may be to hit a certain time. Is our ambition any less worthy than the lead racers' goal to take first place? And is our ambition more worthy than a runner whose goal is to just get across the finish line, completing the 26.2 miles? No. The yardstick is often with oneself rather than how we place in the race or in the world. Just because we don't shoot for the fastest time overall doesn't mean our ambitions are any less important.

Now, setting an aspiration matters in terms of motivation to achieve what we desire. Research has shown that the aspirations we hold for ourselves help us achieve.[3] Paul Arden believes this too—that it's not talent that makes people successful but having a clear ambition and the drive to achieve a goal that leads them to their desired outcome. He writes: "Your vision of where or who you want to be is the greatest asset you have," giving the example of Victoria Beckham, who said she wanted to be as well-known as Persil Automatic, a dominant detergent in Britain.[4] Declaring such clear ambitions can have significant power and influence on our trajectory and inform the level of effort we put against our goals.

For now, ask yourself: What is my aspiration around this ambition at this time? How good do I want to be?

One final point on aspiration: It's okay to have high standards and to strive for excellence in areas that are meaningful to you. It's not uncommon for me to hear concern from coaching clients around push back they get from direct reports or peers around their drive for excellence. This tends to be natural for us ambitious folk, and having high standards isn't wrong. You just have to be clear on what excellence means to you, guard against perfectionist tendencies, and make sure you're striving where it matters, which we dive into next.

What Is Worth the Hard Work?

I made the calculation and choice those late nights working on that client project that the potential reward was worth my hard work. I was motivated to overdeliver on expectations, earn the promotion, and grow in my career.

Despite being a proponent of managing effort, I don't think "hard work" is a four-letter word. In fact, the ambitions that matter often require dedication and perseverance.

I also value personal sustainability. Working hard and sustainability aren't mutually exclusive in my mind. I don't think hard work is bad—we just can't work hard on everything all the time for years on end. And if we are going to work hard on the ambitions that matter, we have to be diligent about managing our effort in order to avoid the overextension, overexhaustion cycle.

I want Sustainable Ambition to be a no-judgment zone. I don't want any of us to feel ashamed of being a hard worker, including me! So I get frustrated when I read articles or attend sessions where hard work gets villainized, where I have to be careful about saying anything that might allude to the fact that I put in effort.

Instead, I love this wisdom shared with poet David Whyte by Benedictine monk Brother David Steindl-Rast: "You know the antidote to exhaustion is not necessarily rest. . . . The antidote to exhaustion is wholeheartedness."[5] That's part of how I frame putting in the hard work—where do I want to be wholehearted in what I'm doing? Where am I so motivated, committed, and determined such that I want to be all in?

Pursuing our ambitions will not always be pleasant, even when we care about our pursuits, as I've previously mentioned. That's normal, so there's nuance here. In my interview with Dr. Sahar Yousef, a cognitive neuroscientist and professor at UC Berkeley's Haas School of Business, she advocated training ourselves to appreciate and reward the hard work: "How do you actually change your mindset to be excited by and motivated by the grind? There, you have to start doing the hard work of talking to yourself. You've got to be aware that the grind in and of itself is amazing. And one of the easiest ways to do that . . . I say easy but take that with a grain of salt . . . is to start a new narrative. You have to start changing your beliefs around hard work."[6]

How do we do that? We need to enjoy the process. Sahar

goes on: "It is not wise to suspend the feelings of happiness, celebration, pride, for the end result.... That is the easiest way to negate growth mindset and to diminish any kind of Sustainable Ambition you might be feeling toward that goal. And I promise you, you will burn out instead.... You need to keep telling yourself that putting in the effort toward a job well done feels good." Because at times our ambitions will call us to demonstrate resolve.

In our interview, endurance runner Jack Hsueh talked about the training he puts in to run races such as the Tahoe Rim Trail 100-mile race and the Tor des Géants. "Putting in the work," as he describes it, doesn't guarantee a successful outcome, but it allows him to have confidence going out on the course and to trust in the fact that he's put in the preparation that will carry him through the race journey.[7] Hard work builds self-efficacy, which further builds our motivation and our confidence.

Another factor that can play into your desire to put in the hard work is wanting to feel you've earned the outcome and the success, to be able to relish in the accomplishment. Putting in the hard work makes it personal, rather than earning an external outcome that may have been easily achieved. Can you put in the desired effort such that you are satisfied with what you've done and the results?

Rafael Nadal, one of the most successful tennis players in the world, offers an example of this. In his autobiography, he wrote, "One lesson I've learned is that if the job I do were easy, I wouldn't derive so much satisfaction from it. The thrill of winning is in direct proportion to the effort I put in before."[8] Nadal also reflected what Jack Hsueh noted about preparation: "I also know, from long experience, that if you make an effort in training when you don't especially feel like making it, the payoff is that you will win games when you are not feeling your best. That is how you win championships, that is what separates the great player from the merely good player. The difference lies in how well you've prepared."[9]

So ask yourself: What do I care enough about to put in the hard work? Where do I want to put in the effort to be prepared and confident? How determined and committed am I because I really want the desired outcome? Where do I want to persist for the personal reward?

I'm not championing workaholism, of course. On the contrary, what I'm advocating is dialing in the right effort for the right ambition, for you.

What Effort Is Desired and Required?

Being intentional about the effort we put toward our ambitions means we inquire and explore how much effort we want to put in *and* how much effort is actually required to accomplish our goal or aspiration.

Our desired effort is influenced by our level of motivation for an ambition, which can also be affected by our aspiration and our desired reward, which is why we ask the other two questions. Recall what I share in Chapter 4—exploring our level of desired effort and level of energy is a good test of our true motivation. The more motivated we are by our goals, the more effort and energy we tend to put into pursuing them. We can also be more committed and find grit and persistence when our goals are Right Ambitions and internally motivated.

Asking ourselves about the required effort helps us make more conscious decisions rather than mindlessly giving each ambition our all. Again, ambitions and goals require different levels of effort. This may seem obvious, but those of us who are hard workers or perfectionists often appreciate reminders and permission to not have to do it all at full force. That's what we're going for here—to allow ourselves to dial down our effort—or to dial it up, if it's warranted and we so choose.

What's also important to note is that the required effort for the same ambition may look different for each of us. It can vary, given our skills, talents, strengths, and more. So keep your eyes on your own effort. We're not all the same. For a particular task, some of us may want or have to put in more effort than others to achieve the desired outcome. Or, based on actual or perceived societal biases, we may believe that we need to put in more effort to get the outcome and results we want.

Finally, we want to keep our effort manageable. An ambition can be hard to achieve. We are better served setting goals that are challenging *and* attainable. Goals on our growth edge will demand dedication, but we want them to have the right amount of stretch and pursue them in a way that is sustainable.

In the end, it's about getting it *just right*—like Goldilocks. Too much relentless striving, focus, and effort against one thing at the cost of all else in one's life can lead to negative outcomes. That turns into unbridled and reckless ambition. But too little ambition and effort can result in stagnation and languishing. It's helpful to home in on what's right for you to flourish in the pursuit of your ambitions.

Check in by asking: What is my level of motivation? What level of effort do I want to put in? What level of effort is required to reach my aspiration?

Figure 9.1. Align your Right Effort Matrix

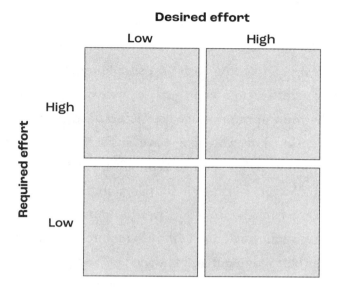

DIAL IN YOUR RIGHT EFFORT

Some people I've worked with have appreciated using a visual tool to help them further investigate the level of effort they want to put against their ambitions and goals. Here, I again rely on the trusty 2 × 2 matrix to evaluate an ambition and its effort using the final motivation question: What effort is desired and required? (See Figure 9.1.) I focus on desired effort because it reflects our motivation and connects to our aspiration and desired reward, the focus of the other two questions.

One person from a workshop acknowledged how this visualization was useful to make sure she put the most effort toward what was most important to her rather than just toward those goals that seemed easiest to do. You might find the same in taking the prioritized life and work ambitions you identify in Chapter 7 and evaluating them using this Right Effort Matrix. Where might you prioritize where you apply your energy when considering your desired level of effort compared to the required level of effort? In addition to using the matrix to map your current ambitions, you can use it on an ongoing basis as a simple mindset check as you experience shifts across your goals or active projects and determine how you want to manage your effort at this time.

Considering how you may have answered the three earlier questions around your level of aspiration, your desired personal reward, and level of motivation for this ambition or goal, ask yourself now: How much effort do I want to put in—a lot or a little? Then think about how much effort is required, from low to high, using your best judgment and knowledge.

The quadrants of the matrix then prompt different strategies you can deploy around dialing in, dialing up, or dialing down your effort depending on where the ambition maps (see Figure 9.2).

Figure 9.2. Strategies to align your Right Effort

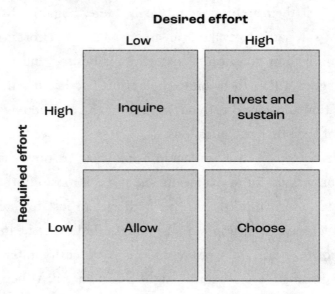

- *Invest and sustain.* High-desired and high-required effort ambitions are where you will invest your energy because you believe the ambitions are worth your hard work. I note *sustain* here as a reminder to make sure you keep yourself sustained for the journey.

- *Choose.* You may have a greater desired effort than what is truly required for an ambition. In this case you have a choice—to indulge in putting in the effort or to dial it back—depending on how good you want to be and if it's worth the hard work. This might be an ambition where you are in your zone of genius, lose yourself in the work, or want to develop mastery. Or you may be overworking because of perfectionism, in which case you might want to ease back.

- *Inquire.* You may have an ambition for which you have low-desired effort, yet it requires high effort. If this is a Right Ambition, explore what's driving your low energy level. An obvious answer could be that you're exhausted or feel overly stretched. Beyond that, a first step is to reconfirm if the goal is still a Right Ambition and if now is the right time to pursue it. If the answer to both is yes, and assuming you can't delay its pursuit, consider ways to dial back your effort. Could you reinterpret the goal to achieve the same outcome more efficiently? Or could you delegate or outsource some of the work? You might feel low energy because you've not made progress. In this case, you might need to tap into tactics to increase your motivation and determine actions to help you gain momentum. Or it could be that you don't feel capable of pursuing the goal. In this situation, consider seeking counsel from a coach, mentor, or advisor to boost confidence in your approach. As you can see, this quadrant and scenario can have multiple explanations, which is why it's important to inquire and examine your circumstances before determining the best course of action.

- *Allow.* It's not necessarily bad if an ambition lands in the low-desired and -required effort quadrant. For a Right Ambition, this could be viewed as a big win—something you desire doesn't actually take a lot of work. Perhaps you can indulge in the ambition by dialing down the effort and enjoying the reward. On the other hand, you can also see a low-desired effort as a signal to confirm whether the goal is truly a Right Ambition and decide to no longer pursue it.

You'll notice in these strategies how Right Ambition, Right Time, and Right Effort start to interact to create Sustainable Ambition. As I've noted, how strong your motivation is around a Right Ambition influences your level of effort and energy for it. Right Time may identify an ambition that you don't have all the time and attention for now but don't want to give up. You may choose to nurture such an ambition, as I discuss in Chapter 8. With Right Effort, you might find that your low-desired effort stems from being overextended and not having the energy for the goal right now. All are plausible and why navigating conflicts across all we want to do isn't as simple as just seeking work-life balance.

Using the matrix isn't formulaic. As a guide, it creates more awareness, and your reflections provide insight. Use your best judgment to be discerning and determine what next steps make the most sense for you. My hope is that being more conscious about these choices can help you start to feel more in control of the level of effort you put toward your ambitions, so you don't feel as though you always have to give everything 110 percent.

> **FREE RESOURCES**
>
> To explore further, you can find a free exercise, Align Your Right Effort, at SustainableAmbition.com/sa-toolkit.

You may wonder how you can tell whether your Right Effort for an ambition might be off. Here are a few clues:

- You're putting in the hard work and feel like you are grinding but not making progress. Explore whether you are working on the right activities to move your ambition forward and if you are being efficient against those tasks.

- You're putting in the hard work but experiencing a lot of frustration. In this case, you are nowhere near feeling that *the grind feels good.* Here you may want to revisit the overall goal, check your motivators, and see if you can link to them to increase your positive energy.

- You find yourself regularly working late hours and sweating the small details on every project, suggesting perfectionism may be at play and worth challenging.

- You're putting effort into a goal that is distracting you from other important priorities, like family and personal relationships, perhaps calling you to revisit how you can protect what's most important in your life.

- You're starting to not show up as your best self or experience health problems, a sign that you might be entering the severe zone and need to address sustainability.

In all these scenarios, but especially in the last, you want to pay attention to when you might be starting to show signs of serious exhaustion or burnout.

PAY ATTENTION—AVOID OVEREXTENSION AND OVEREXHAUSTION

I was having what I've now come to call a "soul day"—one that includes activities I enjoy and that fill up my soul. This day, I had walked almost fifteen thousand steps on the London city streets, combining two loves—London and walking in cities. I started from my home base and journeyed to my first writing destination, a modern, neighborhood coffee shop, combining three other loves—coffee, coffee shops, and time for creative work. From there, I went to my next activity, exploring Charles Dickens's old home for inspiration. After, I had a wonderful lunch in a nearby neighborhood and then was ready to move on to my final writing destination of the day, the British Library.

This was January 2022, and I had finally taken a long-planned London trip after a two-year delay because of the pandemic. The trip was a much-needed extended break. The year before, I had been stretching myself by stepping further into self-employment, testing different methods of client work to see what best fit my portfolio and being mindful to earn enough income. I also had my Sustainable Ambition work and was supporting my parents.

I had sensed that debilitating exhaustion could be on the horizon. While I had my Sustainable Ambition tools in place to help me through the challenging period, I knew I was eating into my reserves and that I would need to rebuild my resilience. Plus, I longed to invest time in my creative ambitions and to have the space to think about ideas and concepts. Thus, London.

For those of us who are ambitious, it's not uncommon to constantly be moving between the edges of working intently on ambitions we care about while leading full lives and then finding that we've stretched ourselves too far. We start to smell the singeing and early signs of what we label as "burnout." In some ways, it's a signal that we are finding the boundaries of what is *just right* for us.

That's why in this chapter I focus on dialing in our effort and why I believe in having a plan to support sustainability in the moment and over time. We want to avoid overextending ourselves to the point of exhaustion. Not keeping our effort dialed in can result in long-term pain. I'm sure if you've ever burned out, you'd agree. It takes so long to recover from burnout that it's worth the effort to avoid it.

That's why it is also important to pay attention. Let me say it again—*pay attention*. People tend to either not recognize the signs of burnout, rationalize overextension for a long time, or ignore the symptoms, letting the effects accumulate until it becomes dire. Check in and see what your body is telling you. Look for physical (e.g., overly fatigued, not sleeping well), mental (e.g., not able to concentrate), and emotional signs of exhaustion (e.g., feeling irritable).

To support you in paying attention, I advocate that you put an appointment on your calendar once a month to assess how you're doing and simply ask yourself: Is how I'm operating right now sustainable? You could also do a quick rating: How would I rate the sustainability of my life with work today? Rate it on a scale of 1 to 5, with 5 = very sustainable, 4 = somewhat sustainable, 3 = neither sustainable nor unsustainable, 2 = somewhat unsustainable, and 1 = not sustainable at all. What does your rating make you think about your Sustainable Ambition now?

Based on your assessment, take the appropriate actions around Right Ambition, Right Time, and Right Effort. As relates to Right Effort, do you need to dial in your effort across your ambitions? Will you need to invest more in your sustaining plan? I provide additional strategies and ideas to consider in the remainder of this part of the book.

You may also wonder if you are already bordering on burnout. Based on what some experts say, be careful not to misdiagnose burnout or rely on your own assessment, as you may get the diagnosis wrong and therefore not know what will resolve matters for you. If you truly think you are experiencing burnout, it's best to see a medical practitioner.

HOW TO DIAL DOWN EFFORT

Dialing down our effort for a goal or ambition isn't easy for most of us. I know I have a habit of approaching my tasks the same way: Do it all well, be methodical, and take the time required. But that's not a wise use of my effort and energy. We need to challenge ourselves to make things easier. Why? Because we rarely question how much effort we should put into an ambition or goal, and we don't dare ourselves to do less.

One method I lean on to help me dial down my effort is from Greg McKeown's book *Effortless*. McKeown advises to invert our approach to our work by asking, "What if this could be easy?"[10] It's a simple prompt to get us to think differently about what's required to accomplish our goal.

Another way to limit the degree of effort is to timebox and give yourself a set amount of time for a task. Any length of time works. I've done thirty minutes for a focused task and then a daylong sprint on a project. This idea of a sprint can be powerful. For one of my coaching clients, it shifted her view of being able to carve out dedicated time to progress a strategic project, resulting in her being able to delegate future work and freeing more of her time.

A final concept to use is the Pareto principle—the idea that 80 percent of outcomes tend to come from 20 percent of inputs—to challenge ourselves to be more efficient. One could think of it as another form of timeboxing, just applied to our effort and energy. What if you challenged yourself to only put in 20 percent of the right effort that would make the most progress and trust that you would deliver 80 percent of the results and outcome you could expect? Wouldn't that be powerful? You can work the model the other way, too, looking to reduce, eliminate, automate, or delegate 80 percent of tasks that aren't worth the effort.

While these are just a few approaches, the point is that we benefit from continually challenging ourselves to dial down our effort, both to manage and to sustain our energy.

• • •

Right Effort is not a one-time activity. Making life and work sustainable is a constant, personal practice that requires course corrections and adjustments. It's a dance to align our effort and energy to our ambitions while we integrate life and work. I don't say that to make it sound impossible; it's just a reality. Our life with work is constantly in flux, and what we need to make things sustainable can change over time. It's better to accept that, so we can feel in control rather than continually be frustrated. The ultimate goal is to create more joy and ease in the process. I know that's ambitious. But that's my hope for all of us.

Dialing in our effort to make the pursuit of our ambitions sustainable is important, but it alone won't result in sustainability. While it can help us avoid becoming overextended, we'd be well served to build our resilience with a sustaining plan. Being conscious about both—managing and sustaining my effort—has been the key to keeping me from falling into overexhaustion several times over the last few years as I navigate my right ambitions at the right time with the right effort. An example was working intensely for a year and then designing a break with energy-boosting activities during my two-week creative sabbatical. I know that not all of us can afford or are in a situation to take such a break like I did. It took me a long time to be in a position to do so. Yet I do believe this approach of building resilience by taking breaks and using a sustaining plan can help you too, and I offer ways in Chapter 10 to make them manageable and doable. Because you'll be in a more powerful position to live the life you desire if you are able to create the conditions to support you in operating at your best.

Chapter 10
• • •

Sustain Your Effort and Yourself

"The most underappreciated leadership strength is the ability to relax and replenish energy." So said Doris Kearns Goodwin, the celebrated presidential biographer, during her MasterClass on presidential history and leadership.[1] She shared how presidents like Abraham Lincoln, Teddy Roosevelt, and Franklin Delano Roosevelt (FDR) identified ways to recover and sustain themselves through their presidencies. For instance, Lincoln enjoyed going to the theater (yes, I do see the irony there), Teddy Roosevelt exercised or did other physical activities two hours every afternoon, and FDR hosted cocktail parties during World War II and took strategic breaks for reflection.

The American presidency is arguably one of the most intense, if not the most intense, jobs in the world. So if presidents can prioritize sustaining activities, can't we?

Like those presidents, we need to manage our energy to sustain our effort and ourselves over time. It's not enough to be discerning about how we use our energy and put the right effort against our ambitions. As humans, we also need to find ways and make time to restore, protect, and support our energy. Sustainability won't just happen. In the book *Wellbeing: The Five Essential Elements*, which I introduce in Chapter 2, the authors write that "the single biggest threat to our own wellbeing tends to be *ourselves*."[2] Ouch! Because of our natural biases, we tend to prioritize short-term benefits over long-term well-being. To be ambitious and sustainably pursue what we want across life and work, we need both a mindset and methods to support our ability to do so.

For mindset, we need to change our belief that being ambitious means being all in and driving all the time. Those of us with workaholic tendencies tend to keep pushing, overextend ourselves, and not prioritize time for recovery.[3] Yet dogged pursuit of ambitions without attention to managing our well-being can negatively affect our health and lead to exhaustion and burnout, as I note in Chapter 9. Instead, we need to build our resilience, so we can consistently pursue our ambitions over time without overextension and overexhaustion. It's about managing our effort at the right level across all we want to do, combined with sustaining activities to keep us operating at our best.

Another mindset shift is to stop thinking that someone else will figure this out for you. If you're not your own boss, it certainly won't be your employer who makes resilience or life-work sustainability magically appear. We need to take responsibility for sustaining ourselves. Why? For one, the demands we juggle span both life and work and stem from our own ambitions and external expectations and commitments. To be sure, if you work for a company, your leaders and manager have a role in helping manage your workload, but they can't manage, and aren't responsible for, your full load. They also won't know, and shouldn't dictate, what will work best to sustain you.

So, yes, we need to manage our employer's demands, but we also need to manage our energy. We need a way to sustain ourselves and build resilience for all we do.

This brings us to the methods. To sustain our effort and ourselves and support our resilience, I advocate two core strategies: (1) pacing ourselves and (2) creating and implementing a sustaining plan.

PACE YOURSELF DAY-TO-DAY

"I'm in slo-mo." I sometimes say this to myself when I've slowed my pace to get focused on my work. I've learned that in these moments of quiet, generally at the end of the day for me (this is how my chronotype—my natural body rhythm—works), I can get my mind to slow down and focus on a project. It's not that I'm necessarily highly efficient and productive, cranking through tasks quickly; it's the opposite. I allow myself to not be hurried and just enjoy the pleasure of putting attention on doing the work.

This is one way I use pacing to create more sustainability for myself. Just as pacing is important in planning our life and work arcs, pacing is also a core sustainability strategy to manage the day-to-day pursuit of our ambitions, goals, and general to-dos across life and work.

Why is pace important? Because day-to-day balance is elusive. In many modern societies, life with work is an endurance event. Our lives tend to be full, especially for those of us who are ambitious. And we tend to operate at high speed. Yet no one other than elite athletes would attempt to run a marathon at a four-and-a-half-minute-per-mile pace. The reality is we can't run a marathon at a sprint: It isn't sustainable. It's a recipe for burnout.

I often hear in my workshops or with clients that they want to feel less rushed and want to create more spaciousness in their life. The practice of pace can help, beyond making choices and prioritizing our focus through the strategies we cover for Right Time.

Busy is a choice. I don't say this to chastise you or to imply being busy is bad. Many of us live active, rich lives. Yet it often takes someone asking us a direct question to shake us out of the societally driven addiction to busyness and operating at a fast pace, traits often touted as status symbols. It can look like what Kristoffer Carter, author of *Permission to Glow*, often says to his clients and shared on my podcast: "When are you going to slow the hell down? Who's going to do this for you? Nobody can do it for you. You have to give yourself the permission."[4]

So here's my suggestion for you: Give yourself the permission to manage your pace for better sustainability. Let's look at three strategies to do so: (1) intentionally set and manage your pace, (2) take breaks of different lengths, and (3) manage sustainability over a longer time horizon.

Intentionally Set and Manage Your Pace

To work with pace, first set your intention, acknowledging what pace you want to operate at during this period. I have you start to think about this in Chapter 7, where you plan your current arc. Setting your pace has no right or wrong. It comes back to being right for you at this time. It's about being conscious of whether you need to operate at a fast pace at this moment and what that might mean for your sustaining plan or putting structures in place to support you. Or do you want to operate at a moderate or slow pace, and what does that mean for how you manage your ambitions and goals?

Setting your pace also requires active management. Of course, ambitious people lead full lives, with full calendars. But it's also helpful to have practices to set your pace and be prepared to intervene and adjust, if needed. I do this regularly when I manage my calendar, but I don't always get it right. I can catch mistakes upon review—where I scheduled too many personal commitments, say—and realize I need to better space out activities, so I don't overstretch myself or not have sufficient time for my commitments. With such awareness, I can adjust and be more thoughtful with my schedule going forward.

My travel is another example of how I use pace to keep my life and work more sustainable. A work trip in 2022 took me to the East Coast for a half-day meeting. I only needed to be there for a night, but leaving early in the morning one day from the West Coast only to fly back late the very next, arriving past midnight, felt rushed and unsustainable for me. To be sure, this wasn't a big decision, but I chose to invest time and money to extend my trip for both work and pleasure and scheduled a side visit to New York City for a few days. I slowed down my pace and did activities that were on my sustaining plan, spending time with friends and enjoying many of my favorite places on earth, like Central Park. I recognize not everyone has the time or resources to make such decisions and investments, but this example illustrates how we can make choices that better control our pace and create experiences that support building resilience.

Finally, when I work with pace, I use the mantra "There will be time." I'm sure I'm not the only one who has an overwhelmingly long daily to-do list or pushes to finish just one more task at the end of a day. I regularly remind myself to cut the list off and pace the to-dos out—there will be time for that, because more often than not, there is. Most tasks don't need to be completed immediately; they need to be paced out to when I'll have the space to give them proper attention and complete them more efficiently. Trust that there will be time. Rather than grind, push tasks off. Allow the right moment, space, or energy to present itself.

I loved how a workshop participant shared, "Do what you can when you can and adjust as needed." That's right. Pace it out.

Take Breaks of Different Lengths

A key strategy for pacing is to embrace taking breaks. This may sound obvious, but many of us don't. For example, 50 percent of knowledge workers rarely or never take breaks during the workday, according to Slack's 2023 Workforce Index, a survey of more than ten thousand global desk workers.[5]

Humans are meant to take breaks and have rest periods. Athletes again offer inspiration. In the book *Peak Performance*, by Brad Stulberg and Steve Magness, they write about Deena Kastor, an American long-distance runner who won the bronze medal in the women's marathon at the 2004 Olympics, as an example of someone who followed a common strategy called "periodization." Generally, periodization helps improve performance by varying between planned cycles of hard work and rest and recovery.

They write how Kastor shared in interviews that what allowed her to dramatically improve her performance wasn't the training and putting in the hard work, though that was also important. It was how she made choices about her recovery. She said it was harder to prioritize recovery periods than doing the training, just like for many of us.[6] But this strategy helped support her achievements and being able to sustainably and successfully run competitively into her forties.

I am a big believer in breaks, particularly of different lengths, from one-minute pauses to full-on sabbaticals and anything in between. Yes, I believe in putting in the hard work (the training), too, as I shared in the last chapter, but not to the point of crowding out sustaining activities.

We may resist taking breaks because we feel pressure to keep doing. The societal narrative that we must plug away at our goals is strong. Yet several research studies have shown that ninety-minute work cycles may sync best with our natural energy levels and enhance our productivity. Plus, research supports the power and importance of breaks to keep us operating at our best—cognitively, emotionally, and socially.[7]

Even short breaks can pack a punch. Shorter pauses of one to ten minutes to disengage from work—whether to move, daydream, or meditate—can improve attention, increase creativity and our ability to solve problems, and reduce exhaustion while improving performance.[8] Practicing mindfulness or taking deep breaths for a short period can help reset and calm our nervous system from a fight-or-flight response and lower our stress levels. Breaks of up to an hour build on these benefits and are important to help us reduce fatigue and avoid burnout.

We may think that we don't have time for breaks during our days, but we often have five- or ten-minute windows. An interesting analysis would be to track how you use such moments and to determine if they help restore you or not. Are those minutes spent scrolling social media? Does that relieve you? It might, but research suggests such passive activities often do not.[9] Could you do something different with that time—like take a walk around the block, read a book, or look at your children's artwork—and experience a different outcome? Nothing says we can't use small windows of time for breaks that truly restore us. With such a mindset, we can find more opportunities to pause than we expect.

We benefit from longer breaks, too, hence why weekends were "invented." You may need to plan a more significant break to create the space you desire. You might carve out a day for an activity that fills you up, such as reading, a hike with friends, an art class, or a class at a local university to learn about a new topic and stretch your mind.

Vacations come into play here as well. Extended time away from work supports our health, overall well-being, and sense of life satisfaction and can give us time with others to strengthen important relationships, among other benefits. Yet, for those who are lucky to have paid vacation time, we often don't take it. Note that if we're burned out, we need more time than the typical two weeks of vacation offered to fully recover.[10]

Longer breaks, like sabbaticals, create space not just for recovery and rejuvenation, but also for reimagination. Given how many of us work these days—intense years of putting in more than forty-hour weeks—I'm surprised more companies don't have formal sabbatical programs to prevent overexhaustion and burnout. Beyond building our resilience, this time away and the space it creates are often needed to allow insights to form about what we truly want next. Or we may need time to invest in re-skilling, like going back to school. If you're fortunate to have the financial runway to support it, consider longer breaks that can sustain you for the long haul.

Some may still resist taking breaks. If that's the case for you, shift your beliefs around pauses by viewing them as a tool that supports, rather than diminishes, your performance and productivity. This mindset shift should include thinking of breaks as critical for your well-being. Periodization works for athletes. It works for us too.[11]

To be more intentional and overcome resistance to taking breaks, it helps to have a plan in place to fight inertia. So next up is creating a Pause and Break Blueprint for yourself.

Exercise: Your Pause and Break Blueprint

In this exercise, you'll take a broader view of pauses from short to long, exploring how you like to take breaks to keep you sustained and build resilience. You'll create a Pause and Break Blueprint, your

Table 10.1. A Pause and Break Blueprint example

Time period	My pause and break approach	Action plan: structure
Year	Two weeks off at end of year	Block on calendar
Quarter	A day hike with my friends	Each quarter, commit to a date with friends and put on calendar
Month	One full day for my creative work	Block on calendar
Week	At least one hour-long walk by myself	Sunday mornings after yoga class
Day	Five deep breaths before the top of each hour during the workday	Set meetings for 25 or 50 minutes to allow time for a pause

go-to guide for taking breaks of different lengths. You'll also reference this as you create your sustaining plan in the next exercise.

Think about how you like to take pauses during your days, weeks, months, quarters, and year. What types of breaks will keep you sustained? For each, consider a structure or trigger that will help you stay committed to the practice of taking the break. This might mean putting an activity formally on your calendar, tying an activity to an existing habit, or planning a break with an accountability partner. See Table 10.1 for an example.

Manage Sustainability over a Longer Time Horizon

Pace also comes into play when managing our longer-term calendars and taking longer breaks. A light bulb went off for me when I interviewed Heather Ainsworth, founder and CEO of Workable Concept, a company that advises leaders on how to help employees with caregiving responsibilities thrive. Heather is someone in my life who has been an inspiration and model of Sustainable Ambition. She is ambitious and highly capable, and she has negotiated work structures throughout her career that have supported her achieving sustainability across life and work. I loved the perspective she shared on my podcast that "balanced and sustainable" isn't about moments in time but rather looking over an eighteen-month time horizon.[12] We can achieve more sustainability when we proactively manage the ups and downs of our effort over a longer period, not just day-to-day.

Why is this a better method? Because it's more realistic. Creating sustainability and pacing ourselves doesn't mean we'll never have to work hard, experience a period of workload intensity, or stretch ourselves. Again, work-life balance sets an expectation that work (or, frankly, life) should never be demanding, yet we know this is a false presumption. It's just not the way our world works, especially today. But consider the past when people worked the land. If a big storm was coming and they needed to prepare the farm and animals to withstand it, they'd get out there and get to work. They wouldn't say, "But I'm done with my eight hours today, and I need balance." At times, work and life come calling when we can't say no.

Although we can't always prevent such demanding periods, we can take back some semblance of control by examining our calendar across a longer time horizon—at minimum, twelve months but up to eighteen. It's another way to put pacing and periodization to work. With better visibility and more awareness, we can consciously pace our effort, allowing for busy times while also planning for recovery and resilience.

The creative sabbatical I shared in the prior chapter is an

example. I had talked with my coach all year about carving out space for both recovery and my creative work. I took shorter day or weekend breaks throughout the year but couldn't block out a significant amount of time, which is why I planned a longer break for early the following year. That was when I was able to fit it in. While I've crafted my work to allow me such flexibility, I also had to compromise. Work cut into the trip unexpectedly. Did I love it? Honestly, no. But for the ability to slow my pace and take the break, I was flexible in this way, too, and fit the work in. I didn't stand firm around my break boundary because the reward was greater than the sacrifice. The benefit of such resilience investments is that they pay dividends in the moment and long after. Simply writing about this trip brings me joy and energizes me now.

A longer-term planning calendar is one way to create a view of how your effort will go up and down over time and inform your resilience-building needs. Making this visual—mapping it out on a calendar you can see in one view in front of you—is beneficial. You can more easily notice when you might need to pace out activities, schedule a longer break for recovery, or plan activities that will sustain you. For example, you might spot when you'll have an intense period where you need to be thoughtful about remaining committed to your sustaining plan. Visualization also makes goals and actions more concrete, and we tend to prioritize and be more committed to activities we put on our calendar.[13] Visualizing future sustaining activities, especially planned after intense work periods, can serve as motivational reminders to help us remain persistent and committed to our goals. For me, what's most important is prioritizing, protecting, and taking the breaks that so many of us tend to skip right on by.

Exercise: Set Your Twelve-Month Plan and Six-Month Horizon

Take time to create, at minimum, a twelve-month view of your upcoming calendar, and consider looking another six months out to develop a snapshot that you can update and adapt as you move forward.

While this is a simple calendaring exercise, it's not one we all naturally do. It will help you gain better visibility into when you'll have demanding periods over the upcoming twelve months and when it will be a good time to build in sustaining activities. This plan can intersect with your Pause and Break Blueprint, too, and perhaps your sustaining plan. To create your plan, follow these steps:

1. *Vision to plan.* Create a twelve-month calendar view on a piece of paper or in an online application you prefer. Map at a high level the core activities you associate with your life and work ambitions and expect to occur during this current twelve-month period.

2. *Map other activities.* Add other events that are already planned for the coming twelve months across your personal and professional life.

3. *Reflect.* What observations do you have regarding your calendar? Use these questions as prompts:
    - How sustainable does your twelve-month plan look?

- When is your schedule or work going to be demanding?
- Are too many activities happening at one time, and can anything be shifted to create better pacing?

4. *Actions for sustainability.* Which activities do you want to mark on your calendar or what actions do you want to note to create sustainability across the twelve months? Use these questions as prompts:
    - What from your Pause and Break Blueprint do you want to put on your calendar for recovery and rejuvenation?
    - What support do you need during high-intensity, fast-paced periods?
    - What do you need to negotiate at work and at home to ensure you achieve sustainability over the year?

5. *Look on the horizon.* Stretch your view out six more months. Based on how the next twelve months look, how can the following six months support both your ambitions and sustainability? How might you pace your activity? Where might you add from your Pause and Break Blueprint?

• • •

We can better sustain both our effort and ourselves by intentionally setting and managing our pace, taking breaks of different lengths, and planning for and managing sustainability over a longer time horizon. Beyond pacing, we also benefit from creating and implementing a sustaining plan.

A PLAN TO SUSTAIN YOURSELF

If we are going to stretch and strive, we need a plan to sustain ourselves. Stretching and striving without a plan is like going off on a long-distance, multiday trek without knowing where you'll take breaks, sleep, or get water. You wouldn't expect nature to miraculously provide for you, make your trek a success, and keep you sustained. You'd plan for that yourself. By the same token, you need to be proactive about managing your energy to pursue your ambitions.

A plan is also crucial because it prompts action. Research shows that while recovery practices improve well-being, we paradoxically neglect them when we need them most.[14] This is why I recommend having a sustaining plan and a minimum viable sustaining plan (MVSP). In a podcast interview with Dr. Marie-Hélène Pelletier, a leadership psychologist, a coach and keynote speaker, and the author of *The Resilience Plan*, she made this point as well—that what typically wears people down is not having a strategic way to ensure they get recharged and sustain themselves.[15] A strategic plan provides structure and helps us commit to these practices within our life context.

For some I've worked with, this mental model of a plan helps them prioritize investing in sustaining themselves before planning other activities. This is a "put your oxygen mask on first" strategy that should complement your right effort as you work toward your ambitions.

With a sustaining plan, we aren't managing our time; rather, we are managing our energy so that we can pursue our prioritized ambitions and tend to important aspects of our life and work without wearing ourselves out. We want to restore, protect, and support our energy, creating a sustainable rhythm between using our energy and replenishing it. All three areas are vital to a sustaining plan.

> We want to restore, protect, and support our energy, creating a sustainable rhythm between using our energy and replenishing it.

Restore: Every day we have a finite amount of energy we can use, and we have a natural bodily cycle of activity followed by recovery. We drain our batteries, and we need to fill them back up. Pretty obvious, right? But beyond sleep, we don't always do it. We can resist investing in recharging, thinking we need to be productive instead. To build our resilience, we need to continually invest in activities and breaks that restore us. But restoration isn't just about slowing down or resting; it's about what fuels our energy.

In her book *Everyday Vitality*, Samantha Boardman advocates that we proactively take positive action to boost our vitality and combat the stress and pressure we experience day to day. She explains that these actions don't need to be arduous or big. Daily micro-activities and uplifting experiences can build our resilience.[16]

And it's important to recognize that we all get energized differently. A friend realized this during the pandemic when he acknowledged that being at home and chilling wasn't what would give him the energy boost he needed. Instead, he noticed he missed being in conversation with others who inspired him and made him think differently. He needed to be engaged in an energizing activity, not a passive one. Adding the right activity that fuels us may take dedicated time, but it can actually boost our energy for all we do. When choosing such activities that will restore your energy, refer to your Right Foundation to identify those tied to your values and what you love to do.

Protect: Yes, we want to restore our energy, but we also want to protect it in the first place by not allowing it to get used in ways that don't serve us. How can we protect our energy? We can avoid activities that exponentially zap it, like those on our loathe list, or set boundaries to keep overcommitment at bay. In other words, we need to get clear on what we will say yes to and no to. Another way to protect our energy is to dial down our effort, giving ourselves grace to not have to be great or perfect at everything. People often love this prompt, and I mean it in a positive way—where will you allow yourself to be bad at things? Yes, we have ambitions around certain areas of our lives, but what are the areas where we don't need to strive or be the best? Where can we let ourselves off the hook? Perhaps we perfectionist types appreciate this permission the most.

Support: The reason to look at what supports us is that I don't believe sustainability is a product of sheer willpower or solitary effort. We operate within a broader context and are affected by external factors. So we need to put in place structures to support our sustainability, both at work and at home. Here it's beneficial to revisit your Horizon Map, considering what matters most now across life and work. The support you'll need to make your life with work sustainable will depend on your current arc priorities, level of ambition, and desired pace. In a situation where you might be leaning in across both life and work, sustainability structures are crucial.

Again, we'll come back to restoring, protecting, and supporting our energy when you create your sustaining plan. But first, a few tips to make your plan stick.

Make It Personal, Prototype, and Practice

There's not a one-size-fits-all approach to building resilience and creating a sustaining plan. It needs to be personal and customized to work for you, so that the activities on your plan align to what you value and what energizes you. Be careful not to put shoulds on your plan! Tailoring the approach to include what matters to you increases the likelihood you'll be motivated to act and follow through.

A sustaining plan doesn't need to be perfect. I suggest you embrace prototyping, an innovation tactic, when you create and implement your plan. Prototyping is a fancy way of saying "test it out." We often don't know what will work for us until we experience it, just like trying on jobs. I love the freedom that prototyping offers. We don't fail; we learn. Test a new energizing activity, a new schedule for your week, a new workout class, or a new way to divide work across your household. Then pause to evaluate. What worked? What didn't? What did you learn? How do you want to optimize? Aim, act, assess, adapt. Repeat.

Prototyping is part of what makes this approach a practice. It's also a practice because you'll need to revisit your plan as you, your ambitions, and your life and work circumstances change. What works well for you at one moment may not work in the future. The key to making a sustaining plan a practice is accepting that changing our behaviors requires intentionality, consistency, and commitment. We humans have ingrained patterns. It takes work to work against them. Plus, we won't always get it right. That's normal. Practice means we learn along the way, and we actively strive to improve. With consistent practice, what we are trying to master gets easier over time.

Commit to a Doable and Realistic Plan

When we create our sustaining plan, we want to make it doable and realistic, so we'll act on it. A caution: We can get ambitious with our sustaining plans. We have all these ideas and want to do all these things! Then, our sustaining plan surprisingly overwhelms us. So build a plan that you can truly commit to and maintain.

The next exercise offers two ways to make your plan more doable and realistic. One way is turning your observations into a weekly plan. The weekly sustaining plan reflects what you can do to keep you sustained over a shorter time horizon and complements the twelve-month plan you created in the prior exercise. As part of this, you'll integrate what you identify in your Pause and Break Blueprint, and you can also consider what you learn in the Where Time and Wish Time exercise in Chapter 8. The overall intent is to identify weekly practices that help you become more resilient and able to show up as your best on a day-to-day basis.

The second way is to create a minimum viable sustaining plan (MVSP). Why? Because we're bound to have intense periods with limited time for our sustaining activities, and because life happens. It's unrealistic and impractical to expect perfection all the time. Instead, we're better served knowing the minimum we need to do to keep us energized and effective. With both, you'll have plans to use during life as usual and demanding time periods.

Then to stick with your plan, try these three strategies. First, when executing your plan, consider a key tip from the habit gurus B. J. Fogg of *Tiny Habits* and James Clear of *Atomic Habits*, and connect a new practice to an existing habit.[17] For example, I'll do five minutes of stretching while I wait for my coffee to brew, or I'll take deep breaths for one minute right after ending a meeting. Second, use a simple tracking system to keep your sustaining plan top of mind and remain accountable to the practice and your routines. Third, be intentional about pausing to check in, reflect, and adjust your plan as needed over time based on what's happening in your life at the moment. Get into a loop of aiming, acting, assessing, and adapting to optimize your plan, so it remains doable and realistic.

KEY AREAS TO EXPLORE AND BUILD INTO YOUR SUSTAINING PLAN

There are a few areas you should consider when creating your sustaining plan. First, think about the four areas that Dr. Marie-Hélène Pelletier highlights in her book, *The Resilience Plan*. She notes that four of the most research-based, powerful areas to consider when building strategic resilience are nutrition, sleep, physical activity (including mindfulness practices), and investment of time in important relationships.[18] Do these four areas show up in your sustaining plan?

Then think about the four areas featured in the book *The Power of Full Engagement: Managing Energy, Not Time, Is the Key to High Performance and Personal Renewal*, by Jim Loehr and Tony Schwartz. The authors note that full engagement requires drawing on four separate but related sources of energy: physical, emotional, mental, and spiritual.[19] While some overlap with the prior list, how do these four areas show up in your sustaining plan?

Exercise: Your Personalized Sustaining Plan and MVSP

Let's create a personalized sustaining plan and an MVSP so you are armed to start embedding sustaining activities as a practice. You'll create the plans by looking for personalized insight across these areas: restore, protect, and support your energy. At the end, you'll have a list of sustaining practices that work best for you and your weekly plan with those practices mapped to your calendar, as appropriate. The exercise helps you set your intentions and determine which practices you'll prototype and then evolve as needed over time.

Workshop participants have found this approach to be affirming, as it allows them to set aside perfectionism and recognize the actions they are already taking that contribute to their sustainability. Let's get started to see what works best for you.

1. *Look back to reflect.* Pull out your calendar from last week to inspire your reflections. Use these prompts to inquire about what helps restore, protect, and support your energy. You could put your reflections into a table like Table 10.2.
    - Restore:
        » I get refueled and recover when . . .
        » I really have fun and enjoy when . . .
        » I get energized when . . .

Table 10.2. Reflections example

	Restore	Protect	Support
Last week reflections	• Energized when: interviewing people 1:1; ideation with a partner • Refueled and recover when: quiet thinking time to self, in community, exercise, out in nature • Have fun and enjoy when: dinner with partner and friends	• Drained when: all-day activity and talking • Boundaries crossed when: start to feel overwhelmed with scheduling demands • Allow grace: making dinner, cleaning house, staying organized	• Feel supported when: friends show up to support me, shared household duties • Life with work is sustainable when: my mornings can be my own
Other reflections	Small moments of joy help sustain me	Need to protect schedule from getting overbooked	Need long breaks alone to think and rejuvenate
Overall observations • I need to balance alone time with people interaction time—need both to restore, protect, and support my energy. • For sustainability, I need long breaks for myself. • Remember that small actions matter and make a big impact.			

- Protect:
    - » I get drained when . . .
    - » I know my boundaries have been crossed when . . .
    - » I can allow myself grace around . . .
- Support:
    - » I feel supported when . . .
    - » I feel like my life with work is sustainable when . . .

2. *Observe.* Consider what you documented. Note any other reflections you'd like to make or overall observations

about what you've learned that can sustain you, including considering the key areas to explore and build into your sustaining plan. Some of what you note will be activities you want to practice or avoid on an ongoing basis. Others will be actions you might want to calendarize, which you'll build into your weekly plan. See Table 10.2 for example observations.

3. *Look forward to create an ideal week.* Considering what you learned about restore, protect, and support: What would a visual schedule of your ideal week look like to reflect your sustaining plan? (See Figure 10.1 for an example.) Make it realistic. Think through questions like these:

    ◦ How many times a week can you do a particular activity?

    ◦ Where will you put in breaks from your Pause and Break Blueprint?

    ◦ What do you want to consider from the Where Time and Wish Time exercise around where you wish you were spending your time?

    ◦ If you want to make sure you have "me time," where are you carving that out each day or in your week?

    ◦ Consider what you learn in Part III about your life nonnegotiables: Where do you want to be firm and put certain activities on your calendar first?

4. *Bring it all together.* With what you've learned, create a sustaining plan for yourself across restore, protect, and support your energy. Note what you would ideally like to do to keep yourself operating at your best. For the protect

Figure 10.1. Example visual schedule of an ideal week

	Mon	Tues	Wed	Thurs	Fri	Sat	Sun
AM	Writing sprint 3x+ per week					Exercise class and run	Coffee and reading
	Exercise when can, thinking time						Thinking time
	• Core, focused working hours • Short breaks, small moments of joy					Out in the neighborhood, park, city	Outside adventure
PM		Coaching and personal calls (personal only 1x per week during this time)				Errands	
	Backup exercise time					Out with partner and/or friends	Wind down and planning
		Yoga	Exercise class				

category in particular, set some boundaries by noting what you will say yes to and no to.

5. *Create your MVSP.* Identify the minimum daily and weekly practices you need to commit to in order to operate at your best. Document these on your weekly plan, too.

6. *Lock it in.* Note a step that can help you commit to acting on your sustaining plan. Also consider putting relevant activities on your calendar to establish a regular practice. See Table 10.3 for an example of steps 4–6.

7. *Prototype your plan.* It's time to get started. Use your plan, including your ideal week visual schedule, as a guide. Practice your actions and continually assess and adapt them over time to optimize what works best given your current circumstances.

Table 10.3. Example of a sustaining plan

Energy management	Sustaining plan	MVSP	Lock it in: action planning
Restore	• Block calendar times for deep work • Pay attention to enjoy small joy moments • Exercise 3–5x/week • Get into park 3–4x/week for walking or running	• Pay attention to enjoy small joy moments • In park at least 1x/week • At least 15 minutes of exercise a day	• At start of week, identify when/where will make exercise and getting into park a priority
Protect	• Be thoughtful about scheduling days/weeks and factoring in recovery time if full days • Continue to allow myself to be bad at dinner and cleaning during intense periods • Say no to evening calls	• Need at least 1 full day/week that isn't full	• Block calendar • Weekly meal planning
Support	• Block mornings as often as possible • Identify resources and ask for help • Schedule extended periods and sprints for creative work	• If don't get mornings, schedule small breaks • Be thoughtful about calendar—protect and pace	• Change calendaring system to protect time • Weekly check-in to plan for needs

Put in Place Work and Home Structures

A final and important part of your sustaining plan is the work and home structures that support making it all a bit more sustainable for you. Structures can include setting boundaries, but more broadly I think of structures as holding up as opposed to pushing back. What will support you as opposed to expending energy to keep forces at bay? Another benefit of structures is that when they start to take hold, they require less energy and effort to maintain the environment that keeps you functioning well. Your structures can help create the sustainability you seek in a way that's realistic and true to your life circumstances.

For work structures, this can look like negotiating with your employer regarding your working hours, including when you'll be available online and when you'll be in the office. An important point around work structures is to remember to ask. Leslie Forde, founder of the organizations Mom's Hierarchy of Needs and Allies at Work—organizations that, respectively, research stress, self-care, and growth for moms and help employers use data to retain working parents—suggests that if you feel vulnerable asking for certain boundaries for yourself at work, band together with others who have similar needs and go to human resources or your manager as a group.[20]

At home, this could mean creating structures around how you make meals or share chores with a partner or roommate. If you're part of a household, don't leave things implicit; make structures explicit, having direct conversations and getting clear on who is doing what or what structures will help the household run smoothly. Make the load appropriate across each person in the household, especially considering people's preferences and strengths.

A more formal example of a home structure is one shared by Neil Pasricha, author of *The Book of Awesome* and *The Happiness Equation*. On the *Knowledge Project* podcast, he shared how he and his family created a family contract and defined "terms for our life." Just as a formal legal contract has terms, like responsibilities, obligations, and promises of each party, what might be terms you'd negotiate for your sustainable life together?[21]

To develop your structures, review the choices you make for your current life and work arc in Chapter 7. With that in mind and what you learned from the questions in the last exercise creating your sustaining plan, think about the support structures you can put in place across life and work to make things more sustainable for yourself.

• • •

At the end of this chapter, my hope is that you now feel in control and ready to commit to managing your energy. No one will create sustainability for you, so I encourage you to practice your sustaining plan to create it for yourself. Please do. Make it personal and right for you. Be intentional and allow your plan to evolve and change, as needed. Because if you are going to stretch and strive, you need a plan to sustain your effort and yourself.

Chapter 11

Allow Yourself to Live and Work Sustainably

"I'm still ambitious . . . [but] you have to build a whole life"—this is where Mara Yale's journey has brought her.[1] Since leaving her job after continual episodes of burnout, as I introduce in Chapter 6, she's restructured her life for more sustainability, and she's proud of what she's built for herself. She embraces her work ambitions, which allow her to engage in multiple disciplines, yet she doesn't want to burn out again. She now pursues her ambitions following the concept of pacing and arcs and allows them to build, grow, and take shape over time. She manages her effort and is proactive about her sustaining activities, like gardening, kayaking, and being present for her kids' sport activities. She's also taken longer sabbaticals, like when her father passed away, and she gave herself a year to not produce and instead allowed time to heal and explore what was next.

One thing Mara doesn't do? She doesn't defend her choices to others. She doesn't succumb to the external pressures of shoulds. Instead, she leans into her experience and sees what comes and what takes shape.

For many of us who are ambitious, Right Effort can be the hardest pillar to navigate. I know it is for me. I can get my right ambitions aligned to motivate my effort and make choices for my current arc. But as a hard worker who is ambitious and likes to achieve, I need to proactively manage myself, prioritizing and being discerning about my effort and energy. With Right Effort, just like the other pillars, emotions can be at play that affect our ability to create sustainability for ourselves.

Overall, my hope and intent with the Sustainable Ambition Method is to help you navigate the conflicts that arise as you pursue your ambitions and to help ease the tension to experience more fulfillment and satisfaction in your life. Instead of believing that pursuing your ambitions must be effortful, perhaps the pursuit can be joyful, easeful, and free of judgment. Perhaps we can allow ourselves to merrily roll along more consciously.

ALLOW A FULL, ENRICHING LIFE

In 2016, as part of a research project, I asked a woman I was interviewing which three adjectives she would use to describe her life. She was a mom with three kids who was also starting a business. The first word she thought of was *busy*. "Oh, but I can't say that," she said, considering it an inappropriate answer, as if it were something to be ashamed of.

Given how I've talked about busyness thus far, declaring that busy is a choice, you can understand her response. We've made *busy* a four-letter word.² Our societal reaction to busyness is a value judgment, which is not what I want. My interview took place after Laura Vanderkam, the time and productivity guru, wrote a *New York Times* article titled "The Busy Person's Lies."³ It's not that I disagree with what Vanderkam reports, which is that if we were to track and have more visibility around where our time goes, we'd be surprised by how we spend it and how we have more time than we may think. With such insight, we can make better choices. This may be true, but the title of the article hints at the emotional challenges one can face when leading a full, rich life. It hit me in my conversation with that mother, and has stayed with me since, that people can feel embarrassed or ashamed about being ambitious or about aspiring to build a whole life, as Mara Yale encouraged.

Most—or likely all—of us want to lead fulfilling, satisfying lives. And some of us want to be and do a lot. It's normal for us to have desires and goals, to pursue what we want for ourselves. My hope through these Sustainable Ambition practices is to give ourselves permission to embrace audacious goals across life *and* work.

And have those ambitions include our personal sustainability. We can sometimes forget that some of the choices we make around what we pursue and fit into our lives can have a positive, dual effect—goals and commitments can be ambitious *and* sustain us. It's not uncommon for people to have this aha moment when they reflect on a year or identify something they want to celebrate—that an accomplishment they are proud of not only checked the box on the goal but also gave them strength. For example, post-pandemic, my sister made it a goal to visit family and friends around the country, reconnecting to the people who matter most to her. This was a life ambition that sustained her through a challenging year. It was a way she prioritized what mattered to her to thrive in life and work. A win all around.

Leading a full life, including activities that support your resilience, creates a flywheel that fuels itself. Saying yes to what truly matters to you in your current arc and in the moment can do that.

Busyness doesn't have to be labeled as *bad*. What's more, we may be mischaracterizing the state of our lives. It could be that, instead, we are leading a fully engaged, wholehearted life. The actress Juliette Binoche described this in a *New York Times* interview in which the journalist asked her "if she always liked to be this busy."[4]

"I wouldn't call myself busy," Binoche objected. "More creative than busy."

The difference, she articulated, was that busyness is like "trying to fill up empty space," whereas being creative "pushes you up into a space where you feel alive and present and discovering and revealing yourself."

Perhaps when we live a wholehearted, full life, we are allowing ourselves to step into our own becoming. We are exploring our identities with a more expansive, curious lens. We are committing to and excited about our pursuits.

What's important in this is that we are conscious of and make choices around how we use our time and effort to build a rich life. In a 2016 *Guardian* article by Oliver Burkeman, he states how, just like busyness, focusing on time and productivity management can serve a purpose—to distract us from asking the important questions, merely *filling up* that empty space: "You can seek to impose order on your inbox all you like—but eventually you'll need to confront the fact that the deluge of messages, and the urge you feel to get them all dealt with, aren't really about technology. They're manifestations of larger, more personal dilemmas. Which paths will you pursue, and which will you abandon? Which relationships will you prioritize, during your shockingly limited lifespan, and who will you resign yourself to disappointing? What matters?"[5]

> Perhaps when we live a wholehearted, full life, we are allowing ourselves to step into our own becoming.

Conflict. Tension. Choices. What do you want in your space? What do you want to be industrious about? Where do you want to focus your time? Where do you want to apply your effort and energy? What matters most now?

Through the work of Sustainable Ambition, you step into making these more conscious choices for yourself. You learn to face your dilemmas.

Nothing to feel bad about here. All that is here is the opportunity to allow yourself to be completely present in the full, enriching life you are creating for yourself, with all its ups and downs, twists and turns, and dualities and contradictions.

ALLOW MORE JOY

Sabrina Moyle was looking for ways to show up in a better way—as an employer, as a mom, as a partner, and as a daughter. "I was really looking for ways to alleviate my own suffering. . . . There were just a lot of aspects of my life that were not really very happy at the time," she said.[6]

Sabrina is a writer and cofounder with her sister, illustrator Eunice Moyle, of Hello!Lucky, a creative studio based in San Francisco known for its letterpress greeting cards and children's books. In the company's early days, Sabrina managed it as any good leader who graduated from business school would—driving to scale the business and make it as profitable as possible. The result? In her words, "It led to just a lot of misery."

But in a new stage of life, Sabrina had an epiphany and identified a disconnect between the role of Hello!Lucky's products in people's lives and how she and her team were feeling. They sold cards that were fun, funny, and playful, and were often a part of people's big life moments, like their weddings. And yet "we were suffering," she said. "We were trying to be part of people's most joyful, important days. . . . But the work itself was draining. . . . It wasn't sustainable."

We ambitious types can easily find ourselves in a similar place because we can be hard driving and hard on ourselves, despite desiring more sustainability. For some of us, it's simply how we're wired. One way to help us find the sustainability we seek is to *allow* more joy in our lives and in our work.

For Sabrina, after a break and time to reevaluate, she established a new mission for the company, focused on how to bring joy, creativity, and connection into the world. She also changed her business model from vertically integrated to focusing exclusively on design and licensing. She made new choices about her personal life, too. "I basically made it my purpose to try to figure out how to live in a more sustainable, intentional, and happy way," she said.

We can do the same, with such intention.

How? Let's play! Yep, play. It's not just for kids. Play has been shown to help humans flourish and feel fulfilled and happy. According to the book *Play*, by Stuart Brown and Christopher Vaughan, we can benefit from the type of play that motivates and is most joyful for us. Yet they caution here, too, similar to what I shared about intrinsic motivation, to not expect the playful activity to *always* be fun.[7]

You might find the ways you prefer to play in the activities you love, from your Right Foundation. By integrating more of these activities into your day-to-day, in both your personal and your professional lives, you can experience more fulfillment, increase your energy, reduce stress, and build your resilience.

Play can also be incorporated into how we structure our activities themselves. In his book *Hidden Potential*, Adam Grant writes about turning the daily grind into something we enjoy. He highlights the solution of combining practice and play and calls it "deliberate play." One of the factors that can contribute to exhaustion, and potentially burnout, is when we lose joy in the process. We can get caught up focusing on the outcome or become so obsessed that we put in too much effort. Deliberate play incorporates joy into our approach and taps into our enthusiasm and excitement for the work at hand. The benefit, as Grant expresses, is that "it's easier to sustain enjoyment and achieve greater things . . . [and] prevent boreout and burnout."[8]

Another way to increase your joy is to connect more regularly to what you love, linking more closely to your intrinsic motivations. Our human brain likes pleasure and enjoyment, which sounds obvious, right? Perhaps not surprisingly, research has found that we are more committed and persistent in pursuing a goal when we enjoy what we are doing.[9] Finding joy in the process matters.[10]

Striving for our ambitions doesn't have to always be difficult or unpleasant. Yes, we need to learn to enjoy the grind, but we are better served making the grind joyful.

In finding joy, it can allow more ease, too.

ALLOW MORE EASE

"Let it be easy, let it be fun." I learned this mantra from my friend Jenny Blake, whom I reference in Chapter 2. I regularly come back to it to remind myself to allow more joy and, especially, more ease because I find that part harder to grant myself. It seems doable to add more fun; ease seems counterintuitive to goal pursuit. But allowing ease is part of Right Effort. How can we step away from achievement and accomplishment having to be hard and instead find more effortlessness in our pursuits? To offer a place to start, I share five strategies to allow more ease: (1) be flexible, (2) work with your energy, (3) build in a buffer, (4) embrace your lack of effort, and (5) go easy on perfectionism.

Be Flexible

We can experience greater well-being in the pursuit of our ambitions if they are motivating and manageable. In contrast, highly stressful projects negatively affect our well-being.[11] One way to ease the stress is to be flexible when our circumstances change. Allow it to be okay if life happens or priorities need to shift. Be willing to reinterpret the goal, the timing, and the effort to create more ease. Don't think you need to remain locked into your original plan and measurement of success. Rigidity doesn't serve us. Be flexible instead and renegotiate with yourself.

Work with Your Energy

Following your energy builds on the concept of flexibility. While at times I push myself to get something done, more often I follow where my natural energy pulls me to focus at the time. What am I motivated to work on in the moment? This approach creates more ease for me.

Working with our natural body rhythms can also help. This is called our chronotype, as I reference in Chapter 10. Set in our late twenties and hard to change, it is a biologically determined circadian rhythm that governs the optimal time we fall asleep and wake up. It also controls our energy levels throughout the day. Knowing your chronotype can help you better understand your optimal working hours, like when you should do focused thinking or creative work and when you'd be better served doing task-oriented work.

Working with your energy rather than against it can help create more ease.

Build in a Buffer

We all naturally work too much. About 20 percent too much, in fact, according to Cal Newport, an MIT-trained computer science professor at Georgetown University who writes about the intersections of technology, work, and the quest to find depth in an increasingly distracted world. He focused on this point in a *New Yorker* article he wrote in 2021, as we started to come out of the pandemic.[12]

One takeaway from the article is that we should give ourselves grace around this tendency to work more, as it is hard to self-regulate our effort. A practical tactic to address this is to build a 20 percent time buffer into our project plans and day-to-day activities. Doing so can create more ease instead of feeling frustrated and stressed when projects continually run over our originally estimated time.

Embrace Your Lack of Effort

If you haven't heard this enough from me yet, let me reassure you that it's okay to dial down your effort, and, if you need it, I'll give you permission to do so. I want to address this again because people often struggle with the concept and with the fear of missing out (FOMO). They ask me, "How can I overcome the feeling that I'm missing out if I don't work at full capacity?"

Start by challenging whether you need to work at full capacity to reach your desired outcomes. Recall what I share in Chapter 9 that not all ambitions are created equal. We don't always have to give everything our maximum effort to reach our desired level of aspiration or success. Another approach is to choose to renegotiate your desired outcome and the associated level of effort you want to put toward a goal.

Otherwise, I get it that it can feel uncomfortable to not accomplish as much or not give your all. Managing this feeling is hard—it's a mind game. What helps is to reframe the story you tell yourself. One option is to believe that the FOMO feeling is a sign you're doing it right. It's along the lines of what James Clear shared in a 2024 newsletter: "You're not focused enough unless you're mourning some of the things you're saying no to."[13]

Or you can shift that feeling of missing out toward what you gain by focusing and managing your effort. Find joy in the choices you've made for yourself and how they align to what motivates and matters most to you now. Appreciate that you are putting the appropriate amount of effort into your goals. Your new definition and measurement of success could include being able to achieve with more ease—that is your desired outcome. FOMO might signal that you've embraced Sustainable Ambition as your new way. Are you really missing out? Or are you ahead based on what matters to you most, including achieving more sustainability? Are you living the life you want?

Go Easy on Perfectionism

Managing perfectionist tendencies isn't easy. I know my own perfectionism can pop up around certain projects that matter to me and I enjoy.

But first, we shouldn't confuse perfectionism with striving for excellence. It's okay to have high standards. Adam Grant writes about perfectionism too in *Hidden Potential*. His counsel is to shift our drive for perfection toward setting our own high standards that are more specific and personal and can help us track our progress and growth: "An objective that's precise and challenging. It focuses your attention on the most important actions and tells you when enough is enough."[14]

Embedded in this approach is remembering to set your own definition of success and gauge the required effort. It's helpful to understand your personal aspiration and what is worth your hard work—to identify what really matters for a project and focus effort and excellence on that, letting go of the minor details that won't move the needle. You can inquire along these lines: How much of your effort is necessary? Where does your effort matter? When can you say, "This is good enough," and cut yourself off?

We can also embrace learning and growth in the process. I've found I experience more freedom in my work by leveraging the innovation principles of prototyping and testing. We can create a first, second, or third rough draft for learning and feedback that will help us move forward through the process more easily, as opposed to getting stuck and grinding away seeking perfection early on.

Shifting our behavioral tendencies is hard, but it starts with awareness. If you realize you're pushing for perfection, get curious. Pause to ask yourself: Am I striving for perfection here? Why might that be? Do I need to be? Do I want to be putting in this much effort? Is this good enough? Then ask: What action do I want to take from here?

ALLOW YOURSELF PEACE WITH GENEROSITY AND GRACE

Part of Sustainable Ambition is an inside job. We can be hard on ourselves. So I'd like to invite you to allow yourself to experience more peace by being generous with yourself and giving yourself grace.

A place to start is to remember that we are human. That's obvious, right? But we don't always remember that, as humans, it's natural to experience conflicts and tensions around what we are called to do, as well as to run into challenges managing our effort.

We humans are also divided selves influenced by our external environment. We have a side that is more rational in nature and a side that operates more intuitively and unconsciously. So we wrestle within ourselves. This idea of a divided self has been explored by ancient philosophers, in Buddhist traditions, and even by economists. Because we are wired this way, it can make decision-making and navigating our wants and desires difficult.

And we humans are complicated beings who also like to try to do a lot. In conversations with several academics, discussing their research and exploring Sustainable Ambition, I found it interesting that they seemed to have more compassion for us as human beings. I interpreted what they had to say as counsel to not take ourselves too seriously and to be more generous and let ourselves off the hook. For example, when speaking to Dr. Ayelet Fishbach about motivation, she shared how we tend to be overly optimistic about all we can do, saying, "It's not really that important to do everything that you put on your plate. . . . You were just trying to do a lot. . . . You're just trying to motivate yourself."[15] She normalized that we'll continually have to-dos that we don't accomplish each day and that we are likely to need more time. That was just us being human—optimistic and eager to accomplish more, always pushing the boundaries of our realities. If that's the case, we don't need to beat ourselves up about it. Instead, the lesson is to give ourselves a break and permission to step into more ease and practice grace.

We lead full lives, and we may be in life stages that stretch us across many dimensions. We do a lot and try to show up as our best. It can be hard to feel we excel at anything when our focus is divided and we are moving in many directions. In such stages, Right Time and Right Effort are critical to help us focus—allowing us to make our worlds smaller and put our attention and effort where we feel it matters most—and to give ourselves permission to lower our bar and not have to excel at everything. We can lean into practices to create more ease, like being flexible, working with our energy, building in a buffer, and the others I share in this chapter.

We can all likely benefit from practicing more self-compassion. Be generous with yourself as you pursue your ambitions. Allow yourself to embrace sustainability and experience more peace by giving yourself grace.

• • •

Right Effort takes dialing in and adjusting over time to achieve sustainable effort and energy. When you're ambitious, it's easy to dial your effort up. The harder act is to get it just right *for you*. My hope is that you can give yourself permission to allow yourself to be ambitious about the life you want and allow more joy and ease in its pursuit.

These are a few questions to help you explore allowing more joy and ease as you sustainably pursue your ambitions with Right Effort:

- How am I pushing myself into a space that feels alive, and am I busy and industrious doing what I want?

- How can I allow and embrace the wholehearted life I'm designing?
- How can I allow and create more joy?
- How can I allow and create more ease?
- How can I be more generous with myself and give myself grace?

Right Ambition. Right Time. Right Effort. Each of these is important on its own, and yet Sustainable Ambition exists at their intersection. By considering and practicing across all three, you can step into a more rewarding, realistic, and resilient approach to achieving personal success and integrating your life and work.

Part V

Practicing Sustainable Ambition

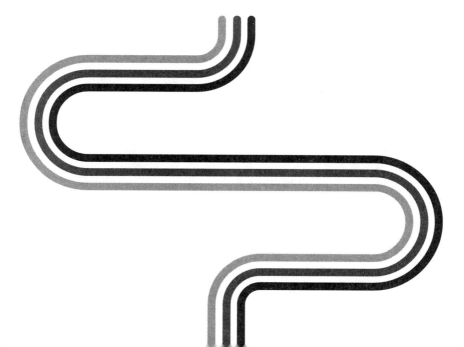

Chapter 12

• • •

Find the Sustainable Ambition Way

On one level, *The West Wing*, the popular late 1990s and early 2000s television series, was a story about ambition—not just of President Josiah (Jed) Bartlet, but of its many characters. I'm a superfan and watch the episodes again and again. The show's aspirational characters are presented as impressive achievers, yet real. Not perfect, human. Watching their stories motivates me to become more ambitious, be deliberate about how I pursue my ambitions, and allow myself to be human too.

Not only does the show inspire me in this way; it speaks to positive aspects of the Sustainable Ambition Method, while also serving as a cautionary tale.

Around Right Ambition, we learn that despite not having thought of being president himself, Bartlet grows into his presidential ambition as he campaigns and starts to win. He buys into the vision of himself as president, finds his purpose often in reciting statistics associated with macro problems to be solved, and ends up valuing and loving the work.

The show is filled with examples of navigating Right Time by making tough choices, such as Abbey Bartlet stepping away from her medical career to serve as First Lady, communications director Toby Ziegler postponing having a baby with his wife, or press secretary C. J. Cregg delaying having a serious relationship until she's out of the White House.

As is often the case, other people, not the lead characters themselves, held up mirrors to illuminate the need to find Right Effort. For C.J., it took former senior White House correspondent Danny Concannon to push her to acknowledge that at some point you have to choose to make a relationship a priority. Later in the series, as the president starts his second term and his multiple sclerosis disability steadily gets worse, it takes the support people around him to force him to decrease his workload and get the rest he needs so he can operate at his best.

While this is a fictional example, you can see elements of the method at work. Up to this point, you've learned how to define goals at any life stage to motivate your effort, how to prioritize them across your life and work to focus your effort, and how you can manage your effort to achieve your personal success while remaining resilient. Now, we're going to build on what you've learned and the work you've completed, bringing Right Ambition, Right Time, and Right Effort together to form the intersection of Sustainable Ambition.

As this demonstrates, the Sustainable Ambition Method is flexible and can be applied on many levels—as a mindset, a method, and a mantra. We've already covered the mindset and how the method can be applied across life and work so that the elements together can help you be sustainably ambitious to create the life you want. In this chapter, you learn how to apply the method to a single ambition or project at a moment in time, perhaps when you need to make a decision about an opportunity or new direction.

We delve into the importance of paying attention and checking in with yourself as you move forward, as your ambitions can shift unexpectedly. When you pause to reflect, you can be more conscious and intentional to ensure you are applying your time and effort to self-defined, meaningful, and motivating goals that are prioritized and aligned to your desired effort and sustained energy. In doing so, you can motivate, focus, and manage your effort for more sustainability to thrive in life and work. Your day-to-day life constantly changes too and will upset your orchestrated plans. For such times, you'll learn how to use a mantra as an easy, quick guide to find your way back to sustainability.

You'll also discover that courage is required on this journey, and your community will be critical to support you along the way.

With all the practices in the book, as well as being mindful of the people you surround yourself with, my hope for you in embracing the Sustainable Ambition Method is that you'll experience more joy, fulfillment, and ease in pursuit of what matters most to you in your life and work.

APPLY THE METHOD TO AN AMBITION

Up to this point, you've applied the method to your life and work ambitions and have looked at your ambitions as they relate to each of the pillars—Right Ambition, Right Time, and Right Effort. Through that process, you've also seen how at times the pillars can interact to help you find the Sustainable Ambition way through.

Now, we'll apply the method against one ambition, goal, or project with all three pillars at play. The method isn't formulaic. Instead, it prompts us to ask the right questions, reflect, and consider several strategies: whether we need to reinterpret or reprioritize the ambition; examine how we might resolve a challenge, particularly around time and effort; or contemplate if we should release the ambition or shift it to another time.

To use the method in this way, choose an ambition or goal to explore and rate it on the three pillar dimensions using a scale of 1 (strongly disagree) to 10 (strongly agree). Then use the following questions to guide how you respond across the three pillars of Right Ambition (want to), Right Time (time to), and Right Effort (energy to). See Figure 12.1 for an example of the tool.

Right Ambition (want to): This ambition is one that I personally want to pursue.

- How much do I want this ambition versus it being a should?
- How meaningful and motivating is this ambition to me?
- How much am I energized by this ambition?

Figure 12.1. The Sustainable Ambition Evaluation Tool

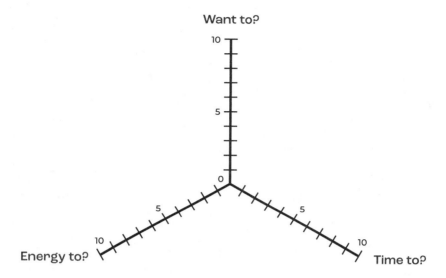

Right Time (time to): This is the right time for me to pursue this ambition.

- Do I have increasing energy for this ambition, aligning with how I wish to spend my time now?
- Is there urgency for me to pursue this ambition now?
- Does this ambition fit into my current arc and align with my desired pace?

Right Effort (energy to): I have the energy to pursue this ambition.

- Do I have the energy to put the desired amount of effort toward my aspiration?
- How determined and committed am I to achieve my ambition and get my desired reward?
- How well can I sustain myself if I pursue this ambition?

At the end of the evaluation, connect the dots across each of the three pillars and reflect on the triangle or wing, if you will, created. (See Figures 12.2 and 12.3 for examples.) How big is the wing? How even is it across its sides? Given the size and shape of the wing, you can ask yourself questions to determine your actions. Will this ambition take flight? Do I have to adjust it to help it fly? Should it not take flight, and what are the implications?

Do you get a sense of Right Ambition? Yes! Right Time? Yes! Right Effort? Yes! You have a Sustainable Ambition that is a self-defined, meaningful, and motivating goal that is right for you now and aligned to your desired effort and sustained energy. Time to go for it and put in the appropriate effort to sustainably pursue it.

You might find lower ratings on one of the dimensions, which suggests you may not want to, it may not be the time to, or you may not have the energy to pursue the ambition. In this situation, you can dig deeper to unpack why and what you want to do to move forward, given what you have rated low and what you've learned through the book about each pillar. What conflict needs to be resolved? How might you reinterpret, prioritize, or choose what matters now and determine your next actions? Can you link the ambition to your Right Foundation and make it a Right Ambition to motivate your effort? Is this an ambition you are ready to prioritize and choose to focus your time and energy on? Or can you coordinate or compromise around it? How can you adjust your effort and pursue the ambition sustainably?

How does this work in practice? Let me share a situation of my own and how I could have used the method and this tool to help me decide, with more ease and a lot less emotional turmoil, whether to take advantage of an unexpected opportunity.

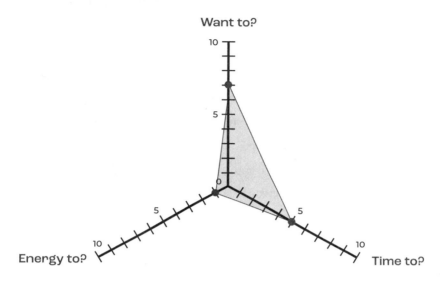

Figure 12.2. A small wing, showing some want-to and time-to but not much energy-to

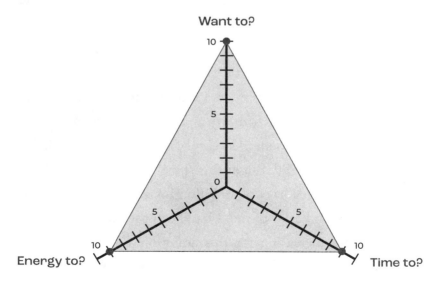

Figure 12.3. A big wing, showing a Sustainable Ambition

In April 2021, I had been contracting with a company for a few months when they approached me about joining their team full time. When I had actively looked for a job a few years back, the role now offered at this consulting firm had been exactly what I wanted. Yet here it was, and instead of being thrilled, I was torn. I should say yes, but I hesitated. Why did I feel so much internal conflict?

These types of decisions are tough! And they can be agonizing. How do we decide? The Sustainable Ambition Method can help us unpack these tensions to gain more insight and help us find a more sustainable path forward. This is how the ratings would have looked for me if I had used the method to help me in the moment.

Want to: 7. My head said I should want this job, but I was resisting. Surprisingly, I wasn't energized by this ambition; nor was I motivated by the role or the title. That was despite the fact that it fit with my values (growth and learning) and how I like to contribute (consulting and helping others succeed), and it offered work I love (strategy). I thought it fit into my vision for my life, yet I felt tension because of the effort that would be required in the role. On to step 2.

Time to: 5. On some level, it was the right time for this opportunity. The decision was urgent, and I needed to pay my bills, just like everyone else. I valued stability, and self-employment still felt unstable to me. It was a senior-level role, and I had the experience. I should want this, right? But at this stage in my life, I just didn't want to step into this level of ambition for another organization that would demand a lot of me. I had been there, done that. My energy was not increasing for this ambition. I'd rather put my energy into creating and building something for myself. It was time for that.

Energy to: 3. This was the crux of the decision. I did not have the energy and was not willing to put in the effort for this level of ambition within this type of firm. Remember—I'm a hard worker. Typically, when a task or job is in front of me, I put myself into it. As a contractor to this firm, I worked hard. I got the job done—always. But I did not have the energy to step into this full-time role. Part of that was because I didn't want to; nor was it time to. I didn't want to have a full-time job that fully consumed me, and consulting firms and agencies consume you. The dollar-per-hour trade-off wasn't worth it to me. I had another ambition where I wanted to put my energy and effort instead—to explore and bring Sustainable Ambition to the world.

Without the method, I took my typical actions to help me decide—the pro/con list and seeking others' opinions and advice. I pretended to step into the role, which left me feeling anxious—that was a sign, to be sure. But I still couldn't comfortably land on a decision.

Eventually, I set a deadline for myself to end the agony and release my energy. I got myself to say no, and yet in that moment, I still wasn't sure if I was making the right decision. If I had done this exercise and connected the dots, I would have more clearly known that the answer was solidly no. In the end, I didn't want to, it wasn't the time to, and I didn't have the energy to. A full-time role in that type of company wasn't my ambition at that time after all. It was time for me to move on to what was next. It was time for a new life and work arc. I learned that I wasn't honoring what my body and my natural resistance was telling me—that I just didn't have the energy for the opportunity. I fought all the signs, instead of listening to my knowing within.

This rational tool would have helped me resolve my conflict and helped make what I wanted more conscious for me. What's more, it would have saved me two weeks of angst-ridden decision-making energy that I could have used on other higher-priority ambitions. I literally spent fourteen days of my life on this decision!

You, too, can evaluate a life or work ambition to uncover insights to help you determine how you want to move forward. Where might you be able to resolve some conflicts you are experiencing and free some of your time and energy with greater conscious clarity around what you want for yourself now?

Here I provide several examples of how Right Ambition (want to), Right Time (time to), and Right Effort (energy to) can apply across different types of ambitions and goals. These are real examples from a colleague, a coaching client, and me.

Example 1

Ambition: A colleague was presented with a significant leadership opportunity at a new company that has the potential to make a big impact in the world. This role was a wow.

- Want to (9): I am drawn to this ambition, and it aligns with my vision, how I want to contribute, and work I love.

- Time to (4): My family isn't stable right now and needs attention. If I take this job, I'll have to address and put in place support for our collective needs.

- Energy to (4): I'm tired after the last three years post-pandemic. I need a break first, and I'd need to put structures in place to make this work for myself and my family.

- Conclusion and action: I'm willing to explore the opportunity because I am called to it. But if I move forward, I will need to put structures in place and request time off before I jump into the role so that I will be fully recovered and have energy to take it on.

Example 2

Ambition: A coaching client started our first call together sharing that they loved their job but needed to make their life and work integration more sustainable.

- Want to (10): I'm thrilled to be in this role and am in the best spot of my career to date.
- Time to (8): I took this job at this time because my kids are older now and don't need me as much. Yet commuting across the country to my job one week each month is challenging for me and my family. I knew this going in, and I'm willing to continue to accept it for now. I just need to make it sustainable.
- Energy to (6): I'm willing to put my energy and effort into this job, but it won't be sustainable if I don't figure out ways to sustain myself and build my resilience.
- Conclusion and action: I'm committed to this ambition and will work on my sustainability plan and put structures in place to ensure this job is sustainable for me and my family.

Example 3

Ambition: I long to take a sabbatical.

- Want to (10): I desperately want to take a sabbatical. I'm burned out and need time to restore myself.

- Time to (3): I feel this is urgent, but I need to be the one to hold a steady job right now as my husband continues to look for his next role.

- Energy to (2): We're not financially ready to take this step. I may want it, but taking a sabbatical right now would cause more stress.

- Conclusion and action: Hold! The sabbatical was not to be at this time, but that didn't mean I didn't need a break. As I stepped into a new job, I negotiated taking three weeks off within my first three months to get a more extended break since I jumped from one job to the other. I was also working in a less intense role and was able to add back more sustaining activities to my days, such as exercise and creative pursuits. I started to build back my resilience stores.

Example 4

Ambition: I still want to take a sabbatical!

- Want to (10): I'm not quite as burned out as I was before, but I still long to take an extended break.

- Time to (8): This upcoming time could be a perfect window where we can pull this off. The flexibility of our work could support this now, and we are financially ready.

- Energy to (8): I want to do this! I'm willing to step into the discomfort the experience will bring, and I'm willing to put in the effort to plan how we can make this work.
- Conclusion and action: All signs point to go! I took a leave from my job and embarked on an eight-month sabbatical. Glorious! But, as should be expected, not without its ups and downs, too.

With this evaluation, making decisions and navigating the conflicts we experience with our ambitions and across life and work can still be hard. My hope is that the method, this tool, and all you've learned in the book can shed more light on your situation, so you can make the right choices for you with more insight and consciousness. You can come back to the method and this tool regularly to evaluate ambitions, determine the best course of action, and save yourself time, energy, and suffering in the process. Conflicts and tensions across our ambitions and goals won't go away. As we, our lives, and the world around us change, the algorithm of our ambitions, life, and work gets reprogrammed repeatedly, leaving us to wrestle with what we want to do now and where we want to put our time, energy, and effort.

PAY ATTENTION AND PLAN FOR SHIFTING AMBITIONS

Paying attention to avoid going on autopilot is part of the Sustainable Ambition practice. The practice calls us to be more conscious about our ambitions and how we are being ambitious. Why is that important? Because it's hard to get Sustainable

Ambition right all the time. As I share at the start of the book, getting it right and navigating toward sustainability requires attentiveness and adaptability. Sometimes having your ambition, timing, or effort off is what helps you figure out what's right for you at this time. Accepting the method as a practice serves as a reminder to continuously reflect and recalibrate, allowing the times you are off to be a part of the learning journey.

When you pause to take stock, you might find that your ambitions are shifting. Expect this. Such evolutions typically happen when we've experienced some change—big or small, foreseen or unforeseen. By paying attention on a regular basis, you are less likely to be surprised and caught off guard. That's why I also encourage you to continually explore and plant seeds around new interests sooner than later, fostering your personal growth.

> Curiosity can help us reclaim and see a richer and fuller view of our ambitions and who we can become.

We can also more easily embrace our ambitions shifting over time when we realize that we don't have to find *a path*. Few of us get on one singular track that is consistent and keeps us going up and up and up. More often, our story unfolds over time, with us being able to see the connecting threads as we reflect back on our past experiences. With this perspective, we can reduce the pressure we can feel to *figure it out* and *have clarity*. We can instead step into Sustainable Ambition and allow for discovery and the progressive growth of our ambitions.

Find confidence and comfort in trusting your curiosity to guide you. It can carry you far. Recall what I share in earlier chapters about thinking about ambitions more broadly. Curiosity can help us reclaim and see a richer and fuller view of our ambitions and who we can become. We may not be able to know what we are passionate about, but asking what we're curious about is easier to uncover. So, what are you curious about now that catches your attention, creates a spark, and is meaningful and motivating to you?

And yes, clarity is good and can help get us into action. But clarity around certain aspects of our path can be elusive. Let me give you a personal example, since I can struggle with this myself. I hold an overall ambition for my life and have goals associated with my long-term vision. I also hold ambitions and goals for the short term. But ask me to tell you exactly what my current efforts will manifest, and my mind goes blank. The midterm view is murky. That's more normal for most of us than we realize. We can hold overarching, bigger, broader views of what we want for our life, but it's hard to know exactly what we want to manifest two, three, or five years out. One year or long-term is easier.

To work with this, I focus on the short term—the current way I want to give, the values I want to prioritize now, what I'm curious about and want to explore at this time, and what I want to master in the coming year. I identify closer-in activities that align with my current goals and ambitions and plant seeds that may turn into a new opportunity I can't foresee now.

Another strategy is to build optionality to facilitate the times our ambitions shift. This is a theme echoed by many podcast guests who have navigated evolving ambitions, allowing them to ebb and flow. What I mean by *optionality* is putting yourself in a position where you have options and aren't locked in. In other words, you can make sustainable lifestyle and career choices. This can include financial decisions that give you more flexibility, like not accumulating a lot of debt or choosing how to live your life day-to-day to keep your financial burn rate low. It can be planting seeds, investing in your potential, and building new skills so you can be more agile negotiating transitions.

I appreciated how Shane Parrish, a Canadian former spy and author of *Clear Thinking*, emphasized this point in a 2022 piece: "One of the most overlooked opportunities in life is how you are positioned when circumstances hit. Good positions create options, while bad positions reduce them. . . . Good positions allow you to master your circumstances rather than be mastered by them."[1]

That's what I mean here—put yourself in a good position to have agency over your life and work. Build optionality.

My husband and I buying our first home was a good demonstration of this. We didn't stretch ourselves and purchased a home we could afford based on one salary. Why? Because we wanted to have optionality. We didn't want to be in a position where we both *had to* be tied to certain jobs to afford our mortgage payment.

As best we can, we want to prepare ourselves, so we aren't blindsided by our shifting ambitions and instead consciously guide that shift. We want to put ourselves in good positions to navigate the changes more easily as they come.

PLAN YOUR PERIODIC CHECK-INS

Making Sustainable Ambition a practice helps us pay attention over time and provides structure to keep us focused on what we're trying to achieve both with our goals and around sustainability.

Practice is important not just because adaptability is required but also because we're human and easily distracted. No judgment here! It's a reality and totally okay. I hear this from people who have done work with Sustainable Ambition. The inertia of life and work can push against us making progress. I experience this too, which is why I come back to the concepts over and over. We can transform and modify what we do by repeatedly acting to master new ideas and behaviors. Practicing the method builds your capacity over time and creates habits where the mindset and the method become more embedded in your routine.

How can we carry the Sustainable Ambition Method with us every day? One way is to be intentional in setting aside time for check-ins, as I suggest at the start of the book. By periodically checking in with ourselves and being aware of what we are experiencing and feeling, we can more likely make adjustments to stay in the healthy, happy, sustainable zone and not fall into the dangerous, severe zone. Such check-ins can take place at a moment in time, monthly, quarterly, or annually.

I advocate that you schedule these sessions on your calendar. In Chapter 9, I also recommend that you calendar a monthly review of your sustainability and sustaining plan to make sure you're not on the border of exhaustion or burnout.

Now I'm suggesting you add an annual check-in to your calendar and, if you'd like, add or align quarterly reviews in the appropriate month, too. This is a way to help you keep these concepts top of mind in your everyday life and pull yourself back from unhelpful habits we can fall into.

Take action now, right at this moment. Literally go schedule the sessions on your calendar, because what gets put on our calendars tends to happen. I encourage you to make this commitment to yourself.

What can you do in these check-ins? I offer options and guidance in the following list.

> **REMINDERS TO PRACTICE SUSTAINABLE AMBITION**
>
> If you'd like more support remembering to practice Sustainable Ambition, sign up for my reminder email series at SustainableAmbition.com/sa-practice. I'll send notes at each quarter and at the end of the year to remind you to check in with yourself and commit to your ambitions and personal sustainability. You can unsubscribe at any time.

Annual Horizon Map Check-In

Conduct an annual check-in reviewing your Horizon Map to see if anything has changed and shifted across your arcs.

Quarterly or Annual Check-In

- At each quarter or the end of a year, check on your overall sustainability and reflect on your Sustainable Ambition. Consider how things are going by using the U-curve of ambition—do you feel you're operating in the stagnant, sustainable, or severe zone? When evaluating, consider the pace you want to be operating at now. Are you ebbing up or down? Either is great, as long as it's right for you.
- Then use these reflection questions to think about where you might be off across Right Ambition, Right Time, and Right Effort:
    - Right Ambition: How am I feeling about my ambitions?

Am I motivated and energized by what I'm pursuing across life and work? Has anything shifted for me?

  - Right Time: How am I doing with my life and work ambitions across my arcs? Am I focused on the right priorities now? Do I need to adjust anything and make different choices? How sustainable is the pace at which I'm operating?

  - Right Effort: Am I on the path to overextension and overexhaustion? How am I doing with managing my day-to-day pace, my effort across my ambitions, my sustaining plan, and my work and home structures? What's working? What's not working?

- Finally, determine the actions you'll take to optimize across the three pillars—Right Ambition, Right Time, and Right Effort—to motivate, focus, and manage your effort. Apply what you've learned from the book to make things *right* for you and to operate in a Sustainable Ambition way.

Evaluation Tool Check-In

Review the alignment of an ambition or goal across the three pillars using the Sustainable Ambition Evaluation Tool I introduce in this chapter. Are you still aligned to Right Ambition, Right Time, and Right Effort?

Other Tools in the Book

I call many of the exercises and insights in the book *practices*, because these are approaches that we can use repeatedly to support us in being sustainably ambitious. When we hit a bump in the road or a roadblock and don't know where to turn, we can come back to these approaches and strategies to find a way forward. In a check-in, go back to sections in the book that align to where you might need to put attention. What exercises or insights can support you in making a choice and taking action to move you forward?

EMBRACE THE MANTRA

"I want work-life balance!" When I hear these words from people, they are often said with longing, as a desperate plea. *Where is it already?* And as I write at the start of the book, I don't think the term serves us.

I'd like to offer an alternative mantra to adopt instead. It's a simple and very doable way to keep the practices in the book alive. Ask yourself in a moment of conflict or tension: *What is the Sustainable Ambition way here?* When all else fails you, come back to this central, guiding question to check in with yourself and define what this means for you to create more fulfillment, joy, and ease in the moment.

Simply pause, ask the question, and answer it to see what ideas you generate. What new action, or inaction even (eliminating something), can you take to move forward and create more sustainability around your ambitions?

You can also use the question as a prompt to run through the three pillars quickly. When I do this, it can look like examining whether I still want to pursue an ambition or goal or instead reinterpret it; recognizing that I need to push the pursuit of some ambitions out, renegotiating a timeline with myself or someone else; or determining that I need to put another break or more sustaining activities on my calendar.

In using any of these approaches I share in this chapter and the book, my hope is that you'll find *your way* with Sustainable Ambition. These journeys aren't easy and will take courage, but they can be easier when we pay attention and practice. What also helps is when we are supported by those around us.

FIND COURAGE AND FOSTER YOUR COMMUNITY

Would *The West Wing*'s Jed Bartlet have ever become president without his good friend Leo McGarry? The presidency wasn't even on Bartlet's radar. It took someone who knew him well to plant the seed of ambition for him, sharing a simple campaign slogan that Leo couldn't get out of his mind for weeks: "Bartlet for America."

Would he have pushed to pursue a second term after his multiple sclerosis became public if it wasn't for his long-time secretary, Dolores Landingham? It took her coming back from the dead (it's a television show) to deliver the final, convincing word: "You know, if you don't wanna run again, I respect that. But if you don't run because you think it's going to be too hard or you think you're gonna lose . . . well, God, Jed, I don't even want to know you."[2]

Courage is often required to step into the ambitions that call us. Throughout my podcast interviews, I've heard this from guests. Why? Because it does take courage to step off the norm of the socialized path and into greater agency with a self-authored mind. It takes courage to step onto a new growth curve and into the unknown. Courage calls us because fear often holds us back.

Sustainable Ambition alone is aspirational. It will challenge you. This quote attributed to Mark Twain reminds us that, at such times, who we surround ourselves with matters and is critical to our success: "Keep away from people who try to belittle your ambitions. Small people always do that, but the really great make you feel that you, too, can become great."[3]

Our ambitions need to be protected and nurtured, and we need to be supported when going through change or taking courageous steps. Your community can support your redefinition of success and your reclaiming of ambition. They can help sustain you when you go through challenging or stretching times, bolstering your resilience. Community lifts you and is your force multiplier.

Academic research supports this thesis.[4] We are heavily peer-influenced. People in our inner circle help shape how we see and feel about the world, what we expect of ourselves, and our overall mood and energy. When we look to step out of the norm and seek to find that courage to do so, it is invaluable to foster a community around us that can champion and support us as we move forward.

How is courage calling you forth, and how can you build your community to support you?

Investing in these supportive relationships could look like contacting a friend or mentor to share your ambition or to create an accountability partner so you take the next step toward it. You might invest in building your network or join a community organization to deepen your connections in an area of interest. Or you might seek out a coach or a mastermind group to help you go further faster. You could even create a circle of friends or a group that meets for check-ins to support each other on your Sustainable Ambition journeys.

I encourage you to commit to at least one action and take a first step to foster your community to support your courage to move forward with what is calling you forth.

> **FOSTER YOUR COMMUNITY**
>
> You can find more tips on building community at SustainableAmbition.com/sa-toolkit.

WHAT'S NEXT?

"What's next?" is a signature phrase of President Bartlet in *The West Wing* and becomes a mantra throughout the series. As a candidate, Bartlet introduces the phrase to his newish staff: "When I ask 'what's next?' it means I'm ready to move on to other things. So, what's next?"[5]

As you move through life and work inflection points, ask yourself this question too.

We are constantly in a state of becoming. We'll set off in a direction and realize we need to make a shift. We push into a new ambition with trepidation and grow into it over time, finding our courage. And we can lean on our community along the way, just as President Bartlet did to win the first election and make it through his second term. What's next?

In the last episode of the series and in the final minutes, we see President Bartlet on inauguration day after the smooth transfer of power and the new president has been sworn in.[6] His job is done. He's a civilian on a plane, flying to his home in New Hampshire.

He's contemplative, looking out to a beautiful blue sky and sunset on the horizon, as the plane makes a turn.

"What are you thinking about?" Abbey asks.

Bartlet replies, "Tomorrow."

You are in charge of your ambitions, success, and sustainability now.

What's next for you?

What ambitions do you hold?

Who do you want to become tomorrow?

Conclusion

• • •

Choose What's Possible beyond What's Next

A clear, blue, brilliant sky. A flock of small birds flying.

"This card is calling you forth."

The tarot card reader revealed the last card after having laid them all out in front of me on a table and turned them over one by one to describe the meaning. I was at a close friend's first book launch party, at a local bookstore, and given the book's paranormal genre, she had a tarot card reader to offer readings as a fun activity for guests.

This final card caught my attention more than the others. In addition to the birds flying in the clear blue sky, it had an image of a bird that sat on a perch in a gilded cage, with the bird's wings slightly open.

"You're being called forth," the tarot card reader said again.

I seek inspiration at times I feel tension or stuck. It doesn't matter if I fully believe in the method or not. Offer me an assessment of any sort, and I'm likely to see what new insights it can offer to help move me forward. I simply think, *Why not?* A tarot card reader is no different. *Who knows how the universe works? Let's have fun and see what I can learn.*

At the time, I was in the midst of a transition and finding my footing. I had stepped into a new career path and questioned my decision. I had pivoted to a should—*I should get e-commerce experience if I want to work in the Bay Area*—hoping it would pave a new, stable direction while checking enough boxes on my list of personal requirements. But the role felt more limiting and restrictive than I expected. At the same time, I longed for more personal ownership and agency, to build something of my own.

My eyes came back to the card, and I studied it longer. The image on the tarot card was unusual in that the bird sat safely inside the cage, but the cage door was wide open. I didn't see that at first, but now upon reflection, I thought, *Why hadn't the bird flown away?*

This card has stayed with me ever since that event. I've searched for it and can't find the exact card that I remember in my mind's eye. Perhaps I saw the inspiration I needed to see in that moment.

The card is similar to a more common tarot card, the Eight of Swords, which in some designs shows such an image of a bird seemingly captive in a cage. The cage can have different meanings, such as remaining safe in our current environments or comfort zone and not embracing change. We may think that we are constrained and restricted, but we aren't, and instead put in place self-imposed barriers. Birds on cards tend to represent freedom, potential, transitions, and new directions in life. The open cage door suggests that it's time for us to get past our limitations, have courage, and take flight. We are free to explore new possibilities, pursue our hopes and dreams, and fully embrace our potential and who we want to become.

I was being called forth. But what mindsets and beliefs held me back? What fears kept me from stepping forward? Who did I want to become? Could I allow myself to take the leap?

As tarot card readings are contextual, I chose the meaning of that card to be that I shouldn't feel confined by traditional norms of crafting what was next for my career. I was scared to leave a well-paying, stable job, but I took the leap and quit. I stepped into self-employment and consulting and explored starting a business with a partner. I allowed myself to step into my desire to build a body of work of my own and to have more personal ownership. I mustered the courage to do so and created and leaned on my community to help me embrace fearlessness and make the leap to fly out of that cage. I'm still on my journey of discovery and embrace the ups and downs that come along with the adventure. But I lean into my Sustainable Ambition practices to help me find more joy and ease along the way.

You're being called forth too. In reading this book, you've pulled the Eight of Swords.

When you started reading it, you may have felt like me at the time of that tarot card reading—a bit stuck and unsure of how to design the life and work you want. You may have been unclear about what you want and who you are, want to be, and want to become. You may have had different perspectives about success and ambition and felt powerless to change your trajectory. You may have come to the book feeling exhausted.

You could have remained safely in the cage of external expectations and norms for ambition and success and remained attached to the unrelenting quest for work-life balance. But you've chosen instead to step into self-authorship, personal reward, and self-defined success and contentedness. You've stepped into a more realistic way of managing the conflict across all you want to do in your life and work, prioritizing what matters most now. You can be more discerning about your effort and build life and work resilience. Not to say it's easy, but you can motivate, focus, and manage your effort to make it all more sustainable.

Right Ambition. Right Time. Right Effort.

You are now ready to jump into and embrace the journey and discovery, allowing yourself to change, grow, and become over time. You can continue to choose and practice Sustainable Ambition to help you experience more joy and ease along the way.

The societal norms that gave you structure and helped you find a path served their purpose, but now you know that they don't need to hold you back.

The door has been open all along.

You had the choice: Remain caged and constrained? Or let yourself be free?

Free of the weight of external rules and expectations.

Free of the need to do it all.

Free of the pressure to drive hard all the time.

The sky is open for you to continue to explore who you want to be and become while dancing with the external world and the winds that swarm around you, searching for the air that will give you lift.

As you proceed, pay attention for and embrace change.

Make yourself uncomfortable.

See possibility rather than barriers.

Be brave.

Now is the time to allow yourself to fully become who you want to be—now and into the future. Step into self-authorship, embrace your full potential, and design the life you want.

Let yourself step outside the cage. Let yourself be ambitious. Let yourself trust that you can spread your wings, that the air will catch you, and that you will find lift. Trust that you now know how to make it all work in a way that is right for you. Trust that your community will let you take the lead and support you. And when you need it, they'll also encourage you, offer guidance as you navigate the changing winds, and allow you to draft. Remember, too—I'm on this journey with you and here to be a champion as part of your community, cheering you on and supporting your Sustainable Ambition now and into the future.

So, from this blue sky, what's possible beyond what's next?

What new perspectives and possibilities can you see from here?

What new dreams might you have or allow to take shape for tomorrow and beyond?

What will your ambitions grow into next?

Stay engaged. Sustain your ambition. Step into new adventures. Choose to enjoy the journey and to dance with the changing winds. It's normal to be nervous. Shift that anxious energy to excitement. Choose to join the other birds soaring and dancing in the sky. Dancing with the wind. Dancing with what comes and enjoying the ride.

Right Ambition. Right Time. Right Effort. You've been transformed, and it's time to emerge and make the leap, to step into being free. The sky is open for exploration and discovery.

Sure, you may not know where the leap and changing winds will take you. Trust the flight path will reveal itself and that you will shape the narrative along the way. Search for the joy in the journey.

The sky is yours.

It's time to fly.

Off you go!

Be free.

Acknowledgments

• • •

When I ran my first marathon, I didn't tell many people. My thinking: Keep expectations *low*. I didn't want to have to announce to my coworkers after the fact that I didn't hit a certain time or reach a certain goal. This has been my way in the past—being shy to share goals and keeping ambitions to myself. But I now know this isn't the better way. As I note in the book, community is critical to both the pursuit of our ambitions and our well-being. So on this book journey, I stretched myself to be more inclusive, allowed myself to be seen, and invited people to support me. The book has been an interesting creative and personal adventure—one, not surprisingly, with plot twists, tests, and conflict. I am forever grateful to my community, those who gave me energy and cheered me on to the end of this part of the story and who, in doing so, have helped me find my own freedom and flight.

To those whose stories are featured in the book: I'm forever grateful for your generosity in letting me share your personal story with others so that they can learn from you and your experiences.

To my *Sustainable Ambition* podcast guests: The podcast and being in conversation with you is one of the most joyful activities of this creative journey. Thank you for allowing me the privilege to connect with, be in community with, and learn from you.

To the researchers and authors who inspire me and inform my work and to all who do research on success, ambition, motivation, and associated fields related to Sustainable Ambition: I appreciate your curiosity and the insights you offer to help us know our humanity better.

To those who have been on this book journey with me, including workshop participants, advance readers, and my coaching clients: I am appreciative of your interest in Sustainable Ambition and your willingness to prototype and practice with me and to allow me to learn with you. Your contribution to this book and my work is invaluable. With deep gratitude, I thank you.

To those joining this Sustainable Ambition journey: Thank you for being courageous in choosing this path and for, I hope, sharing the Sustainable Ambition message with others. With each new person who embraces, practices, and models Sustainable Ambition, we are more likely to shift dominant narratives, demonstrate a new way of viewing success and ambition, and make it easier for all of us to truly thrive in life and work.

To my book community: I couldn't have done this project without the support of Anjanette "AJ" Harper, my developmental editor, guide, and author of *Write a Must-Read*. For me to call AJ my coach is not sufficient. This idea first came to life in AJ's book workshop, and then she went above and beyond in supporting its development. AJ, I can't thank you enough for encouraging me to step into authorship as part of my self-authorship journey and creating space for me to develop my writing craft. I'm inspired to continue my creative exploration and endeavors. "Onward!" as you would say. I also wouldn't be at this step without the cheerleading of Laura Stone. Your positive enthusiasm is a gift and blessing. And to all in the Top Three Book Authors' Club and community, thank you for always providing input and encouragement. I can unequivocally say that this book would not be in readers' hands without the guidance and moral support from this community.

To Jenny Blake: I thank you for seeing the spark of an idea around Sustainable Ambition and encouraging me to immediately claim it and make haste in getting it out into the world. I am also ever appreciative of your generosity in sharing knowledge. My podcast and this book would not exist without your teaching.

To my creative mentors and cheerleaders Philip VanDusen, Evette Davis, Karin Carrington, and John O'Meara: Thank you for seeing me as a creative person and encouraging me to follow this ambition that was calling me.

To my coaches on this journey: I need support to keep me moving forward just like everyone else, and my coaches have been crucial to keeping me in action and committed to my ambitions. Thank you for listening to me, helping me through rough patches, and being cheerleaders all the way to the finish line of the book and beyond.

To those who shared their book-writing experiences with me: I'm grateful for all the insights, as they shaped my approach and helped me have the endurance to keep going.

To all my friends: Thank you for your support of me always, even if I was too shy still, as I tend to be, to share this ambition with you until the end.

To my family: This book is a manifestation of the support I've always been given by my parents and siblings, who seem to delight in my ambitions. They've never tried to quash them or tell me a goal wasn't possible or that I wasn't capable. Quite to the contrary, my parents stretched to give me opportunity. I have also learned from watching many of them with their own creative endeavors, which have inspired me to pursue my own. I'm especially grateful to my sister, Marguerite Oneto, who has been my partner in other endurance events. She's been walking alongside me on this book-writing journey and has been a sounding board and reader along the way. Marguerite, I couldn't have done it without you.

Finally, to my husband: I thank my partner in this endurance event and creative experience of life, Jess Wilson, who gives me the courage and unconditional support to keep going and to pursue and invest in my creative endeavors. He naturally embraces Sustainable Ambition and has been a teacher for me, as well as the main person I lean on to help me stay committed to my practice. The best Sustainable Ambitions are the ones we pursue together. Jess, having you as a partner in life is the best choice I've ever made.

Sustainable Ambition Tools and Resources

• • •

To ensure you can practice Sustainable Ambition and make progress on what matters most to you, here are a number of tools and resources to help you implement the method and support your journey.

- *The Sustainable Ambition Toolkit:* Get templates, tools, resources, and more at SustainableAmbition.com/sa-toolkit.

- *The Sustainable Ambition Assessment:* This online assessment can help you determine where you want to put your attention as you start to implement the method across Right Ambition, Right Time, and Right Effort. While there is value in applying the method sequentially, you may find you need or want to put more immediate attention toward a particular area. You can find the assessment or send it to a friend at SustainableAmbition.com/sa-assess.

- *The Sustainable Ambition Evaluation Tool:* This online evaluation tool can help determine if an ambition, goal, or project is a Sustainable Ambition. This is an online version of the tool I share in Chapter 12. You can find the evaluation tool or send it to a friend at SustainableAmbition.com/sa-evaluation.

- *Practice reminders:* If you'd like reminder emails for practicing Sustainable Ambition over time, sign up at SustainableAmbition.com/sa-practice.

- *Self-coaching questions:* As another form of a check-in, find a self-coaching guide you can use yourself or to coach others on optimizing their Sustainable Ambition in the moment. Find the guide at SustainableAmbition.com/sa-selfcoach.

- *Book club or circle group:* Do this work with others through a book club or personal or professional circle of friends or colleagues. Use facilitator guides at SustainableAmbition.com/sa-guide.

- *Newsletter:* Sign up for my biweekly newsletter to get the latest tips, ideas, and tools on Sustainable Ambition at SustainableAmbition.com/subscribe.

- *Podcast:* Subscribe and listen to the *Sustainable Ambition* podcast on your favorite podcast player or at SustainableAmbition.com/podcast.

- *Other Sustainable Ambition books:* Track your Sustainable Ambition progress over time with the *Sustainable Ambition 12-Month Workbook + Planner* or explore your curiosity with *My Little Book of Curiosity*. Learn more at SustainableAmbition.com/books.

HELP BRING SUSTAINABLE AMBITION TO LIFE

I would be grateful if you'd help others discover Sustainable Ambition and create a movement where more of us can thrive in life and work. If you're so inclined, please consider the following:

- Rate and review *Sustainable Ambition* on Amazon, Goodreads, or wherever you purchased your book.
- Give a gift copy to a friend, family member, or colleague.
- Recommend the book for your book club or create a circle to be each other's community and force multipliers.
- Share your ahas and what you love on social media by tagging #SustainableAmbition and #SustainableAmbitionBook.
- Send your favorite episode of the *Sustainable Ambition* podcast to those ambitious people around you who want to thrive in life and work.

Go Deeper with Sustainable Ambition

• • •

FOR INDIVIDUALS

If you'd like to take the principles further and work with a coach one-on-one or in a group setting, learn more at SustainableAmbition.com/coaching.

FOR COMPANIES, ORGANIZATIONS, AND CONFERENCES

Sustainable Ambition concepts and practices can be applied in organizations and companies and presented at conferences. Visit SustainableAmbition.com/organizations to learn more. Offerings include:

- Keynote speaking
- Interactive workshops and master classes
- Discounted rates for bulk book purchases
- Sustainable Ambition train-the-trainer and content licensing

Sustainable Ambition Quick Reference

• • •

- *Sustainable Ambition mindset:* Use the mindset to see if you're guiding your actions consistently with the method. It consists of three parts: (1) being conscious about the ambitions you choose and using self-defined success as your guide, (2) realigning toward what matters most now across life and work and taking responsibility for making courageous choices, and (3) building resilience, knowing that sustainability is a constant, personal practice.

- *Sustainable Ambition Method:* Sustainable Ambition lives at the intersection of three elements, aligning the right ambition at the right time with the right effort (see Figure 1.2). The method can be applied at any moment in time against your life and work ambitions or against a single ambition.

- *Sustainable Ambition meaning:* Sustainable Ambition is a collection of self-defined, meaningful, motivating goals that are most important and right for you now and are aligned to your desired effort and sustained energy. The meaning serves as a check for applying the method—it's the outcome you should expect. It can also serve as an evaluation to see if you're on track.

- *Right Ambition:* It is self-defined and aligns with your personal definition of success, not society's. It is rooted in what you want, not what you should want, and is about achieving in a way that is personally rewarding to you, focusing on your own fulfillment and satisfaction. With this lens, the question becomes: What do *you want* to do?

- *Right Time:* It considers life and work together and means courageously choosing where you want to put your attention based on what matters most in your life and work now. It points you to prioritize and pace your ambitions accordingly and asks you to accept and understand that life and work are naturally integrated and that time is finite. The question becomes: What is it time to do?

- *Right Effort:* It is being discerning about the level of effort you put toward your ambitions rather than treating them equally, and about how you manage your effort and energy to make your life and work sustainable. It calls you to take responsibility and puts you back in control to make your life and work integration sustainable, acknowledging that just like time, effort and energy are finite. It calls you to be judicious about where and how you optimally use your effort and have a plan for how you restore, protect, and support your energy and effort and build your resilience. The question becomes: What do you have the effort and energy to do?

Recommended Reading

Success

- *The Formula: The Universal Laws of Success*, by Albert-László Barabási
- *Status Anxiety*, by Alain de Botton

Right Ambition

- *How Will You Measure Your Life?* by Clayton M. Christensen
- *Get It Done: Surprising Lessons from the Science of Motivation*, by Dr. Ayelet Fishbach
- *Great at Work: How Top Performers Work Less and Achieve More*, by Morten T. Hansen
- *The Big Leap: Conquer Your Hidden Fear and Take Life to the Next Level*, by Gay Hendrick
- *Conscious Business: How to Build Value through Values*, by Fred Kofman
- *All the Gold Stars: Reimagining Ambition and the Ways We Strive*, by Rainesford Stauffer
- *What Do You Want Out of Life?* by Valerie Tiberius

Right Time

- *The Long Game: How to Be a Long-Term Thinker in a Short-Term World*, by Dorie Clark
- *Unfinished Business: Women Men Work Family*, by Anne-Marie Slaughter

Right Effort

- *It's Not How Good You Are, It's How Good You Want to Be*, by Paul Arden
- *Free Time: Lose the Busywork, Love Your Business*, by Jenny Blake
- *Everyday Vitality: Turning Stress into Strength*, by Samantha Boardman
- *Four Thousand Weeks: Time Management for Mortals*, by Oliver Burkeman
- *The Sweet Spot: How to Find Your Groove at Home and Work*, by Christine Carter
- *Never Not Working: Why the Always-On Culture Is Bad for Business—and How to Fix It*, by Malissa Clark
- *Hidden Potential: The Science of Achieving Great Things*, by Adam Grant
- *The Power of Full Engagement: Managing Energy, Not Time, Is the Key to High Performance and Personal Renewal*, by Jim Loehr and Tony Schwartz
- *Essentialism: The Disciplined Pursuit of Less*, by Greg McKeown

- *Effortless: Make It Easier to Do What Matters Most*, by Greg McKeown
- *The Resilience Plan: A Strategic Approach to Optimizing Your Work Performance and Mental Health*, by Dr. Marie-Hélène Pelletier

For Career Optimizers and Explorers

- *Pivot: The Only Move That Matters Is Your Next One*, by Jenny Blake
- *Working Identity: Unconventional Strategies for Reinventing Your Career*, by Herminia Ibarra
- *Designing Your Life: How to Build a Well-Lived, Joyful Life*, by Bill Burnett and Dave Evans
- *The Portfolio Life: How to Future-Proof Your Career, Avoid Burnout, and Build a Life Bigger Than Your Business Card*, by Christina Wallace
- *One Person, Multiple Careers: The Original Guide to the Slash Career*, by Marci Alboher

Other

- *Me, Myself, and Us: The Science of Personality and the Art of Well-Being*, by Dr. Brian Little
- *Wellbeing: The Five Essential Elements*, by Tom Rath and Jim Harter
- *Flow: The Psychology of Optimal Experience*, by Mihaly Csikszentmihalyi

Notes

CHAPTER 1

1. Gail O'Hara, "Alain de Botton," *Kinfolk* 15, March 3, 2015, pp. 131–132.
2. Bianca Bosker, "Sheryl Sandberg: 'There's No Such Thing as Work-Life Balance,'" *Huffpost*, April 7, 2012, https://www.huffpost.com/entry/sheryl-sandberg_n_1409061.
3. "Life-Work Integration," Thrive Global, https://thriveglobal.com/categories/life-work-integration/.
4. *Merriam-Webster*, s.v. "ambition," accessed November 5, 2024, https://www.merriam-webster.com/dictionary/ambition.
5. Andreas Hirschi and Daniel Spurk, "Striving for Success: Towards a Refined Understanding and Measurement of Ambition," *Journal of Vocational Behavior* 127 (June 2021), https://www.sciencedirect.com/science/article/pii/S000187912100049X.
6. Timothy Judge and John Kammeyer-Mueller, "On the Value of Aiming High: The Causes and Consequences of Ambition," *Journal of Applied Psychology* 97, no. 4 (2012): 758–775.
7. Alex Crees, "Study: Ambitious People Unhappier, Don't Live as Long," *Fox News*, October 28, 2015, https://www.foxnews.com/health/study-ambitious-people-unhappier-dont-live-as-long.
8. "The Inverted-U Theory," MindTools, accessed October 1, 2024, https://www.mindtools.com/ax20nkm/the-inverted-u-theory.

9. Brian Little, *Me, Myself, and Us: The Science of Personality and the Art of Well-Being* (New York: PublicAffairs, 2012), 202.

10. Albert-László Barabási, *The Formula: The Universal Laws of Success* (Boston: Little, Brown, 2018), 14.

11. Barabási, *The Formula*, 13, 14.

12. Sonja Lyubomirsky and Laura King, "The Benefits of Frequent Positive Affect: Does Happiness Lead to Success?" *Psychological Bulletin* 131, no. 6 (2005): 803–855.

13. Arthur Brooks, "If You Want Success, Pursue Happiness," *The Atlantic*, October 13, 2022, https://www.theatlantic.com/family/archive/2022/10/prioritizing-happiness-before-success/671714/.

14. Jenny Blake, "On Yes! to Free Time and High Net Freedom with Jenny Blake," *Sustainable Ambition* (podcast), episode 48, February 23, 2022, https://sustainableambition.com/sapodcast/48.

CHAPTER 2

1. Dominic DeMarco, "On Following Your Own Path and Success for the 99% with Dominic DeMarco," *Sustainable Ambition* (podcast), episode 54, April 19, 2022, https://sustainableambition.com/sapodcast/54. All quotations from Dominic in this section come from this podcast episode.

2. Alain de Botton, *Status Anxiety* (New York: Pantheon, 2004), 251.

3. Adam Grant, *Hidden Potential: The Science of Achieving Greater Things* (New York: Viking, 2023), 79–80.

4. Rainesford Stauffer, *All the Gold Stars: Reimagining Ambition and the Ways We Strive* (New York: Hatchette, 2023), 2.

5. Stauffer, *All the Gold Stars*, 166.

6. Andreas Hirschi and Daniel Spurk, "Striving for Success: Towards a Refined Understanding and Measurement of Ambition," *Journal of Vocational Behavior* 127 (June 2021), https://www.sciencedirect.com/science/article/pii/S000187912100049X.

7. Tom Rath and Jim Harter, *Wellbeing: The Five Essential Elements* (New York: Gallup Press, 2010), 7–8, 10–11.

8. Stauffer, *All the Gold Stars*, 254–255.

9. Colleen Walsh, "Winfrey: Failure Is Just Movement," *Harvard Gazette*, May 30, 2013, https://news.harvard.edu/gazette/story/2013/05/winfrey-failure-is-just-movement/.

10. Ligaya Mishan, "When Women Artists Choose Mothering over Making Work," *New York Times Style Magazine*, December 1, 2023, https://www.nytimes.com/2023/12/01/t-magazine/mothers-artists-working-women.html.

11. Jeffrey Kluger, "Ambition: Why Some People Are Most Likely to Succeed," *Time*, November 6, 2005, https://time.com/archive/6596659/ambition-why-some-people-are-most-likely-to-succeed/.

12. Stauffer, *All the Gold Stars*, 2.

13. Robert Kegan and Lisa Laskow Lahey, *An Everyone Culture: Becoming a Deliberately Developmental Organization* (Boston: Harvard Business Review Press, 2016), 62–63.

14. Kegan and Lahey, *An Everyone Culture*, 76.

15. David Brown, "On a Year Off and Deviating from the Norm with David Brown," *Sustainable Ambition* (podcast), episode 9, February 23, 2021, https://sustainableambition.com/sapodcast/9.

16. "*On the Shortness of Life*: Book Summary, Key Questions, and Best Quotes," *Daily Stoic*, accessed October 1, 2024, https://dailystoic.com/on-the-shortness-of-life-seneca/.

CHAPTER 3

1. Eva Dienel, "On Creating the Life I Want with Christine Bader and Eva Dienel," *Sustainable Ambition* (podcast), episode 16, April 27, 2021, https://sustainableambition.com/sapodcast/16. All quotations by Eva in this chapter come from this podcast episode.

2. Bridget Jones, "On Managing Your $ to Support Your Life with Bridget Jones," *Sustainable Ambition* (podcast), episode 14, April 6, 2021, https://sustainableambition.com/sapodcast/14.

3. Clayton Christensen, "How Will You Measure Your Life?" *Harvard Business Review*, July–August 2010, https://hbr.org/2010/07/how-will-you-measure-your-life.

4. Roy Baumeister and Kathleen Vohs, "Pragmatic Prospection: How and Why People Think about the Future," *Review of General Psychology* 20, no. 1 (2016): 3–16.

5. Mathew Harris and Caroline Brett, "Personal Stability from Age 14 to Age 77 Years," *Psychology and Aging* 31, no. 8 (2016): 862–874.

6. Sangil Lee, Trishala Parthasarathi, and Joseph Kable, "The Ventral and Dorsal Default Mode Networks Are Dissociably Modulated by the Vividness and Valence of Imagined Events," *Journal of Neuroscience* 41, no. 24 (June 2021): 5243–5250.

7. Barbara Medea, Theodoros Karapanagiotidis, Mahiko Konishi, Cristina Ottaviani, Daniel Margulies, Andrea Bernasconi, Neda Bernasconi, Boris C. Bernhardt, Elizabeth Jefferies, and Jonathan Smallwood, "How Do We Decide What to Do? Resting-State Connectivity Patterns and Components of Self-Generated Thought Linked to the Development of More Concrete Personal Goals," *Experimental Brain Research* 236 (July 2016): 2469–2481.

8. Benjamin Baird, Jonathan Smallwood, Michael D. Mrazek, Julia W. Y. Kam, Michael S. Franklin, and Jonathan W. Schooler, "Inspired by Distraction: Mind Wandering Facilitates Creative Incubation," *Psychological Science* 23, no. 10 (August 2012), https://journals.sagepub.com/doi/abs/10.1177/0956797612446024.

9. Rebecca Williams, "On Clarifying, Claiming, and Communicating Your Why with Rebecca Williams," *Sustainable Ambition* (podcast), episode 4, December 27, 2020, https://sustainableambition.com/sapodcast/4.

10. Brent Rosso, Kathryn Dekas, and Amy Wrzesniewski, "On the Meaning of Work: A Theoretical Integration and Review," *Research in Organizational Behavior* 30 (2010): 91–127.

11. Bryan Dik, Zinta Byrne, and Michael Steger, *Purpose and Meaning in the Workplace* (Washington, DC: American Psychological Association, 2013).

12. Carol Ryff, "The Benefits of Purposeful Life Engagement on Later-Life Physical Function," *JAMA Psychiatry* 74, no. 10 (2017): 1046–1047.

13. Stacey Schaefer, Jennifer Morozink Boylan, Carien M. van Reekum, Regina C. Lapate, Catherine J. Norris, Carol D. Ryff, and Richard J. Davidson, "Purpose in Life Predicts Better Emotional Recovery from Negative Stimuli," *PLoS One* 8, no. 11 (2013), https://www.ncbi.nlm.nih.gov/pmc/articles/PMC3827458/.

14. Morten Hansen, *Great at Work: The Hidden Habits of Top Performers* (New York: Simon and Schuster, 2018), 90–91.

15. Naina Dhingra and Bill Schaninger, "The Search for Purpose at Work," *McKinsey Podcast*, June 3, 2021, https://www.mckinsey.com/capabilities/people-and-organizational-performance/our-insights/the-search-for-purpose-at-work.

16. Fred Kofman, "How to Succeed beyond Your Wildest Dreams," LinkedIn, July 31, 2015, https://www.linkedin.com/pulse/how-succeed-beyond-your-wildest-dreams-33-fred-kofman/.

17. Kennon Sheldon and Andrew Elliott, "Goal Striving, Need Satisfaction, and Longitudinal Well-Being: The Self-Concordance Model," *Journal of Personality and Social Psychology* 76, no. 3 (1999), https://selfdeterminationtheory.org/SDT/documents/1999_SheldonElliot.pdf.

18. Valerie Tiberius, "How Theories of Well-Being Can Help Us Help," *Journal of Practical Ethics* 2, no. 2 (2014), http://www.jpe.ox.ac.uk/wp-content/uploads/2014/12/JPE0011-Tiberius.pdf.

19. Valerie Tiberius, *What Do You Want out of Life? A Philosophical Guide to Figuring Out What Matters* (Princeton, NJ: Princeton University Press, 2023), xvi.

20. Art Markman, "On Smart Strategies to Be Fulfilled at Work with Art Markman," *Sustainable Ambition* (podcast), episode 66, July 19, 2022, https://sustainableambition.com/sapodcast/66. All quotations from Art in this chapter come from this interview.

21. Mike Trigg, "On the Novel Bit Flip and Ambition in Silicon Valley," *Sustainable Ambition* (podcast), episode 81, October 11, 2022, https://sustainableambition.com/sapodcast/81.

22. Ayelet Fishbach, *Get It Done: Surprising Lessons from the Science of Motivation* (New York: Hachette, 2022), 66.

23. Edward Deci, Richard Koestner, and Richard Ryan, "A Meta-analytic Review of Experiments Examining the Effect of Extrinsic Rewards on Intrinsic Motivation," *Psychological Bulletin* 125, no. 6 (November 1999): 627–668.

24. Christopher Niemiec, Richard Ryan, and Edward Deci, "The Path Taken: Consequences of Attaining Intrinsic and Extrinsic Aspirations in Post-college Life," *Journal of Research in Personality* 43, no. 3 (June 2009): 291–306.

25. Barry Schwartz and Amy Wrzesniewski, "Internal Motivation, Instrumental Motivation, and Eudaimonia," in *Handbook of Eudaimonic Well-Being*, ed. J. Vittersø (Switzerland: Springer International, 2016), 123–134.

CHAPTER 4

1. Eva Dienel, "On Creating the Life I Want with Christine Bader and Eva Dienel," *Sustainable Ambition* (podcast), episode 16, April 27, 2021, https://sustainableambition.com/sapodcast/16.

2. Ayelet Fishbach, *Get It Done: Surprising Lessons from the Science of Motivation* (New York: Hachette, 2022), 24–25.

3. Clayton Christensen, "How Will You Measure Your Life?" *Harvard Business Review*, July–August 2010, https://hbr.org/2010/07/how-will-you-measure-your-life.

4. Edward Deci and Richard Ryan, *Intrinsic Motivation and Self-Determination in Human Behavior* (New York: Plenum Press, 1985).

5. Fishbach, *Get It Done*, 37.

CHAPTER 5

1. Amil Niazi, "Losing My Ambition," *New York Magazine*, March 25, 2022, https://www.thecut.com/2022/03/post-pandemic-loss-of-ambition.html.

2. Jack Bauer, Dan McAdams, and Jennifer Pals, "Narrative Identity and Eudaimonic Well-Being," *Journal of Happiness Studies* 9 (November 2006): 81–104.

3. Ruth Gotian, "On the Success Factor: A Blueprint for High Performance with Ruth Gotian," *Sustainable Ambition* (podcast), episode 60, June 7, 2022, https://sustainableambition.com/sapodcast/60.

4. Gay Hendricks, *The Big Leap: Conquer Your Hidden Fear and Take Life to the Next Level* (New York: HarperOne, 2009).

5. Ayelet Fishbach, *Get It Done: Surprising Lessons from the Science of Motivation* (New York: Hachette, 2022), 92.

6. Katie Ceccarini, "On Building Endurance for Work + Life and Effective Leadership with Katie Ceccarini," *Sustainable Ambition* (podcast), episode 32, September 28, 2021, https://sustainableambition.com/sapodcast/32.

7. Dorie Clark, *The Long Game: How to Be a Long-Term Thinker in a Short-Term World* (Brighton, MA: Harvard Business Review Press, 2021).

8. Fishbach, *Get It Done*, 92.

9. "The Inverted-U Theory," MindTools, accessed October 1, 2024, https://www.mindtools.com/ax20nkm/the-inverted-u-theory.

10. Brian Little, *Me, Myself, and Us: The Science of Personality and the Art of Well-Being* (New York: PublicAffairs, 2012), 197.

11. Daniel Kahneman and Angus Deaton, "High Income Improves Evaluation of Life but Not Emotional Well-Being," *Proceedings of the National Academy of Sciences (PNAS)* 107, no. 38 (August 2010): 16489–16493; Ed Diener and Robert Biswas-Diener, "Will Money Increase Subjective Well-Being?" *Social Indicators Research* 57, no. 2 (February 2002): 119–169.

12. Luke Burgis, *Wanting: The Power of Mimetic Desire in Everyday Life* (New York: St. Martin's Press, 2021).

13. Tobias Weaver, "How to Use Voluntary Discomfort Like a Stoic," Orion Philosophy, October 20, 2023, https://orionphilosophy.com/how-to-use-voluntary-discomfort-like-a-stoic/.

14. "The Favorite Stoic Exercises of Tim Ferris, Arianna Huffington, Robert Greene, and More," *Daily Stoic*, accessed October 1, 2024, https://dailystoic.com/favorite-stoic-exercises/; Lucius Seneca, *Letters from a Stoic: Seneca's Moral Letters to Lucilius*, trans. Richard Mott Gummere (Vrindavan, India: Classy, 2023), 31.

15. Jack Hsueh, "On Finding Motivation in Loving the Journey with Ultra-marathoner Jack Hsueh," *Sustainable Ambition* (podcast), episode 62, June 21, 2022, https://sustainableambition.com/sapodcast/62.

16. Scott Raab, "What I've Learned: Michael J. Fox," *Esquire*, December 16, 2007, https://www.esquire.com/entertainment/interviews/a4045/michaeljfox0108/.

CHAPTER 6

1. Christine Bader, "On Creating the Life I Want with Christine Bader and Eva Dienel," *Sustainable Ambition* (podcast), episode 16, April 27, 2021, https://sustainableambition.com/sapodcast/16.

2. Christine Bader, "An Update from Christine: Living the Life I Want," *The Life I Want* (blog), September 28, 2022, https://www.thelifeiwant.co/blog/2022/9/28/christine-departs.

3. Clarence So, Zoom interview by the author, May 28, 2024. All quotations from Clarence in this chapter come from this interview.

4. Mara Yale, Zoom interview by the author, July 22, 2023. All quotations from Mara in this chapter come from this interview.

5. Doug Milliken, "Self-Defined Career Success with Doug Milliken," *Sustainable Ambition* (podcast), episode 119, November 15, 2023, https://sustainableambition.com/sapodcast/119. All other information about Doug in this chapter comes from this interview.

6. "Breaking Down Burnout in the Workplace," Mayo Clinic, April 6, 2023, https://mcpress.mayoclinic.org/mental-health/breaking-down-burnout-in-the-workplace/.

7. Herminia Ibarra, *Working Identity: Unconventional Strategies for Reinventing Your Career* (Boston: Harvard Business School Press, 2004), 11.

CHAPTER 7

1. Sahar Yousef, "On Becoming Superhuman and Avoiding Reckless Ambition with Sahar Yousef," *Sustainable Ambition* (podcast), episode 51, March 22, 2022, https://sustainableambition.com/sapodcast/51. All quotations from Sahar in this chapter come from this interview.

2. "Time Is What Keeps Everything from Happening at Once," Quote Investigator, July 6, 2019, https://quoteinvestigator.com/2019/07/06/time/.

3. Geoff Tanner, "On Starting Your Second Life Now with Geoff Tanner," *Sustainable Ambition* (podcast), episode 1, December 27, 2020, https://sustainableambition.com/sapodcast/1.

4. Mike Murgatroyd, "On Good Risk, Lifestyle Design, and Courage to Step off the Path with Mike Murgatroyd," *Sustainable Ambition* (podcast), episode 35, October 19, 2021, https://sustainableambition.com/sapodcast/35.

5. Albert-László Barabási, *The Formula: The Universal Laws of Success* (Boston: Little, Brown, 2018).

CHAPTER 8

1. Ayelet Fishbach, "The Power of Designing Your Motivation and Ambition with Ayelet Fishbach," *Sustainable Ambition* (podcast), episode 114, September 6, 2023, https://sustainableambition.com/sapodcast/114.

2. Jordan Etkin, Joannis Evangelidis, and Jennifer Aaker, "Pressed for Time? Goal Conflict Shapes How Time Is Perceived, Spent, and Valued," *Journal of Marketing Research* 52, no. 3 (June 2015), https://journals.sagepub.com/doi/10.1509/jmr.14.0130.

3. Christina Wallace, "The Benefits of a Portfolio Life: Fulfillment beyond Work with Christina Wallace," *Sustainable Ambition* (podcast), episode 104, May 3, 2023, https://sustainableambition.com/sapodcast/104. All quotations from Christina in this chapter come from this interview.

4. Valerie Jarrett, "Working Women: Valerie Jarrett and the Importance of Mentorship," *Michelle Obama: The Light Podcast*, September 30, 2020, https://podcasts.apple.com/us/podcast/working-women-valerie-jarrett-importance-mentorship/id1532956108?i=1000493064975.

5. Ashley Whillans, "Time for Happiness," *Harvard Business Review*, January 24, 2019, https://hbr.org/2019/01/time-for-happiness?ab=seriesnav-bigidea.

6. Kira Newman, "Why You Never Seem to Have Enough Time," *Greater*

Good Magazine, March 13, 2019, https://greatergood.berkeley.edu/article/item/why_you_never_seem_to_have_enough_time.

7. Graeme Massie, "'I've Got Nothing Left in the Tank': Jacinda Arden's Resignation Speech in Full," *The Independent*, January 19, 2023, https://www.independent.co.uk/world/jacinda-ardern-resignation-prime-minister-new-zealand-speech-b2265319.html.

8. Massie, "'I've Got Nothing Left.'"

9. Karyn Flynn, "Navigating Identity Shifts and Embracing New Beginnings with Karyn Flynn," *Sustainable Ambition* (podcast), episode 118, November 1, 2023, https://sustainableambition.com/sapodcast/118.

10. Oliver Burkeman, *Four Thousand Weeks: Time Management for Mortals* (New York: Farrar, Straus and Giroux, 2021), 68–69.

CHAPTER 9

1. Henry David Thoreau, letter to H. G. O. Blake, November 16, 1857, quoted in "The Henry David Thoreau Mis-Quotation Page," Walden Woods Project, accessed September 30, 2024, https://www.walden.org/what-we-do/library/thoreau/mis-quotations/.

2. Paul Arden, *It's Not How Good You Are, It's How Good You Want to Be* (London: Phaidon Press, 2003).

3. Warn Lekfuangfu and Reto Odermatt, "All I Have to Do Is Dream? The Role of Aspirations in Intergenerational Mobility and Well-Being," *European Economic Review* 148 (September 2022), https://www.sciencedirect.com/science/article/abs/pii/S0014292122001143.

4. Arden, *It's Not How Good You Are*, 4.

5. David Whyte, "10 Questions That Have No Right to Go Away," *Oprah Winfrey Network*, June 15, 2011, https://www.oprah.com/oprahs-lifeclass/poet-david-whytes-questions-that-have-no-right-to-go-away_1/2.

6. Sahar Yousef, "On Becoming Superhuman and Avoiding Reckless Ambition with Sahar Yousef," *Sustainable Ambition* (podcast), episode 51, March 22, 2022, https://sustainableambition.com/sapodcast/51. All quotations from Sahar in this chapter come from this interview.

7. Jack Hsueh, "On Finding Motivation in Loving the Journey with Ultra-marathoner Jack Hsueh," *Sustainable Ambition* (podcast), episode 62, June 21, 2022, https://sustainableambition.com/sapodcast/62.

8. Rafael Nadal and John Carlin, *Rafa* (New York: Hachette Books, 2011), 238.

9. Nadal and Carlin, *Rafa*, 238.

10. Greg McKeown, *Effortless: Make It Easier to Do What Matters Most* (New York: Crown Currency, 2021), 27.

CHAPTER 10

1. "Doris Kearns Goodwin," MasterClass, accessed October 1, 2024, https://www.masterclass.com/classes/doris-kearns-goodwin-teaches-us-presidential-history-and-leadership.

2. Tom Rath and Jim Harter, *Wellbeing: The Five Essential Elements* (New York: Gallup Press, 2010), 11.

3. Malissa Clark, *Never Not Working: Why the Always-On Culture Is Bad for Business—and How to Fix It* (Boston: Harvard Business Review Press, 2024), 24.

4. Kristoffer Carter, "On Permission to Glow and Epic Leadership with Kristoffer Carter," *Sustainable Ambition* (podcast), episode 29, September 7, 2021, https://sustainableambition.com/sapodcast/29.

5. "The Surprising Connection between After-Hours Work and Decreased Productivity," *Slack*, December 5, 2023, https://slack.com/blog/news/the-surprising-connection-between-after-hours-work-and-decreased-productivity.

6. Brad Stulberg and Steve Magness, *Peak Performance: Elevate Your Game, Avoid Burnout, and Thrive with the New Science of Success* (New York: Rodale Books, 2017), 37–38.

7. Ferris Jabr, "Why Your Brain Needs More Downtime," *Scientific American*, October 15, 2013, https://www.scientificamerican.com/article/mental-downtime/.

8. Kirsten Weir, "Give Me a Break," *Monitor on Psychology* 50, no. 1 (January 2019), https://www.apa.org/monitor/2019/01/break; Emma Schootstra, Dirk Deichmann, and Evgenia Dolgova, "Can 10 Minutes of Meditation Make You More Creative?" *Harvard Business Review*, August 29, 2017, https://hbr.org/2017/08/can-10-minutes-of-meditation-make-you-more-creative; Zhanna Lyubykh and Duygu Biricik Gulseren, "How to Take Better Breaks at Work, According to Research," *Harvard Business Review*, May 31, 2023, https://hbr.org/2023/05/how-to-take-better-breaks-at-work-according-to-research.

9. Samantha Boardman, *Everyday Vitality: Turning Stress into Strength* (New York: Viking, 2021), 64.

10. Art Markman, *Bring Your Brain to Work: Using Cognitive Science to Get a Job, Do It Well, and Advance Your Career* (Boston: Harvard Business Review Press, 2019), 183.

11. Sabine Sonnentag, Laura Venz, and Anne Casper, "Advances in Recovery Research: What Have We Learned? What Should Be Done Next?" *Journal of Occupational Health Psychology* 22, no. 3 (2017): 365–380.

12. Heather Ainsworth, "On Building Better Work-Life Integration with Heather Ainsworth," *Sustainable Ambition* (podcast), episode 2, December 27, 2020, https://sustainableambition.com/sapodcast/2.

13. Emily Balcetis, "You 2.0: The Mind's Eye," *Hidden Brain* (podcast), August 10, 2020, https://hiddenbrain.org/podcast/you-2-0-the-minds-eye/.

14. Sabine Sonnentag, "The Recovery Paradox: Portraying the Complex Interplay between Job Stressors, Lack of Recovery, and Poor Well-Being," *Research in Organizational Behavior* 38 (2018): 169–185.

15. Marie-Hélène Pelletier, "Building Resilience: Practical Strategies for Personal and Professional Well-Being with Marie-Helene Pelletier," *Sustainable Ambition* (podcast) episode 126, February 21, 2024, https://sustainableambition.com/sapodcast/126.

16. Boardman, *Everyday Vitality*, 65–69.

17. B. J. Fogg, *Tiny Habits: The Small Changes That Change Everything* (Boston: Houghton Mifflin Harcourt, 2020); James Clear, *Atomic Habits: An Easy and Proven Way to Build Habits and Break Bad Ones* (New York: Avery, 2018).

18. Marie-Hélène Pelletier, *The Resilience Plan: A Strategic Approach to Optimizing Your Work Performance and Mental Health* (Vancouver, BC: Page Two, 2024).

19. Jim Loehr and Tony Schwartz, *The Power of Full Engagement: Managing Energy, Not Time, Is the Key to High Performance and Personal Renewal* (New York: Free Press, 2003).

20. Leslie Forde, "On Keeping Your Energy and Spirit Intact with Leslie Ford," *Sustainable Ambition* (podcast), episode 19, May 25, 2021, https://sustainableambition.com/sapodcast/19.

21. Neil Pasricha, "Neil Pasricha: Happy Habits," *Knowledge Project* (podcast), episode 72, December 24, 2019, https://fs.blog/knowledge-project-podcast/neil-pasricha/.

CHAPTER 11

1. Mara Yale, Zoom interview by the author, July 22, 2023.

2. Lee Carter, "You'd Be a Lot Happier If You Stop Saying You're So Busy," *Fast Company*, April 3, 2022, https://www.fastcompany.com/90735704/youd-be-a-lot-happier-if-you-stop-saying-youre-so-busy.

3. Laura Vanderkam, "The Busy Person's Lies," *New York Times*, May 13, 2016, https://www.nytimes.com/2016/05/15/opinion/sunday/the-busy-persons-lies.html.

4. Sasha Weiss, "Juliette Binoche," *New York Times*, October 16, 2021, https://www.nytimes.com/interactive/2021/10/14/t-magazine/juliette-binoche-film-greats.html.

5. Oliver Burkeman, "Why Time Management Is Ruining Our Lives," *The Guardian*, December 22, 2016, https://www.theguardian.com/technology/2016/dec/22/why-time-management-is-ruining-our-lives.

6. Sabrina Moyle, "Living a More Sustainable, Intentional, Happy Life with Sabrina Moyle," *Sustainable Ambition* (podcast), episode 110, July 12, 2023, https://sustainableambition.com/sapodcast/110. All quotations from Sabrina in this chapter come from this interview.

7. Stuart Brown and Christopher Vaughan, *Play: How It Shapes the Brain, Opens the Imagination, and Invigorates the Soul* (New York: Penguin Random House, 2009).

8. Adam Grant, *Hidden Potential: The Science of Achieving Greater Things* (New York: Viking, 2023), 93–94.

9. Mihaly Csikszentmihalyi, *Flow: The Psychology of Optimal Experience* (New York: Harper Perennial, 2008).

10. Kaitlin Woolley and Ayelet Fishbach, "The Experience Matters More Than You Think: People Value Intrinsic Incentives More Inside Than Outside an Activity," *Journal of Personality and Social Psychology* 109, no. 6 (2015): 968–982.

11. Brian Little, *Me, Myself, and Us: The Science of Personality and the Art of Well-Being* (New York: PublicAffairs, 2012), 197.

12. Cal Newport, "Why Do We Work Too Much?" *New Yorker*, August 30, 2021, https://www.newyorker.com/culture/office-space/why-do-we-work-too-much.

13. James Clear, "3-2-1: Starting the New Year the Right Way, How to Stay Focused, and a Lesson on Long-Term Thinking," *James Clear* (blog), January 4, 2024, https://jamesclear.com/3-2-1/january-04-2024.

14. Grant, *Hidden Potential*, 73.

15. Ayelet Fishbach, "The Power of Designing Your Motivation and Ambition with Ayelet Fishbach," *Sustainable Ambition* (podcast), episode 114, September 6, 2023, https://sustainableambition.com/sapodcast/114.

CHAPTER 12

1. Shane Parrish, "Simple Acts," *Brain Food*, October 23, 2022, https://fs.blog/brain-food/october-23-2022/.

2. *The West Wing*, season 2, episode 22, "Two Cathedrals," directed by Thomas Schlamme, written by Aaron Sorkin, aired May 16, 2001.

3. "Keep away from People Who Try to Belittle Your Ambitions," Quote Investigator, March 23, 2013, https://quoteinvestigator.com/2013/03/23/belittle-ambitions/.

4. Emily Balcetis, "You 2.0: The Mind's Eye," *Hidden Brain* (podcast), August 10, 2020, https://hiddenbrain.org/podcast/you-2-0-the-minds-eye/.

5. *The West Wing*, season 2, episode 2, "In the Shadow of Two Gunman, Part II," directed by Thomas Schlamme, written by Aaron Sorkin, aired October 4, 2000.

6. *The West Wing*, season 7, episode 22, "Tomorrow," directed by Christopher Misiano, written by Aaron Sorkin and John Wells, aired May 14, 2006.

About the Author

• • •

KATHY ONETO is a coach, speaker, and facilitator committed to helping people thrive on their terms, in both life and work. She is also a strategy executive who bridges her two worlds by applying strategic approaches to life and work decisions and practices.

Kathy is the founder of Sustainable Ambition® and host of the *Sustainable Ambition* podcast. Her mission is to champion more expansive views of success and ambition and to help people craft a life with work that offers more joy, satisfaction, and fulfillment and allows them to be ambitious with more adventure, ease, and peace.

Kathy started asking questions at a young age about success, ambition, and navigating life and work and has used her career as a touchstone to make decisions at different stages. Looking back on her experiences, she realized she had been intuitively practicing what would become the Sustainable Ambition Method. Today, she works with clients and company employees to apply the method, helping them find personal motivation in their goals, architect their next life and work arcs, and manage their effort for more resilience and sustainability.

As a strategist, Kathy has had a twenty-five-year career working across business, branding, innovation, and talent. In her work today, she helps organizations navigate ambiguity and uncertainty by uncovering insight, finding clarity to move forward on what matters, and taking sustained action.

Proud of her public education, Kathy has a BS in commerce from the University of Virginia and received her MBA from the University of California, Berkeley's Haas School of Business. Her writing has appeared in *Fast Company*, *Brandingmag*, and *MediaPost*. She's been a guest lecturer at the business schools at Berkeley, the University of San Francisco, Duke University, and the University of Colorado.

Kathy lives in San Francisco with her husband and the fog. As a former triathlete and marathon runner, she's happiest building up her resilience outdoors—running in Golden Gate Park, walking the streets of her city or ones she's traveled to, or reading with the sun on her face. You can connect with her at KathyOneto.com and SustainableAmbition.com.